PREFACE

In the rapidly evolving world of data management, Snowflake stands out as a cutting-edge platform that challenges engineers to master its unique capabilities. This series is designed to rigorously evaluate your knowledge of Snowflake through a series of targeted Q&A exercises, reinforcing your understanding and sharpening your expertise in preparation for the SnowPro certifications. Even without your intent to get a certification, this book will sharpen your skills to tackle any real-life Snowflake warehouse problems by reinforcing your textbook prior learning.

We'll begin with foundational topics such as data loading and unloading—essential skills for managing data pipelines efficiently. From there, we'll test your comprehension of Snowflake's architecture, including warehouses and the dynamic allocation of compute resources. Concepts like results caching will also be explored, focusing on their role in optimizing query performance.

Further sections will examine secured views and materialized views, probing your understanding of Snowflake's data security mechanisms and query optimization techniques. You'll be challenged on role-based access control (RBAC) strategies, Snowpipe for automated data ingestion, and advanced features like data cloning for backup and testing scenarios.

As the series progresses, you'll tackle questions on schema design, external tables, the Snowflake data marketplace, CRUD operations, and time travel—key elements for recovering historical data and managing changes. Additionally, micropartitions, a cornerstone of Snowflake's storage and performance efficiency, will be a focal point, along with data modeling best practices for scalable design.

Each Question #builds upon previous concepts to ensure a holistic assessment of your knowledge. This isn't just preparation for the SnowPro certification; it's an opportunity to validate your ability to tackle real-world challenges in Snowflake's data ecosystem, positioning you as a top-tier Snowflake engineer.

You will be presented with sets of five multiple-choice questions (MCQs) at a time, each of which may have one or more correct answers. The answers and detailed explanations are provided five questions later. This format ensures that there are no visual cues near the questions, encouraging deeper thought and challenging your grasp of the subject. At the same time, the answers remain close enough that you don't need to search far, striking the perfect balance between challenge and accessibility.

Kapil Srivastava
Dec 2024

Three decades of dredging data

Table of Contents

I.	DATA LOAD/UNLOAD	4
II.	SNOWFLAKE STAGES	28
III.	WAREHOUSES	73
IV.	SNOWFLAKE STREAMS	94
V.	SNOWFLAKE TASKS	113
VI.	SNOWPIPE	129
VII.	DATA CLONING	145
VIII.	RESULTS CACHING	159
IX.	SECURED VIEWS	172
X.	MATERIALIZED VIEWS	183
XI.	ROLE BASED ACCESS CONTROL	197
XII.	SNOWFLAKE SCHEMA	209
XIII.	EXTERNAL TABLES	222
XIV.	DATA MARKETPLACE	236
XV.	CRUD TRANSACTIONS	250
XVI.	TIME TRAVEL	265
XVII.	MICROPARTITIONS	292
XVIII.	DATA MODELING	306

DATA LOAD/UNLOAD

Question #1:
You need to unload data from the orders table into an internal stage named @mystage/unload.
Which command sequence is correct?
Options:
A. COPY INTO @mystage/unload FROM orders;
B. PUT orders INTO @mystage/unload;
C. UNLOAD INTO @mystage/unload FROM orders;
D. COPY INTO 's3://mybucket/orders/' FROM orders;

Question #2:
You have a local file sales.csv that you want to load into a Snowflake table called sales. Which of the following steps is correct?
Options:
A. COPY INTO sales FROM 'sales.csv';
B. PUT file://sales.csv @mystage/load; followed by COPY INTO sales FROM @mystage/load/sales.csv;
C. COPY INTO sales FROM @mystage/load/sales.csv;
D. LOAD file://sales.csv INTO sales;

Question #3:
You need to export data from the employees table to an external S3 bucket. What is the correct command?
Options:
A. COPY INTO 's3://mybucket/employees/' FROM employees STORAGE_INTEGRATION = s3_integration;
B. COPY INTO 's3://mybucket/employees/' FROM employees;
C. UNLOAD INTO 's3://mybucket/employees/' FROM employees;
D. PUT employees INTO 's3://mybucket/employees/';

Question #4:
You need to validate that a file data.csv has been successfully uploaded to the internal stage @mystage/load. Which command should you use?
Options:
A. SELECT * FROM @mystage/load;
B. LIST @mystage/load;

C. DESCRIBE @mystage/load;
D. VALIDATE @mystage/load/data.csv;

Question #5:
You want to load data from an external S3 bucket into a Snowflake table inventory. What is the correct command?
Options:
A. COPY INTO inventory FROM 's3://mybucket/inventory.csv' STORAGE_INTEGRATION = s3_integration;
B. PUT 's3://mybucket/inventory.csv' @mystage/load;
C. LOAD INTO inventory FROM 's3://mybucket/inventory.csv';
D. COPY INTO inventory FROM @mystage/load/inventory.csv;

Answers and Explanations

Question #1:
Correct Answer: A. COPY INTO @mystage/unload FROM orders;
Explanation:

A: Correct. The COPY INTO command is used to export data from a table to a stage;
B: Incorrect. The PUT command uploads files to a stage, but it cannot directly operate on table data;
C: Incorrect. UNLOAD is not a valid Snowflake command; unloading is done using COPY INTO
D. D: Incorrect. This refers to an external S3 bucket, not the internal stage specified in the question

Question #2:
Correct Answer: B. PUT file://sales.csv @mystage/load; followed by COPY INTO sales FROM @mystage/load/sales.csv;
Explanation:

A: Incorrect. COPY INTO cannot directly access local files.
B: Correct. The PUT command uploads the local file to a stage, and COPY INTO loads the data into the table.
C: Incorrect. The PUT step is missing.
D: Incorrect. LOAD INTO is not a valid Snowflake command.

Question #3:
Correct Answer: A. COPY INTO 's3://mybucket/employees/' FROM employees STORAGE_INTEGRATION = s3_integration;
Explanation:

A: Correct. The STORAGE_INTEGRATION parameter ensures secure access to the S3 bucket.
B: Incorrect. The STORAGE_INTEGRATION parameter is mandatory for exporting to an external S3 bucket.
C: Incorrect. UNLOAD is not a valid Snowflake command.
D: Incorrect. The PUT command is not used for exporting table data.

Question #4:
Correct Answer: B. LIST @mystage/load;
Explanation:

A: Incorrect. You cannot query data directly from a stage using SELECT.
B: Correct. The LIST command lists files in a stage.
C: Incorrect. DESCRIBE is not used for checking stage files.
D: Incorrect. VALIDATE is not a valid Snowflake command.

Question #5:
Correct Answer: A. COPY INTO inventory FROM 's3://mybucket/inventory.csv' STORAGE_INTEGRATION = s3_integration;
Explanation:

A: Correct. The COPY INTO command with STORAGE_INTEGRATION is required for securely loading data from S3.
B: Incorrect. PUT cannot upload files directly from an external S3 bucket.
C: Incorrect. LOAD INTO is not a valid Snowflake command.
D: Incorrect. This assumes the file is already in an internal stage, which is not mentioned in the scenario.

Question #6:
You are tasked with unloading a large amount of data (several petabytes) from a Snowflake table big_table to an S3 bucket for long-term storage. Which of the following commands are correct?
Options:
A. COPY INTO 's3://mybucket/big_table/' FROM big_table STORAGE_INTEGRATION = s3_integration;
B. UNLOAD INTO 's3://mybucket/big_table/' FROM big_table;
C. COPY INTO 's3://mybucket/big_table/' FROM big_table;
D. PUT @big_table TO 's3://mybucket/big_table/';

Question #7:
You need to load a massive amount of petabyte-scale data from a CSV file stored on an S3 bucket into Snowflake. Which commands are correct?
Options:
A. COPY INTO target_table FROM 's3://mybucket/large_data.csv' FILE_FORMAT = (TYPE = 'CSV');
B. PUT 's3://mybucket/large_data.csv' @mystage/load; followed by
COPY INTO target_table FROM @mystage/load/large_data.csv FILE_FORMAT = (TYPE = 'CSV');
C. LOAD INTO target_table FROM 's3://mybucket/large_data.csv';
D. COPY INTO target_table FROM 's3://mybucket/large_data.csv';

Question #8:
You are unloading a massive dataset from Snowflake to an S3 bucket for archival purposes.

The table big_data_table contains several petabytes of data. Which commands are appropriate?

Options:

A. COPY INTO 's3://mybucket/archived_data/' FROM big_data_table FILE_FORMAT = (TYPE = 'CSV');
B. PUT big_data_table TO 's3://mybucket/archived_data/';
C. COPY INTO 's3://mybucket/archived_data/' FROM big_data_table;
D. COPY INTO 's3://mybucket/archived_data/' FROM big_data_table STORAGE_INTEGRATION = s3_integration;

Question #9:

To load data from a large number of files stored in an S3 bucket into Snowflake's analytics table, which commands are appropriate?

Options:

A. COPY INTO analytics FROM 's3://mybucket/files/*.csv' FILE_FORMAT = (TYPE = 'CSV');
B. PUT 's3://mybucket/files/*.csv' @mystage/analytics; followed by
COPY INTO analytics FROM @mystage/analytics/*.csv;
C. COPY INTO analytics FROM @mystage/analytics/*.csv FILE_FORMAT = (TYPE = 'CSV');
D. COPY INTO analytics FROM 's3://mybucket/files/*.csv';

Question #10:

You want to load petabyte-scale data from a compressed CSV file stored in an S3 bucket into Snowflake. What is the correct command?

Options:

A. COPY INTO target_table FROM 's3://mybucket/compressed_data.csv.gz' FILE_FORMAT = (TYPE = 'CSV', COMPRESSION = 'GZIP');
B. PUT 's3://mybucket/compressed_data.csv.gz' @mystage/load; followed by
COPY INTO target_table FROM @mystage/load/compressed_data.csv.gz FILE_FORMAT = (TYPE = 'CSV', COMPRESSION = 'GZIP');
C. COPY INTO target_table FROM 's3://mybucket/compressed_data.csv.gz';
D. COPY INTO target_table FROM @mystage/load/compressed_data.csv.gz;

Answers and Explanations

Question #6:
Correct Answers:
A. COPY INTO 's3://mybucket/big_table/' FROM big_table STORAGE_INTEGRATION = s3_integration;
C. COPY INTO 's3://mybucket/big_table/' FROM big_table;

Explanation:

A: Correct. This command uses a storage integration for secure access while unloading data from Snowflake to S3.
C: Correct. This is another valid approach for unloading data but without specifying a storage integration, which might work if your account has direct S3 access.
B: Incorrect. UNLOAD is not a valid Snowflake command.
D: Incorrect. PUT is used for uploading files to a stage, not for exporting table data.

Question #7:
Correct Answers:

A. COPY INTO target_table FROM 's3://mybucket/large_data.csv' FILE_FORMAT = (TYPE = 'CSV');

B. PUT 's3://mybucket/large_data.csv' @mystage/load; followed by
COPY INTO target_table FROM @mystage/load/large_data.csv FILE_FORMAT = (TYPE = 'CSV');

Explanation:

A: Correct. This directly loads CSV data from S3 into Snowflake, specifying the file format.
B: Correct. This two-step process involves uploading data to a Snowflake stage (PUT) and then loading it using COPY INTO.
C: Incorrect. LOAD INTO is not a valid Snowflake command.
D: Incorrect. This command is missing the required FILE_FORMAT specification.

Question #8:
Correct Answers:

A. COPY INTO 's3://mybucket/archived_data/' FROM big_data_table FILE_FORMAT = (TYPE = 'CSV');

D. COPY INTO 's3://mybucket/archived_data/' FROM big_data_table STORAGE_INTEGRATION = s3_integration;

Explanation:

A: Correct. It specifies the file format when exporting the table data.
D: Correct. This command securely exports data using a storage integration.
B: Incorrect. PUT uploads files to a stage, not an S3 bucket.
C: Incorrect. This lacks format or integration parameters needed for large-scale exports.

Question #9:
Correct Answers:

A. COPY INTO analytics FROM 's3://mybucket/files/*.csv' FILE_FORMAT = (TYPE = 'CSV');

C. COPY INTO analytics FROM @mystage/analytics/*.csv FILE_FORMAT = (TYPE = 'CSV');

Explanation:

A: Correct. This loads data directly from S3 with a specified file format.
C: Correct. This loads files from an internal stage into Snowflake.
B: Incorrect. While valid, using PUT is unnecessary if loading directly from S3.
D: Incorrect. The FILE_FORMAT specification is mandatory for CSV files.

Question #10:
Correct Answers:

A. COPY INTO target_table FROM 's3://mybucket/compressed_data.csv.gz' FILE_FORMAT = (TYPE = 'CSV', COMPRESSION = 'GZIP');

B. PUT 's3://mybucket/compressed_data.csv.gz' @mystage/load; followed by
COPY INTO target_table FROM @mystage/load/compressed_data.csv.gz FILE_FORMAT = (TYPE = 'CSV', COMPRESSION = 'GZIP');

Explanation:

A: Correct. This handles both CSV format and GZIP compression.
B: Correct. This method uploads the compressed file to a stage before loading it.
C: Incorrect. It does not specify compression, leading to possible errors.
D: Incorrect. Without specifying the file format and compression, this command may fail.

Question #11

You are exporting data from the sales table to an external S3 bucket. To minimize costs, what should you consider while running the export?
Options:

A. Use COPY INTO with the MAX_FILE_SIZE parameter to create larger files.
B. Set the MAX_FILE_SIZE to a very low value (e.g., 1 MB).
C. Use compression, such as GZIP, in the COPY INTO command.
D. Export only required columns and rows instead of the entire table.

Question #12

When loading large files from an external S3 bucket into a Snowflake table, how can you optimize costs and performance?
Options:

A. Split the files into smaller chunks before loading.
B. Use AUTO_COMPRESSION during the COPY INTO process.
C. Use COPY INTO without specifying a file format.
D. Enable parallelism by using multiple threads in the COPY INTO command.

Question #13

You are performing a bulk load of historical data from an internal stage into the orders_archive table. How can you reduce compute costs?
Options:

A. Use a small warehouse size if the load time is not critical.
B. Pause the warehouse immediately after the load completes.
C. Use a multi-cluster warehouse to speed up the load.
D. Load all data at once to minimize warehouse usage time.

Question #14

You need to export multiple tables to an external stage for backup, but you want to minimize costs. What should you do?
Options:

A. Export all tables as a single, large file.
B. Use COPY INTO with partitioning based on table data.
C. Enable OVERWRITE = TRUE to replace old files during export.

D. Use the same file format for all tables to avoid multiple processing charges.

Question #15

You need to load real-time streaming data into Snowflake with cost-efficiency in mind. Which approaches are valid?
Options:

A. Use Snowpipe with AUTO_INGEST.
B. Use a large warehouse to process small batches frequently.
C. Use COPY INTO periodically for larger batches.
D. Use compression when staging the data files.

Answers and Explanations

Question #11
Correct Answers:
A, C, D
Explanation:
A: Larger files reduce the number of file operations in S3, leading to lower costs.
B: Incorrect. Smaller files increase the number of file operations, leading to higher costs due to more frequent reads/writes.
C: Compression (e.g., GZIP) reduces file size, thus lowering both storage and transfer costs.
D: Exporting only the required columns and rows reduces the amount of data processed, cutting down unnecessary costs.

Question #12
Correct Answers:
A, B, D
Explanation:
A: Splitting the files into smaller chunks allows Snowflake to process data in parallel, improving performance and reducing processing time.
B: AUTO_COMPRESSION optimizes storage by automatically applying the best compression algorithm, lowering storage costs.
C: Incorrect. Not specifying a file format will cause the COPY INTO process to fail, as Snowflake requires a defined file format.
D: Enabling parallelism using multiple threads speeds up the load process, enhancing performance and efficiency, reducing overall time and cost.

Question #13
Correct Answers:
A, B
Explanation:
A: Using a small warehouse reduces compute costs, even if it means a longer load time. This is a cost-effective approach when time is not critical.
B: Pausing the warehouse after the load completes eliminates idle compute costs.
C: Incorrect. Multi-cluster warehouses are more expensive and generally unnecessary for

historical loads, which do not require the extra capacity.
D: Incorrect. Loading all data at once increases the likelihood of performance issues (e.g., warehouse overloading), which may require retries, thus increasing costs.

Question #14
Correct Answers:
B, D
Explanation:
A: Incorrect. Exporting all tables as a single, large file can make the export process inefficient, as large files take more time and resources to process.
B: Partitioning data during export optimizes processing and future query performance, helping to minimize costs in the long run.
C: Incorrect. Overwriting old files increases the number of write operations, adding unnecessary costs.
D: Using the same file format for all tables ensures that Snowflake does not need to process multiple formats, reducing the overhead and associated costs.

Question #15
Correct Answers:
A, C, D
Explanation:
A: Snowpipe with AUTO_INGEST efficiently processes data as it arrives, reducing warehouse compute costs by only activating the necessary compute resources when required.
B: Incorrect. Using a large warehouse to process small batches frequently is inefficient, as the large warehouse incurs high costs for frequent, small operations.
C: Using COPY INTO periodically for larger batches reduces the frequency of compute operations, leading to cost savings by avoiding frequent triggering of compute resources.
D: Compression during staging reduces the file size, leading to lower storage and transfer costs, making the process more cost-efficient.

Question #16:
You try to unload data from the customers table to an external S3 bucket using the following command, but it fails:
COPY INTO 's3://mybucket/customers/' FROM customers;
What could be the reasons for this failure? (Select all that apply)
Options:
A. The table customers does not exist.
B. The S3 bucket mybucket is not accessible due to permission issues.
C. The STORAGE_INTEGRATION parameter is missing.
D. Snowflake stages do not support unloading to S3 buckets.

Question #17:
While loading data from an internal stage, you receive the following error:
File not found in stage @mystage/load.
What could be the causes? (Select all that apply)
Options:
A. The file was never uploaded to the stage.
B. The stage name @mystage/load is incorrect.

C. The file name was not specified in the COPY INTO command.
D. The stage is not accessible due to insufficient privileges.

Question #18:
You are loading data from a CSV file into a Snowflake table, and some rows are failing due to formatting issues. What steps can you take to resolve this? (Select all that apply)
Options:
A. Use the ON_ERROR option with CONTINUE.
B. Use the ON_ERROR option with SKIP_FILE.
C. Use the FILE_FORMAT option to define the correct file structure.
D. Modify the table schema to accommodate all rows.

Question #19:
You attempt to load a JSON file into a Snowflake table using the COPY INTO command but encounter a parsing error. What actions can you take? (Select all that apply)
Options:
A. Specify the FILE_FORMAT as JSON.
B. Use the MATCH_BY_COLUMN_NAME option.
C. Verify that the JSON file contains valid JSON syntax.
D. Set the ON_ERROR parameter to SKIP_FILE.

Question #20:
During a data unload to an internal stage, the process fails with the error:
Insufficient storage space.
What can you do?
Options:
A. Delete older files in the stage to free up space.
B. Compress the data before unloading it.
C. Increase your Snowflake storage allocation.
D. Use an external stage instead.

Answers and Explanations

Question #16
Correct Answer: B, C
Explanation:
B is correct because permission issues with the S3 bucket may prevent Snowflake from accessing it.
C is correct because a missing STORAGE_INTEGRATION parameter is necessary for accessing external storage such as S3 in Snowflake.
A is incorrect because if the customers table does not exist, the error message would specifically indicate this, not a failure related to unloading to S3.
D is incorrect because Snowflake supports unloading to S3 buckets via the COPY INTO command when correctly configured.

Question #17
Correct Answer: A, B, D
Explanation:
A is correct because the file might not have been uploaded to the stage, which would result in the error.

B is correct because the stage name @mystage/load could be incorrect or misspelled, causing the file not to be found.
D is correct because insufficient privileges can prevent access to the stage, leading to the error.
C is incorrect because not specifying the file name in the COPY INTO command would typically result in a different error related to missing file specifications, not a "file not found" error.

Question #18
Correct Answer: A, C
Explanation:
A is correct because the ON_ERROR option with CONTINUE allows Snowflake to continue processing rows even if some rows fail due to formatting issues.
C is correct because using the correct FILE_FORMAT option helps Snowflake understand the file's structure, ensuring proper loading.
B is incorrect because SKIP_FILE skips the entire file, not individual problematic rows.
D is incorrect because modifying the table schema may not resolve all formatting issues in the file, which should be handled by defining the correct file format.

Question #19
Correct Answer: A, C
Explanation:
A is correct because specifying the FILE_FORMAT as JSON ensures that Snowflake correctly parses the JSON data during the load.
C is correct because verifying that the JSON file contains valid syntax is essential for preventing parsing errors.
B is incorrect because MATCH_BY_COLUMN_NAME is not relevant for fixing parsing errors with JSON data, as it is used for aligning column names between the file and table during the load.
D is incorrect because ON_ERROR=SKIP_FILE skips the entire file when errors occur, which may not be the desired solution if the goal is to fix the parsing issue.

Question #20
Correct Answer: A, C
Explanation:
A is correct because deleting older files in the internal stage can free up storage space and resolve the error.
C is correct because increasing your Snowflake storage allocation would provide more space for the unload process.
B is incorrect because compressing the data does not directly address the issue of insufficient storage space.
D is incorrect because using an external stage does not inherently resolve the issue of insufficient internal stage storage.

Question #21
You need to unload data from the sales table into an S3 bucket with gzip compression. Which commands will achieve this?
Options:

A. COPY INTO 's3://mybucket/sales/' FROM sales FILE_FORMAT=(TYPE=CSV COMPRESSION=GZIP) STORAGE_INTEGRATION=s3_integration;
B. COPY INTO @mystage/unload/sales FILE_FORMAT=(TYPE=CSV COMPRESSION=GZIP);
C. COPY INTO 's3://mybucket/sales/' FROM sales FILE_FORMAT=(TYPE=CSV) STORAGE_INTEGRATION=s3_integration;
D. COPY INTO @mystage/unload/sales FILE_FORMAT=(TYPE=CSV);

Question #22
You are loading a compressed gzip file from an internal stage into the customers table.
Which commands will accomplish this?
Options:
A. COPY INTO customers FROM @mystage/load/customers.csv.gz FILE_FORMAT=(TYPE=CSV COMPRESSION=GZIP);
B. COPY INTO customers FROM @mystage/load/customers.csv FILE_FORMAT=(TYPE=CSV COMPRESSION=GZIP);
C. COPY INTO customers FROM 'file://customers.csv.gz' FILE_FORMAT=(TYPE=CSV COMPRESSION=GZIP);
D. COPY INTO customers FROM @mystage/load/customers.csv.gz FILE_FORMAT=(TYPE=CSV);

Question #23
You need to unload data from the products table into an internal stage as zlib-compressed files.
Which commands are valid?
Options:
A. COPY INTO @mystage/unload/products FILE_FORMAT=(TYPE=CSV COMPRESSION=ZLIB);
B. COPY INTO @mystage/unload/products FILE_FORMAT=(TYPE=CSV);
C. COPY INTO @mystage/unload/products FILE_FORMAT=(TYPE=CSV COMPRESSION=NONE);
D. COPY INTO @mystage/unload/products FILE_FORMAT=(TYPE=CSV COMPRESSION=GZIP);

Question #24
You are loading a zlib-compressed file from an external S3 bucket into the inventory table.
Which commands are valid?
Options:
A. COPY INTO inventory FROM 's3://mybucket/inventory.csv.zlib' FILE_FORMAT=(TYPE=CSV COMPRESSION=ZLIB) STORAGE_INTEGRATION=s3_integration;
B. COPY INTO inventory FROM 's3://mybucket/inventory.csv' FILE_FORMAT=(TYPE=CSV COMPRESSION=ZLIB) STORAGE_INTEGRATION=s3_integration;
C. PUT 's3://mybucket/inventory.csv.zlib' @mystage/load; followed by COPY INTO inventory FROM @mystage/load/inventory.csv.zlib;
D. COPY INTO inventory FROM 's3://mybucket/inventory.csv.zlib' FILE_FORMAT=(TYPE=CSV) STORAGE_INTEGRATION=s3_integration;

Question #25
You are loading multiple specific gzip-compressed files from an internal stage into the orders

table.
Which commands can you use?
Options:
A. COPY INTO orders FROM @mystage/load/ FILES=('file1.csv.gz', 'file2.csv.gz') FILE_FORMAT=(TYPE=CSV COMPRESSION=GZIP);
B. COPY INTO orders FROM @mystage/load/ PATTERN='.*\.csv\.gz' FILE_FORMAT=(TYPE=CSV COMPRESSION=GZIP);
C. COPY INTO orders FROM @mystage/load/ FILE_FORMAT=(TYPE=CSV COMPRESSION=GZIP);
D. COPY INTO orders FROM @mystage/load/ FILES=('file1.csv', 'file2.csv') FILE_FORMAT=(TYPE=CSV COMPRESSION=NONE);

Answers and Explanations

Question #21
Correct Answers:
A, B
Explanation:
A: Correct. Exports data to an external S3 bucket with gzip compression, specifying the correct compression type.
B: Correct. Exports data to an internal stage with gzip compression, also specifying the compression type.
C: Incorrect. Missing COMPRESSION=GZIP, so it won't apply gzip compression.
D: Incorrect. Missing COMPRESSION=GZIP, so gzip compression won't be applied.

Question #22
Correct Answers:
A, B
Explanation:
A: Correct. Specifies gzip compression and correctly references the file in the internal stage.
B: Correct. Even if the file name doesn't include .gz, the COMPRESSION=GZIP ensures the file is decompressed correctly.
C: Incorrect. The file:// protocol is not valid for referencing files in Snowflake.
D: Incorrect. Missing COMPRESSION=GZIP, so gzip decompression won't be applied.

Question #23
Correct Answers:
A, D
Explanation:
A: Correct. Uses ZLIB compression to unload data to an internal stage.
B: Incorrect. Specifies no compression, which is not the intended behavior for zlib-compressed files.
C: Incorrect. Specifies no compression, which is not valid for unloading zlib-compressed files.
D: Correct. GZIP is also a valid compression option for unloading data, though different from zlib.

Question #24
Correct Answers:
A, B
Explanation:
A: Correct. Specifies ZLIB compression and correctly references the file in the external S3 bucket.
B: Correct. Snowflake can decompress .csv files with ZLIB compression even without the .zlib extension.
C: Incorrect. The PUT command is used to load local files to internal stages, not for accessing external S3 files.
D: Incorrect. Missing COMPRESSION=ZLIB, which is necessary for loading zlib-compressed files.

Question #25
Correct Answers:
A, B
Explanation:
A: Correct. Specifies the specific files to load and applies gzip decompression to them.
B: Correct. Uses a regex pattern to match .csv.gz files and apply gzip decompression.
C: Incorrect. Without specifying files or patterns, the command will load unintended files from the stage.
D: Incorrect. No compression specified, which is not suitable for gzip-compressed files.

Question #26
You have two CSV files, file1.csv and file2.csv, stored in an internal stage @mystage/load, and you need to load their data into a table called combined_sales. Which command should you use?
Options:
A. COPY INTO combined_sales FROM @mystage/load/;
B. COPY INTO combined_sales FROM @mystage/load/file1.csv, @mystage/load/file2.csv;
C. PUT file1.csv, file2.csv INTO combined_sales;
D. LOAD INTO combined_sales FROM @mystage/load/file1.csv, @mystage/load/file2.csv;

Question #27
You have structured data files in both CSV and JSON formats stored in the S3 bucket s3://mybucket/data/. You need to load all these files into a Snowflake table all_data. What is the correct command?
Options:
A. COPY INTO all_data FROM 's3://mybucket/data/' FILE_FORMAT = (TYPE = 'CSV, JSON');
B. COPY INTO all_data FROM 's3://mybucket/data/' FILE_FORMAT = (TYPE = 'CSV');
C. COPY INTO all_data FROM 's3://mybucket/data/' FILE_FORMAT = (TYPE = 'JSON');
D. COPY INTO all_data FROM 's3://mybucket/data/' FILE_FORMAT = (TYPE = 'CSV'), (TYPE = 'JSON');

Question #28
You are loading data from multiple Parquet files located in the S3 path s3://mybucket/parquet_data/ into a Snowflake table called analytics. Which COPY INTO

clause is needed for efficient parallel loading?

Options:

A. COPY INTO analytics FROM 's3://mybucket/parquet_data/' FILE_FORMAT = (TYPE = 'PARQUET');
B. COPY INTO analytics FROM 's3://mybucket/parquet_data/' FILE_FORMAT = (TYPE = 'CSV');
C. COPY INTO analytics FROM 's3://mybucket/parquet_data/' FILE_FORMAT = (TYPE = 'PARQUET') PARALLEL = TRUE;
D. COPY INTO analytics FROM 's3://mybucket/parquet_data/' FILE_FORMAT = (TYPE = 'PARQUET') MAX_PARALLEL = 4;

Question #29

You have staged files in @mystage/load that contain inconsistent date formats. You want to load this data into the transactions table, ensuring all dates are converted to the format YYYY-MM-DD. What should you do?

Options:

A. COPY INTO transactions FROM @mystage/load FILE_FORMAT = (TYPE = 'CSV', DATE_FORMAT = 'YYYY-MM-DD');
B. COPY INTO transactions FROM @mystage/load FILE_FORMAT = (TYPE = 'CSV') ON_ERROR = 'DATE_CONVERT';
C. COPY INTO transactions FROM @mystage/load FILE_FORMAT = (TYPE = 'CSV', DATE_FORMAT = 'MM/DD/YYYY');
D. COPY INTO transactions FROM @mystage/load;

Question #30

You are loading data from two S3 buckets, s3://sourcebucket/data1/ and s3://sourcebucket/data2/, into a single Snowflake table called consolidated_data. What is the best approach?

Options:

A. COPY INTO consolidated_data FROM 's3://sourcebucket/data1/', 's3://sourcebucket/data2/' FILE_FORMAT = (TYPE = 'CSV');
B. COPY INTO consolidated_data FROM 's3://sourcebucket/data1/' FILE_FORMAT = (TYPE = 'CSV'); COPY INTO consolidated_data FROM 's3://sourcebucket/data2/' FILE_FORMAT = (TYPE = 'CSV');
C. COPY INTO consolidated_data FROM 's3://sourcebucket/data/' FILE_FORMAT = (TYPE = 'CSV');
D. COPY INTO consolidated_data FROM @mystage/load;

Answers and Explanations:

Question #26:
Correct Answer: A
Explanation:
A is correct because the COPY INTO command loads data from a stage, and by specifying the folder path (@mystage/load/), Snowflake will load all files from that location.
B is incorrect because Snowflake does not support specifying multiple files directly in the COPY INTO command.
C is incorrect because the PUT command is used for uploading files to a stage, not for loading them into a table.
D is incorrect because LOAD INTO is not a valid Snowflake command.

Question #27:
Correct Answer: A
Explanation:
A is correct because Snowflake allows specifying multiple file formats (CSV and JSON) in a single FILE_FORMAT clause, enabling loading from both file types in the same command.
B is incorrect because this command will only load CSV files and ignore JSON files.
C is incorrect because this command will only load JSON files, ignoring CSV files.
D is incorrect because file formats should be specified together in a single FILE_FORMAT clause, not separately.

Question #28:
Correct Answer: A
Explanation:
A is correct because Snowflake automatically handles parallel loading for COPY INTO commands when loading data from Parquet files. No additional parallelism options are needed.
B is incorrect because the files are in Parquet format, not CSV.
C is incorrect because Snowflake does not use a PARALLEL option in the COPY INTO command.
D is incorrect because MAX_PARALLEL is not a valid option for the COPY INTO command in Snowflake.

Question #29:
Correct Answer: A
Explanation:
A is correct because the DATE_FORMAT option ensures that all date fields are converted to the specified format (YYYY-MM-DD) when loading data.
B is incorrect because ON_ERROR handles errors but does not convert date formats.
C is incorrect because this command uses the wrong date format (MM/DD/YYYY) instead of YYYY-MM-DD.
D is incorrect because without specifying DATE_FORMAT, no date conversion will take place during the loading process.

Question #30:
Correct Answer: B
Explanation:
A is incorrect because Snowflake does not allow specifying multiple S3 paths in a single COPY INTO command.
B is correct because separate COPY INTO commands must be issued for each S3 bucket to load data into the same table.
C is incorrect because the S3 paths data1/ and data2/ must be specified individually.
D is incorrect because the files are not staged in @mystage/load, but are stored in the S3 buckets.

Question #31
You need to load a CSV file products.csv into a Snowflake table products and apply a

transformation to convert all product_name values to uppercase during the load. Which command should you use?
Options:

A. COPY INTO products FROM @mystage/load/products.csv FILE_FORMAT = (TYPE = 'CSV') ON_ERROR = 'CONTINUE';
B. COPY INTO products FROM @mystage/load/products.csv FILE_FORMAT = (TYPE = 'CSV') TRANSFORM = 'UPPER(product_name)';
C. COPY INTO products (product_name) FROM (SELECT UPPER(product_name) FROM @mystage/load/products.csv) FILE_FORMAT = (TYPE = 'CSV');
D. COPY INTO products (product_name) FROM @mystage/load/products.csv FILE_FORMAT = (TYPE = 'CSV') INCLUDE_TRANSFORM = TRUE;

Question #32
You have a JSON file data.json staged in @mystage/load. You want to load this file into a table events but extract only the event_id and event_date fields during the process. What is the correct command?
Options:

A. COPY INTO events FROM @mystage/load/data.json FILE_FORMAT = (TYPE = 'JSON') ON_ERROR = 'CONTINUE';
B. COPY INTO events (event_id, event_date) FROM (SELECT event_id, event_date FROM @mystage/load/data.json) FILE_FORMAT = (TYPE = 'JSON');
C. COPY INTO events (event_id, event_date) FROM @mystage/load/data.json FILE_FORMAT = (TYPE = 'JSON');
D. COPY INTO events FROM (SELECT event_id, event_date FROM @mystage/load/data.json) FILE_FORMAT = (TYPE = 'JSON');

Question #33
You want to transform data while unloading it from the sales table into a CSV file staged at @mystage/unload. Specifically, you want to exclude all sales records with a total amount below 1000. Which command should you use?
Options:

A. COPY INTO @mystage/unload/sales.csv FROM (SELECT * FROM sales WHERE total_amount >= 1000) FILE_FORMAT = (TYPE = 'CSV');
B. COPY INTO @mystage/unload/sales.csv FROM sales WHERE total_amount >= 1000 FILE_FORMAT = (TYPE = 'CSV');
C. COPY INTO @mystage/unload/sales.csv FROM sales FILE_FORMAT = (TYPE = 'CSV') EXCLUDE_CONDITION = 'total_amount < 1000';
D. EXPORT INTO @mystage/unload/sales.csv FROM (SELECT * FROM sales WHERE total_amount >= 1000) FILE_FORMAT = (TYPE = 'CSV');

Question #34
You have an Avro file staged at @mystage/load and want to load its data into the inventory table. What should you ensure before executing the COPY INTO command?
Options:

A. Create a file format of type AVRO.
B. Use the default file format.
C. Convert the Avro file to CSV format first.
D. Apply a schema validation using VALIDATE FILE.

Question #35

You want to load data into the transactions table from a staged file, but the table has a column load_date that must be populated with the current date for every record. How can this be achieved?
Options:

A. Use a default value for the load_date column in the table definition.
B. COPY INTO transactions FROM @mystage/load FILE_FORMAT = (TYPE = 'CSV') INCLUDE_COLUMN = 'load_date';
C. COPY INTO transactions (columns_except_load_date) FROM @mystage/load FILE_FORMAT = (TYPE = 'CSV'); UPDATE transactions SET load_date = CURRENT_DATE;
D. COPY INTO transactions FROM (SELECT *, CURRENT_DATE AS load_date FROM @mystage/load) FILE_FORMAT = (TYPE = 'CSV');

Answers and Explanations:

Question #31:
Correct Answer: C
Explanation:
C is correct because the COPY INTO command allows for transformations like UPPER(product_name) directly in the SELECT query, which ensures that the product_name values are converted to uppercase during the load.
Why others are wrong:
A: This simply loads the data without any transformations applied to product_name.
B: TRANSFORM is not a valid parameter for the COPY INTO command.
D: There is no parameter called INCLUDE_TRANSFORM in Snowflake; this option is invalid.

Question #32:
Correct Answer: B
Explanation:
B is correct because it extracts only the event_id and event_date fields using a SELECT query, ensuring only those fields are loaded into the events table.
Why others are wrong:
A: This option loads the entire JSON file without extracting specific fields, which doesn't meet the requirements.
C: You cannot directly specify the columns for a JSON file load without using a query to extract the fields.
D: While this uses a query, the COPY INTO syntax here is invalid because the table columns aren't explicitly defined.

Question #33:
Correct Answer: A
Explanation:

A is correct because it filters the records using a SELECT query that includes the condition WHERE total_amount >= 1000, ensuring only the qualifying records are exported.
Why others are wrong:
B: This syntax is invalid because conditions like WHERE total_amount >= 1000 cannot directly follow the FROM clause in COPY INTO.
C: EXCLUDE_CONDITION is not a valid parameter in Snowflake's COPY INTO command.
D: Snowflake does not support an EXPORT command. The correct command for exporting is COPY INTO.

Question #34:
Correct Answer: A
Explanation:
A is correct because Snowflake requires creating a specific file format of type AVRO to load Avro files. This ensures the file's structure and schema are correctly interpreted during the load.
Why others are wrong:
B: The default file format doesn't support Avro files. A custom Avro file format must be created.
C: Converting Avro files to CSV is unnecessary and inefficient when Snowflake natively supports Avro with the correct file format.
D: VALIDATE FILE is used to check staged files' accessibility and structure but doesn't eliminate the need for an appropriate file format.

Question #35:
Correct Answer: D
Explanation:
D is correct because it assigns the current date to the load_date column dynamically using a SELECT query during the load. This approach directly addresses the requirement.
Why others are wrong:
A: While a default value for load_date can be set in the table definition, this is not part of the COPY INTO command and doesn't meet the dynamic assignment requirement.
B: INCLUDE_COLUMN is not a valid Snowflake parameter.
C: Splitting the load and update into two steps is inefficient and not the correct approach when it can be handled in a single step.

Question #36
You need to load a CSV file containing customer data from @mystage/load/customers.csv into a Snowflake table customers, but some rows in the file have missing email values. What should you do to skip only those problematic rows during the load process?

Options:
A. COPY INTO customers FROM @mystage/load/customers.csv FILE_FORMAT = (TYPE = 'CSV') ON_ERROR = 'CONTINUE';
B. COPY INTO customers FROM @mystage/load/customers.csv FILE_FORMAT = (TYPE = 'CSV') ERROR_ON_NULL = 'email';
C. COPY INTO customers FROM (SELECT * FROM @mystage/load/customers.csv WHERE email IS NOT NULL) FILE_FORMAT = (TYPE = 'CSV');

D. COPY INTO customers FROM @mystage/load/customers.csv FILE_FORMAT = (TYPE = 'CSV') SKIP_NULLS = TRUE;

Question #37

You are loading a Parquet file sales.parquet staged in @mystage/load into a Snowflake table sales. The file includes a column sale_date formatted as a string, but you need to convert it to a DATE format during the load. Which command should you use?

Options:
A. COPY INTO sales FROM (SELECT TO_DATE(sale_date, 'YYYY-MM-DD') AS sale_date FROM @mystage/load/sales.parquet) FILE_FORMAT = (TYPE = 'PARQUET');
B. COPY INTO sales FROM @mystage/load/sales.parquet FILE_FORMAT = (TYPE = 'PARQUET') TRANSFORM = 'TO_DATE(sale_date, "YYYY-MM-DD")';
C. COPY INTO sales FROM @mystage/load/sales.parquet FILE_FORMAT = (TYPE = 'PARQUET') ON_ERROR = 'CONTINUE';
D. COPY INTO sales (sale_date) FROM (SELECT TO_DATE(sale_date) FROM @mystage/load/sales.parquet) FILE_FORMAT = (TYPE = 'PARQUET');

Question #38

You want to load data from multiple staged files into a single Snowflake table orders. How can you ensure that Snowflake loads data from all files with the same prefix orders_?

Options:
A. COPY INTO orders FROM @mystage/load FILES = ('orders_') FILE_FORMAT = (TYPE = 'CSV');
B. COPY INTO orders FROM @mystage/load PATTERN = '.orders_.' FILE_FORMAT = (TYPE = 'CSV');
C. COPY INTO orders FROM @mystage/load PATTERN = 'orders_.' FILE_FORMAT = (TYPE = 'CSV');
D. COPY INTO orders FROM @mystage/load FILE_FORMAT = (TYPE = 'CSV') RECURSIVE = TRUE;

Question #39

You need to load a CSV file into Snowflake, but the file includes a header row that should be ignored during the load process. What parameter should you include in the COPY INTO command?

Options:
A. COPY INTO my_table FROM @mystage/load FILE_FORMAT = (TYPE = 'CSV') HEADER = TRUE;
B. COPY INTO my_table FROM @mystage/load FILE_FORMAT = (TYPE = 'CSV') SKIP_HEADER = 1;
C. COPY INTO my_table FROM @mystage/load FILE_FORMAT = (TYPE = 'CSV') ON_ERROR = 'SKIP_HEADER';
D. COPY INTO my_table FROM @mystage/load FILE_FORMAT = (TYPE = 'CSV') OMIT_HEADER = TRUE;

Question #40

You are loading data from a JSON file into Snowflake but need to map a nested field $.customer.id to the customer_id column in your table. How should you write the COPY INTO command?

Options:
A. COPY INTO my_table FROM @mystage/load FILE_FORMAT = (TYPE = 'JSON') COLUMN_MAPPING = 'customer_id:$.customer.id';
B. COPY INTO my_table (customer_id) FROM @mystage/load FILE_FORMAT = (TYPE = 'JSON') ON_ERROR = 'CONTINUE';
C. COPY INTO my_table FROM @mystage/load FILE_FORMAT = (TYPE = 'JSON') PARSE_JSON = '$.customer.id';
D. COPY INTO my_table (customer_id) FROM @mystage/load FILE_FORMAT = (TYPE = 'JSON');

Question #36

Correct Answer: A
Explanation:

Option A is correct because ON_ERROR = 'CONTINUE' will skip rows with errors (like missing email values) and continue loading the other rows.
Option B is incorrect because ERROR_ON_NULL is not a valid parameter in Snowflake.
Option C is incorrect because filtering rows with a query before loading is unnecessary when using ON_ERROR = 'CONTINUE'.
Option D is incorrect because SKIP_NULLS is not a valid parameter in Snowflake.

Question #37

Correct Answer: A
Explanation:

Option A is correct because it uses a SELECT query to apply the TO_DATE transformation to the sale_date column during the load.
Option B is incorrect because TRANSFORM is not a valid parameter in Snowflake's COPY INTO command.
Option C is incorrect because the transformation isn't being applied, and there's no support for applying TO_DATE in the COPY INTO command without using a SELECT.
Option D is incorrect because TO_DATE requires a format specifier for date conversion, and using it without specifying the format would result in an error.

Question #38

Correct Answer: C
Explanation:

Option C is correct because it uses the PATTERN parameter with a regex to filter files with names starting with orders_ and ending with any characters, which is the intended way to load all relevant files.
Option A is incorrect because the FILES parameter requires a specific file name, not a pattern.
Option B is incorrect because the regex used in the pattern would be too broad and could match unintended files.
Option D is incorrect because RECURSIVE is not a valid parameter for COPY INTO.

Question #39

Correct Answer: B
Explanation:

Option B is correct because SKIP_HEADER is the correct Snowflake parameter to skip header rows during the load process.
Option A is incorrect because HEADER is not a valid parameter in Snowflake.
Option C is incorrect because ON_ERROR is for handling row errors, not for skipping header rows.
Option D is incorrect because OMIT_HEADER is not a valid parameter.

Question #40

Correct Answer: D
Explanation:

Option D is correct because Snowflake automatically maps JSON paths to the target columns if the column names match, allowing you to load the nested field directly from the JSON structure.
Option A is incorrect because COLUMN_MAPPING is not a valid option in Snowflake's COPY INTO.
Option B is incorrect because ON_ERROR does not handle mapping for nested fields.
Option C is incorrect because PARSE_JSON is not a valid parameter for COPY INTO.

Question #41
You have a JSON file staged in @mystage/load containing nested objects, such as:

{

 "order_id": 123,

 "customer": {

  "name": "John Doe",

  "email": "john.doe@example.com"

 }

}

You want to load the order_id and customer.name into a table orders. What is the correct command?

Options:
A. COPY INTO orders (order_id, customer_name) FROM @mystage/load FILE_FORMAT = (TYPE = 'JSON');
B. COPY INTO orders (order_id, customer_name) FROM @mystage/load FILE_FORMAT = (TYPE = 'JSON') PARSE_JSON = TRUE;
C. COPY INTO orders (order_id, customer_name) FROM (SELECT VALUE, VALUE.name FROM @mystage/load) FILE_FORMAT = (TYPE = 'JSON');
D. COPY INTO orders (order_id, customer_name) FROM (SELECT PARSE_JSON(data), PARSE_JSON(data).name FROM @mystage/load) FILE_FORMAT = (TYPE = 'JSON');

Question #42
You need to extract and load the array elements from a staged JSON file into a table products. The JSON contains:

{

  "products": [

    {"id": 1, "name": "Laptop"},

    {"id": 2, "name": "Mouse"}

  ]

}

How do you load each id and name as separate rows?

Options:
A. COPY INTO products FROM @mystage/load FILE_FORMAT = (TYPE = 'JSON') FLATTEN_ARRAY = TRUE;
B. COPY INTO products (id, name) FROM (SELECT VALUE.id, VALUE.name FROM TABLE(FLATTEN(INPUT => @mystage/load))) FILE_FORMAT = (TYPE = 'JSON');
C. COPY INTO products (id, name) FROM (SELECT id, name FROM @mystage/load) FILE_FORMAT = (TYPE = 'JSON');
D. COPY INTO products FROM (SELECT VALUE.products.id, VALUE.products.name FROM @mystage/load) FILE_FORMAT = (TYPE = 'JSON');

Question #43
You are unloading data from a Snowflake table orders into a JSON file. The orders table contains columns order_id and details (a VARIANT column storing nested JSON). What is the correct command to ensure the unloaded file retains the nested JSON structure?

Options:
A. COPY INTO @mystage/unload/orders.json FROM orders FILE_FORMAT = (TYPE = 'JSON');

B. COPY INTO @mystage/unload/orders.json FROM (SELECT order_id, TO_JSON(details) AS details FROM orders) FILE_FORMAT = (TYPE = 'JSON');
C. COPY INTO @mystage/unload/orders.json FROM (SELECT TO_JSON(order_id, details) FROM orders) FILE_FORMAT = (TYPE = 'JSON');
D. COPY INTO @mystage/unload/orders.json FROM orders FILE_FORMAT = (TYPE = 'JSON') RETAIN_NESTING = TRUE;

Question #44

A staged JSON file contains inconsistent keys in its objects. Some objects have a price key, while others do not. You want to load this data into the products table without errors. What option should you use?

Options:

A. COPY INTO products FROM @mystage/load FILE_FORMAT = (TYPE = 'JSON') ON_ERROR = 'CONTINUE';
B. COPY INTO products FROM @mystage/load FILE_FORMAT = (TYPE = 'JSON') NULL_ON_ERROR = TRUE;
C. COPY INTO products FROM @mystage/load FILE_FORMAT = (TYPE = 'JSON') VALIDATE_KEYS = TRUE;
D. COPY INTO products FROM (SELECT COALESCE(VALUE, 0) AS price FROM @mystage/load) FILE_FORMAT = (TYPE = 'JSON');

Question #45

You want to unload a Snowflake table customers into a staged JSON file, but only include rows where the status is active. What is the correct command?

Options:

A. COPY INTO @mystage/unload/customers.json FROM customers FILE_FORMAT = (TYPE = 'JSON') WHERE status = 'active';
B. COPY INTO @mystage/unload/customers.json FROM (SELECT * FROM customers WHERE status = 'active') FILE_FORMAT = (TYPE = 'JSON');
C. COPY INTO @mystage/unload/customers.json FROM customers FILE_FORMAT = (TYPE = 'JSON') FILTER = 'status = active';
D. COPY INTO @mystage/unload/customers.json FROM customers FILE_FORMAT = (TYPE = 'JSON') STATUS_FILTER = 'active';

Answers and Explanations

41. Correct Answer: C.
Explanation:

A: Incorrect. This command doesn't handle nested JSON parsing.
B: Incorrect. PARSE_JSON is a function, not a parameter for COPY INTO.
C: Correct. This uses the VALUE: notation to extract fields from JSON.
D: Incorrect. PARSE_JSON is unnecessary when using the VALUE: notation.

42. Correct Answer: B.
Explanation:

A: Incorrect. FLATTEN_ARRAY is not a valid parameter for COPY INTO.
B: Correct. The FLATTEN function is used to handle arrays within JSON.
C: Incorrect. This doesn't address the array structure in JSON.
D: Incorrect. FLATTEN is required to handle the nested array.

43. Correct Answer: B.
Explanation:
A: Incorrect. This would flatten the VARIANT column into a string.
B: Correct. The TO_JSON function ensures the nested structure is retained.
C: Incorrect. TO_JSON cannot be applied to multiple columns simultaneously.
D: Incorrect. RETAIN_NESTING is not a valid parameter.

44. Correct Answer: A.
Explanation:

A: Correct. This skips problematic rows and continues loading other records.
B: Incorrect. NULL_ON_ERROR is not a valid parameter.
C: Incorrect. VALIDATE_KEYS is not a valid Snowflake parameter.
D: Incorrect. This approach requires explicit transformation logic.

45. Correct Answer: B.
Explanation:

A: Incorrect. WHERE is not a valid parameter for COPY INTO.
B: Correct. Using a SELECT statement allows filtering rows based on status.
C: Incorrect. FILTER is not a valid parameter for COPY INTO.
D: Incorrect. STATUS_FILTER is not a valid parameter.

SNOWFLAKE STAGES

Question 1:

You are tasked with loading data from an external Amazon S3 stage into Snowflake. Which of the following steps are required for a successful load?

A. Create an external stage in Snowflake that specifies the S3 bucket URL and access credentials.

B. Ensure that the S3 bucket objects are encrypted using server-side encryption with customer-managed keys (SSE-CMK).

C. Use the COPY INTO command to load data from the stage into a Snowflake table.

D. Define a file format that matches the structure of the data files in the S3 bucket.

Question 2:

Which of the following statements are true about Snowflake internal stages?

A. They support automatic data compression for better storage management.

B. Data loaded into internal stages must be in a CSV format only.

C. Internal stages are created by default for every user and table in Snowflake.

D. They are accessible only by the user who created them unless explicitly shared.

Question 3:

When unloading data from Snowflake to an external stage, which of the following are correct considerations?

A. Specify a file format that matches the table's structure.

B. Set an encryption key within the COPY INTO command for additional security.

C. Confirm that you have read permissions on the external stage.

D. Use AUTO_COMPRESS = TRUE if you want Snowflake to compress the data on export.

Question 4:

You want to create a secure external stage to load data into Snowflake from Azure Blob Storage. Which of the following configurations are necessary?

A. Specify the storage account name and access key in the stage definition.

B. Create a storage integration object in Snowflake to manage credentials securely.

C. Define a file format to ensure data is parsed correctly during the load process.

D. Enable ENCRYPTION=TRUE in the stage to secure data at rest.

Question 5:

Which of the following are true regarding external stages in Snowflake?

A. External stages can be used to load data from both Amazon S3 and Azure Blob Storage.

B. You can use the same external stage to both load data into and unload data from Snowflake.

C. All files in an external stage must be JSON-formatted for Snowflake compatibility.

D. Each cloud storage provider requires a unique configuration for external stages in Snowflake.

Answers and Explanations:

Question 1:

Correct Answer: A, C, D

Explanation:

A. Correct: Creating an external stage is essential for connecting Snowflake to the S3 bucket.

C. Correct: The COPY INTO command loads data from the stage into a Snowflake table.

D. Correct: A compatible file format is required to interpret the data correctly.

B. Incorrect: While server-side encryption is supported, using SSE-CMK is not a requirement for Snowflake. Instead, Amazon S3 supports multiple encryption options, and Snowflake can interact with these options depending on permissions and bucket policies.

Question 2:

Correct Answer: A, C

Explanation:

A. Correct: Snowflake automatically compresses files stored in internal stages to optimize storage.

C. Correct: Snowflake provides default internal stages for every user and table, simplifying data loading and unloading.

B. Incorrect: Snowflake supports multiple file formats for data loading, not just CSV. It includes formats like JSON, PARQUET, and AVRO.

D. Incorrect: Internal stages are private by default, but access is controlled by Snowflake's role-based access control (RBAC) system rather than individual ownership.

Question 3:

Correct Answer: A, D

Explanation:

A. Correct: Defining a file format is necessary so that Snowflake can write the data in a structure that external systems can interpret.

D. Correct: The AUTO_COMPRESS parameter allows data to be compressed during export, reducing storage costs and transfer times.

B. Incorrect: Snowflake handles encryption for stages at the storage layer, so setting a separate encryption key within COPY INTO isn't needed unless specified by the stage configuration.

C. Incorrect: Instead of needing read permissions, you typically require write permissions on the external stage for unloading data.

Question 4:

Correct Answer: A, B, C

Explanation:

A. Correct: When creating a stage to connect to Azure Blob Storage, you need to provide the storage account and key to authorize access.

B. Correct: Using a storage integration in Snowflake allows for secure handling of access credentials, minimizing hard-coded sensitive information.

C. Correct: Specifying a file format is required to control how Snowflake interprets and parses data during the loading process.

D. Incorrect: ENCRYPTION=TRUE is not required in the stage definition since Snowflake automatically manages encryption. Azure Blob Storage handles encryption at rest, and Snowflake does not need this additional parameter for external stages.

Question 5:

Correct Answer: A, B, D

Explanation:

A. Correct: Snowflake supports external stages for data loading from Amazon S3, Azure Blob Storage, and Google Cloud Storage.

B. Correct: An external stage can be used bidirectionally, meaning you can load data into Snowflake or unload data from Snowflake to the same stage.

D. Correct: Each cloud provider has unique configuration requirements, like different authentication mechanisms and stage properties.

C. Incorrect: Snowflake supports multiple file formats for external stages, including CSV, JSON, Parquet, Avro, and ORC. JSON is not a mandatory format for data compatibility.

Question 6:

You are using a named internal stage to store data temporarily. Which of the following statements about this process are true?

A. Named internal stages require explicit permissions to read or write data.

B. Data in named internal stages is compressed by default to save storage.

C. Named internal stages support only the Parquet format for data files.

D. Named internal stages are accessible globally across all roles.

Question 7:

Which actions are valid when working with external stages in Snowflake?

A. Copying data from an external stage to another Snowflake account's stage directly.

B. Loading data into Snowflake tables using COPY INTO from an external stage.

C. Listing files within an external stage using the LIST command.

D. Granting role-based access control on the stage for security.

Question 8:

When configuring an external stage in Snowflake to connect to Google Cloud Storage, which of the following steps are necessary?

A. Specify the Google Cloud project ID in the external stage definition.

B. Define a file format compatible with the data being loaded.

C. Create a storage integration to securely manage Google Cloud credentials.

D. Use ENCRYPTION=TRUE in the stage configuration for secure data transfer.

Question 9:

Which statements about unloading data to an internal stage in Snowflake are correct?

A. The COPY INTO command supports multiple formats, including CSV and JSON.

B. Data in an internal stage can be viewed directly without unloading it first.

C. Data in an internal stage is automatically compressed if specified in the COPY INTO command.

D. You can list files in an internal stage using the LIST command.

Question 10:

When using a named stage in Snowflake to stage data files, which of the following statements are accurate?

A. Named stages can store files for an unlimited amount of time.

B. Named stages allow data sharing between Snowflake accounts.

C. You must define a file format when loading data from a named stage.

D. Named stages can be referenced using the @ symbol followed by the stage name.

Answers and Explanations:

Question 6:

Correct Answers: A, B

Explanation:

A. Access to named internal stages is controlled by Snowflake's role-based permissions, so explicit permissions are required.

B. Data in internal stages is automatically compressed by Snowflake to optimize storage costs.

C. Snowflake's internal stages support multiple file formats, such as CSV, JSON, Parquet, Avro, and ORC; Parquet is not the only supported format.

D. Access to named internal stages is restricted to the role permissions set on the stage, not universally accessible across all roles.

Question 7:

Correct Answers: B, C, D

Explanation:

B. COPY INTO is commonly used to load data from an external stage into Snowflake tables.

C. The LIST command can be used to view files in an external stage, which is helpful for verifying data availability.

D. Snowflake allows you to manage access to stages via role-based access control for secure data handling.

A. Snowflake does not support direct data transfer between stages of different Snowflake accounts. Data sharing across accounts must be handled through specific sharing mechanisms or by exporting and re-importing data.

Question 8:

Correct Answers: B, C

Explanation:

B. A file format is essential to parse data correctly during loading.

C. A storage integration object securely manages Google Cloud credentials, eliminating the need to include sensitive data in the stage definition.

A. The Google Cloud project ID is not required in the stage definition; instead, the storage integration manages all necessary credential information.

D. ENCRYPTION=TRUE is not necessary for secure transfer, as Snowflake and Google Cloud manage encryption through their respective services.

Question 9:

Correct Answers: A, C, D

Explanation:

A. The COPY INTO command supports multiple data formats, allowing for flexibility in data handling.

C. Data can be compressed during export by setting the appropriate options in the COPY INTO command.

D. The LIST command allows you to view files within an internal stage.

B. You cannot view data directly within an internal stage; data must be moved or queried within a table after loading.

Question 10:

Correct Answers: C, D

Explanation:

C. Defining a file format is essential for interpreting data when loading from a named stage.

D. Named stages are referenced using the @ symbol followed by the stage name, e.g., @my_stage.

A. Files in a named stage are subject to retention limits based on Snowflake's storage policies and may incur storage charges.

B. Named stages do not support direct sharing between Snowflake accounts; data sharing requires secure data sharing mechanisms or cross-account access.

Question 11:

What are the correct steps for unloading data from Snowflake into an S3 external stage with encryption enabled?

Options:

A. Define an external stage pointing to the S3 bucket with the ENCRYPTION parameter set to TRUE.

B. Set up a storage integration to manage access permissions.

C. Specify a file format for the exported data.

D. Use COPY INTO with the OVERWRITE=TRUE option to replace existing data.

Question 12:

Which of the following are true when configuring file formats for data loading from a stage in Snowflake?

Options:

A. You can specify compression settings in the file format for efficient storage.

B. Only CSV format is supported when loading from a stage.

C. File formats can specify specific parsing options, like field delimiters.

D. File format settings are optional; Snowflake will automatically detect file formats.

Question 13:

Which of the following statements best describes how Snowflake handles data loading from an external stage?

Options:

A. Data from external stages is loaded into Snowflake tables directly without the need for transformation.

B. External stages require a file format to define how data files are parsed during loading.

C. Snowflake automatically encrypts data loaded from external stages if the external storage uses SSE-C (Server-Side Encryption with Customer-Managed Keys).

D. Data from external stages must be copied into an internal stage before loading into tables.

Question 14:

What is a key characteristic of named stages in Snowflake?

Options:

A. Named stages provide direct data sharing capabilities across Snowflake accounts.

B. They are automatically created for every user and table within Snowflake.

C. Named stages must be explicitly created and can be managed by users with appropriate permissions.

D. Named stages support only CSV and JSON file formats for data loading.

Question 15:

Which statement is true regarding Snowflake internal stages?

Options:

A. Internal stages are designed for data storage external to Snowflake, like AWS S3.

B. Data in internal stages can only be accessed by the user who created it.

C. Snowflake automatically compresses data stored in internal stages to save space.

D. Only JSON-formatted data can be stored in internal stages.

Answers and Explanations:

Question 11:

Correct Answers: B, C

Explanation:

B is correct because a storage integration provides secure access to the S3 bucket without embedding sensitive information directly in the configuration.

C is correct because specifying a file format ensures that the exported data is structured properly when it is unloaded.

A is incorrect because encryption at the external stage level is not required; Snowflake handles encryption during transfer to external locations.

D is incorrect because the OVERWRITE=TRUE option is optional and only necessary if you want to replace existing data in the S3 bucket.

Question 12:

Correct Answers: A, C

Explanation:

A is correct because compression settings can be included in the file format to optimize storage and reduce the load time.

C is correct because file formats allow specifying parsing options like delimiters, escape characters, and date formats, which are crucial for correct data loading.

Incorrect Option Explanation:

B is incorrect because Snowflake supports a variety of formats, including CSV, JSON, Parquet, ORC, and Avro.

D is incorrect because Snowflake generally requires a defined file format for complex data structures; automatic detection may not work properly for complex cases.

Question 13:

Correct Answer: B

Explanation:

B is correct because a file format is necessary to define how data from external stages should be parsed when loaded into Snowflake tables.

A is incorrect because data from external stages may require transformation depending on the structure and need of the target table, and this can be done within the COPY INTO command.

C is incorrect because Snowflake does not automatically encrypt based on external storage's encryption settings; encryption must be managed by the storage provider (like S3) and is not handled automatically by Snowflake.

D is incorrect because data from an external stage can be directly loaded into Snowflake tables without copying it into an internal stage.

Question 14:

Correct Answer: C

Explanation:

C is correct because named stages must be explicitly created and can be managed by users with the proper permissions. These stages are not automatically created by Snowflake.

Incorrect Option Explanation:

A is incorrect because named stages do not directly support data sharing across Snowflake accounts. Data sharing requires separate configuration.

B is incorrect because default stages are automatically created for users and tables, but named stages must be explicitly created.

D is incorrect because named stages support multiple file formats (CSV, JSON, Parquet, etc.), not just CSV and JSON.

Question 15:

Correct Answer: C

Explanation:

C is correct because Snowflake automatically compresses data stored in internal stages to reduce storage costs.

A is incorrect because internal stages are part of Snowflake's storage, not external storage solutions like S3.

B is incorrect because access to internal stages is managed by role-based access control (RBAC), not limited to the user who created it.

D is incorrect because internal stages can store various file formats, including CSV, JSON, Parquet, and others.

Question 16:

A data pipeline in Snowflake is implemented using a task that processes new data from a table. The task is set up with a schedule but does not seem to execute. What could be the reason for this behavior?

Options: A. The task has been created without specifying a SQL statement to execute.

B. The task requires a parent task to be completed before it can execute.

C. The task is not enabled.

D. The warehouse associated with the task is suspended.

Question 17:

Which of the following statements about external stages is correct?

Options:

A. External stages allow data to be loaded directly into Snowflake tables without a specified file format.

B. They provide a secure way to store data temporarily within Snowflake's storage layer.

C. External stages require configuration of credentials to access cloud storage locations.

D. Data in external stages is automatically compressed by Snowflake upon loading.

Question 18:

When unloading data from Snowflake to an external stage, which configuration is essential for correct file parsing?

Options:

A. Setting the stage compression to AUTO_COMPRESS=TRUE.

B. Defining a file format that matches the expected data structure.

C. Enabling encryption by setting ENCRYPTION=TRUE in the COPY INTO statement.

D. Setting up read permissions on the external stage bucket.

Question 19:

When setting up a stage in Snowflake to load data from Amazon S3, which of the following are necessary configurations?

Options:

A. Defining a file format to parse the data correctly.

B. Specifying the AWS region where the S3 bucket resides.

C. Setting up encryption within the Snowflake stage definition.

D. Providing the IAM role or access credentials required to access the S3 bucket.

Question 20:

You are setting up an external stage in Snowflake to load data from Google Cloud Storage (GCS). Which of the following configurations are required?

Options:

A. Setting up a storage integration to manage access credentials securely.

B. Defining a URL for the GCS bucket location.

C. Enabling encryption within Snowflake's stage settings.

D. Configuring the GCS bucket policy to allow read-only access for Snowflake's service account.

Answers and Explanations:

Question 16:

Correct Answer: C, D

Explanation:

C is correct because tasks in Snowflake do not execute unless they are explicitly enabled.

D is correct because if the associated warehouse is suspended, the task cannot execute as it requires compute resources.

A is incorrect because a task cannot be created without a SQL statement; it would fail at creation.

B is incorrect because not all tasks require a parent task; this depends on how the task chain is configured.

Question 17:

Correct Answer: C

Explanation:

Correct Answer: Option C: External stages require credentials to connect and access data from cloud storage services like S3, Azure Blob Storage, or Google Cloud Storage.

Option A: External stages need a file format specified to ensure proper data parsing when loaded into Snowflake.

Option B: External stages point to data stored outside Snowflake rather than within Snowflake's internal storage.

Option D: Data compression for external stages is managed by the external storage provider, not Snowflake.

Question 18:

Correct Answer: B

Explanation:

Correct Answer: Option B: Defining a file format is essential to ensure that data is correctly structured and parsed during the unloading process.

Option A: Compression is optional and does not affect file parsing; it only influences storage efficiency.

Option C: Encryption settings are managed by the external storage provider, so ENCRYPTION=TRUE is not necessary.

Option D: Read permissions are relevant for loading data but are not required for unloading data to the external stage.

Question 19:

Correct Answer: A, D

Explanation:

Correct Answers:

Option A: COPY INTO is the primary command used to load data from a stage into a table.

Option D: A file format can be defined within the COPY INTO command to specify parsing rules, like delimiters and null handling.

Option B: Both internal and external stages support data loading into Snowflake tables.

Option C: Data transformations can be applied within the COPY INTO command by specifying SQL expressions to manipulate data during the load.

Question 20:

Correct Answer: A, D

Explanation:

Correct Answers:

Option A: A storage integration securely manages access credentials, helping avoid hardcoding sensitive information.

Option D: The GCS bucket must have a policy allowing Snowflake's service account read-only access for data loading.

Option B: The GCS bucket location is defined through the integration and stage configuration; a direct URL is not specified in the Snowflake stage.

Option C: Encryption is managed by Google Cloud, and Snowflake does not require a specific encryption setting for the stage.

Question 21:

Which of the following are true about using stages in Snowflake to unload data?

You must define a file format to specify how data should be structured when unloaded.

The COPY INTO command can be used to export data from Snowflake to an external stage.

Unloading data is limited to internal stages only.

You need to configure a storage integration for unloading data to an external stage.

Select 2 answers:

A. You must define a file format to specify how data should be structured when unloaded.

B. The COPY INTO command can be used to export data from Snowflake to an external stage.

C. Unloading data is limited to internal stages only.

D. You need to configure a storage integration for unloading data to an external stage.

Question 22:

When using internal stages in Snowflake, which statements are correct?

Data in an internal stage is compressed by default to save storage costs.

Internal stages support storing files in multiple formats, such as CSV, JSON, and Parquet.

Data in internal stages must be explicitly encrypted using ENCRYPTION=TRUE.

Data from internal stages is accessible across all Snowflake accounts by default.

Select 2 answers:

A. Data in an internal stage is compressed by default to save storage costs.

B. Internal stages support storing files in multiple formats, such as CSV, JSON, and Parquet.

C. Data in internal stages must be explicitly encrypted using ENCRYPTION=TRUE.

D. Data from internal stages is accessible across all Snowflake accounts by default.

Question 23:

When creating an external stage in Snowflake that points to an Amazon S3 bucket, which of the following configurations are mandatory?

Setting up a storage integration with the necessary IAM role for S3 access.

Defining the file path in the S3 bucket.

Specifying the AWS region where the S3 bucket is located.

Including the access key and secret key directly in the stage definition.

Select 2 answers:

A. Setting up a storage integration with the necessary IAM role for S3 access.

B. Defining the file path in the S3 bucket.

C. Specifying the AWS region where the S3 bucket is located.

D. Including the access key and secret key directly in the stage definition.

Question 24:

Which statements about data loading from an external stage in Snowflake are correct?

A file format must be defined for loading structured data like JSON or Parquet.

Data transformations can be applied during the load process using SQL expressions in the COPY INTO statement.

Data loading is only possible from public external stages.

Snowflake automatically removes loaded files from external stages after the data load.

Select 2 answers:

A. A file format must be defined for loading structured data like JSON or Parquet.

B. Data transformations can be applied during the load process using SQL expressions in the COPY INTO statement.

C. Data loading is only possible from public external stages.

D. Snowflake automatically removes loaded files from external stages after the data load.

Question 25:

In Snowflake, when unloading data to a Google Cloud Storage (GCS) stage, which configurations are essential?

Setting up a storage integration to handle GCS credentials securely.

Defining a FILE_FORMAT for the exported data.

Specifying the OVERWRITE=TRUE option to remove existing files in the GCS bucket.

Enabling encryption explicitly within the stage definition.

Select 2 answers:

A. Setting up a storage integration to handle GCS credentials securely.

B. Defining a FILE_FORMAT for the exported data.

C. Specifying the OVERWRITE=TRUE option to remove existing files in the GCS bucket.

D. Enabling encryption explicitly within the stage definition.

Answers and Explanations:

Question 21:

Correct Answers: B,D

Explanation:

B is correct because the COPY INTO command is used to unload data to external stages (like S3, GCS).

D is correct because you need a storage integration to handle credentials for external stages.

A is incorrect because defining a file format is not always necessary for unloading data.

C is incorrect because unloading can also happen from external stages, not just internal stages.

Question 22:

Correct Answers: A,B

Explanation:

A is correct because Snowflake automatically compresses data in internal stages to save on storage costs.

B is correct because internal stages support multiple data formats.

C is incorrect because internal stages do not require explicit encryption; Snowflake handles it automatically.

D is incorrect because internal stages are accessible only within the same Snowflake account.

Question 23:

Correct Answers: A,B

Explanation:

A is correct because a storage integration is required for Snowflake to access Amazon S3 securely.

B is correct because you must define the file path in the S3 bucket to indicate where the data is located.

C is incorrect because Snowflake automatically detects the AWS region of the S3 bucket.

D is incorrect because including access keys directly in the stage definition is discouraged due to security concerns.

Question 24:

Correct Answers: A,B

Explanation:

A is correct because file formats ensure structured data (like JSON, Parquet) is properly parsed during loading.

B is correct because SQL expressions can be used for data transformations while loading from external stages.

C is incorrect because data can be loaded from both public and private external stages.

D is incorrect because Snowflake does not automatically remove files from external stages after loading.

Question 25:

Correct Answers: A,B

Explanation:

A is correct because a storage integration is needed for securely managing GCS credentials.

B is correct because defining a file format is necessary to structure the data when exporting to GCS.

C is incorrect because OVERWRITE=TRUE is optional and only needed if you want to replace existing files.

D is incorrect because encryption for GCS is managed by Google Cloud and does not need to be specified in the Snowflake stage.

Question 26:

Which of the following statements are correct about file retention policies for stages in Snowflake?

Select 2 answers:

A. Internal stages have retention policies based on Snowflake's storage model.

B. Files in named stages are automatically deleted after a specified period.

C. Snowflake charges for storage of files in internal stages.

D. External stages do not incur Snowflake storage costs, as data is stored outside of Snowflake.

Question 27:

Which statements accurately describe how stages are used for data unloading in Snowflake?

Select 2 answers:

A. You can specify multiple file formats when unloading data to a stage.

B. The COPY INTO command is used to unload data from a Snowflake table to a stage.

C. Only internal stages support data unloading in Snowflake.

D. Unloading data to an external stage requires setting up a storage integration.

Question 28:

Which of the following actions can be performed directly on data stored in an external stage in Snowflake?

Select 2 answers:

A. Use SQL queries to transform data stored in an external stage.

B. Load data from the external stage into a Snowflake table.

C. Define a file format for data parsing when loading from the external stage.

D. Directly delete data from an external stage using Snowflake SQL commands.

Question 29:

When setting up a named internal stage for secure file storage in Snowflake, which configurations are necessary?

Select 2 answers:

A. Specify the data file format used for loading data from the stage.

B. Set access control permissions for the stage to manage role-based access.

C. Provide encryption settings to secure the data within the stage.

D. Indicate the cloud storage provider (S3, Azure, or GCS) for storing the stage's data.

Question 30:

In Snowflake, what is required when setting up a stage to load data from Microsoft Azure Blob Storage?

Select 2 answers:

A. A storage integration to securely handle Azure credentials.

B. The path to the container and directory within Azure Blob Storage.

C. Defining a URL to the specific file in the storage container.

D. Including the encryption key in the stage definition.

Answers and Explanations:

Question 26:

Correct Answers: A, D

Explanation:

A. Internal stages follow Snowflake's storage policies, including retention limits for data files.

D. External stages do not incur storage costs from Snowflake, as the data remains in external storage systems (e.g., AWS S3, GCS, Azure).

B. Named stages do not automatically delete files after a specified period; file deletion must be managed manually or through external tools.

C. Snowflake does charge for data stored in internal stages, which are part of Snowflake's managed storage.

Question 27:

Correct Answers: B, D

Explanation:

B. The COPY INTO command is used to unload data from Snowflake tables to both internal and external stages.

D. A storage integration is required to manage credentials when unloading data to external stages.

A. Only one file format can be specified when unloading data to maintain data consistency.

C. Data unloading is supported for both internal and external stages in Snowflake.

Question 28:

Correct Answers: B, C

Explanation:

B. Snowflake allows loading data from an external stage directly into a Snowflake table.

C. Defining a file format is necessary when loading data from an external stage to correctly interpret the file's structure.

A. SQL transformations cannot be applied directly to data in an external stage; transformations are performed while loading the data.

D. Data in an external stage cannot be deleted directly through Snowflake; this must be done using cloud storage provider tools.

Question 29:

Correct Answers: A, B

Explanation:

A. A file format must be defined for data loading from the stage to ensure that the data is parsed correctly.

B. Access control permissions are necessary to restrict or grant access to the stage based on user roles.

C. Snowflake automatically encrypts data stored in internal stages, so manual encryption configuration is not required.

D. Internal stages use Snowflake-managed storage, so specifying an external cloud storage provider is unnecessary.

Question 30:

Correct Answers: A, B

Explanation:

A. A storage integration is necessary to securely handle Azure credentials when loading data from Azure Blob Storage.

B. The path to the container and directory is required to locate data within Azure Blob Storage.

C. A URL to a specific file is not required; specifying the container path is sufficient.

D. Azure Blob Storage handles encryption on its own, so including an encryption key in Snowflake's stage definition is unnecessary.

Question 31:

Which of the following is true about temporary stages in Snowflake?

Select 4 answers:

A) Temporary stages are deleted automatically when the session ends.

B) They can be used to store data temporarily for ETL operations within a single session.

C) Temporary stages can be shared between sessions by users with the appropriate role.

D) They are only available to the user who created them.

Question 32:

When unloading data to an external stage on Amazon S3, which configurations are essential?

Select 2 answers:

A) A storage integration to manage access credentials.

B) A file format to structure the data in a consistent way.

C) Defining encryption settings within the stage to secure data during the unload process.

D) Setting OVERWRITE=TRUE to replace existing files.

Question 33:

Which actions can be performed with named stages in Snowflake?

Select 4 answers:

A) Loading data into tables using the COPY INTO command.

B) Setting up role-based access controls to manage permissions.

C) Sharing the stage directly with another Snowflake account.

D) Unloading data from tables to the stage.

Question 34:

Which of the following are true about accessing external stages from Snowflake?

Select 4 answers:

A) Snowflake requires a storage integration to securely access external stages.

B) Data in an external stage can only be accessed from within the same Snowflake account.

C) External stages can be accessed using an external cloud provider's identity and access management (IAM) roles.

D) Data from external stages can be read into Snowflake tables using the COPY INTO command.

Question 35:

When loading data into a table from an internal stage, which options are available to specify data parsing rules?

Select 4 answers:

A) Defining a FILE_FORMAT as part of the stage configuration.

B) Setting a FILE_FORMAT option within the COPY INTO command.

C) Embedding parsing rules directly in the data file.

D) Using the default FILE_FORMAT settings if no custom format is specified.

Answers and Explanations:

Question 31:

Correct Answers: A, B, D

Explanation:

A is correct because temporary stages are removed automatically at the end of the session.

B is correct because temporary stages are often used for storing data during ETL workflows within a session.

D is correct because temporary stages are private to the session and the user who created them, providing data isolation.

C is incorrect because temporary stages cannot be shared across sessions; they are session-specific and isolated to the user who created them.

Question 32:

Correct Answers: A, B

Explanation:

A is correct because a storage integration securely manages access credentials when connecting to Amazon S3.

B is correct because specifying a file format ensures the data is structured correctly when written to the external stage.

C is incorrect because encryption settings are handled by S3, not specifically by Snowflake during the unload process.

D is incorrect because OVERWRITE=TRUE is only required if you want to replace existing files; it's not a mandatory setting.

Question 33:

Correct Answers: A, B, D

Explanation:

A is correct because the COPY INTO command is used to load data from named stages into Snowflake tables.

B is correct because role-based access controls can be set on named stages to manage user permissions.

D is correct because data can be unloaded from Snowflake tables to named stages using the COPY INTO command.

C is incorrect because named stages cannot be shared across Snowflake accounts. Data sharing requires different mechanisms such as the use of Snowflake data sharing features.

Question 34:

Correct Answers: A, C, D

Explanation:

A is correct because Snowflake requires a storage integration to securely manage credentials when accessing external stages.

C is correct because external stages can be accessed using the cloud provider's IAM roles (e.g., AWS IAM roles for S3) with the appropriate storage integration.

D is correct because data can be read into Snowflake tables from external stages using the COPY INTO command.

B is incorrect because external stages can be accessed by other Snowflake accounts if the correct permissions are set on the external cloud storage.

Question 35:

Correct Answers: A, B, D

Explanation:

A is correct because a file format can be defined as part of the stage configuration to specify parsing rules.

B is correct because a file format can also be specified directly in the COPY INTO command.

D is correct because if no custom file format is specified, Snowflake will use default parsing rules.

C is incorrect because parsing rules cannot be embedded directly in the data file; they must be set through file formats in Snowflake.

Question 36:

Which statements are correct about file retention and expiration policies for internal stages?

Select 4 answers:

A) Internal stages have configurable file retention policies based on role permissions.

B) Data in a temporary stage is automatically removed when the session ends.

C) Named stages persist data until manually deleted.

D) Files in internal stages can only be removed by users with the ACCOUNTADMIN role.

Question 37:

Which of the following are true about using an external stage with Google Cloud Storage (GCS) in Snowflake?

Select 3 answers:

A) A storage integration is required to securely manage GCS credentials.

B) The URL to the GCS bucket is defined in the external stage.

C) Only CSV file formats are supported for loading data from GCS into Snowflake.

D) Snowflake can directly load JSON, Parquet, and CSV files from GCS.

Question 38:

What statements are true about unloading data to an internal stage in Snowflake?

Select 2 answers:

A) Data can be unloaded in multiple formats, such as CSV and Parquet.

B) The COPY INTO command can be used to unload data from a Snowflake table to an internal stage.

C) Unloaded data is automatically compressed to reduce storage costs.

D) Data in internal stages is accessible to all Snowflake users by default.

Question 39:

When loading data from Amazon S3 to a Snowflake table using an external stage, which configurations are essential?

Select 2 answers:

A) Defining a storage integration with appropriate permissions.

B) Specifying the S3 bucket URL in the external stage configuration.

C) Setting up a private endpoint in Snowflake for S3 access.

D) Using an encryption key to decrypt the data stored in S3.

Question 40:

Which statements describe best practices for loading large data volumes from an external stage in Snowflake?

Select 3 answers:

A) Use a multi-part file format to reduce the load time.

B) Specify parallel loading options to optimize performance.

C) Load all data in a single transaction to minimize session use.

D) Limit file sizes to ensure efficient parsing and memory usage.

Answers and Explanations:

Question 36:

Correct Answers: B, C

Explanation:

B is correct because data in temporary stages is automatically removed when the session ends.

C is correct because named stages persist data until explicitly deleted.

A is incorrect because file retention policies are determined by the stage type (e.g., temporary or named) and not role-based permissions.

D is incorrect because files in internal stages can be removed by users with sufficient permissions, not just the ACCOUNTADMIN role.

Question 37:

Correct Answers: A, B, D

Explanation:

A is correct because a storage integration is required to securely manage credentials when using an external stage with GCS.

B is correct because the URL to the GCS bucket is part of the external stage definition.

D is correct because Snowflake supports multiple file formats, including JSON, Parquet, and CSV, for loading from GCS.

C is incorrect because Snowflake supports multiple formats (not just CSV) when loading data from GCS.

Question 38:

Correct Answers: A, B

Explanation:

A is correct because data can be unloaded to internal stages in multiple formats like CSV and Parquet.

B is correct because the COPY INTO command is used for unloading data from Snowflake tables to internal stages.

C is incorrect because compression of unloaded data is not automatic; it must be explicitly specified.

D is incorrect because data in internal stages is not automatically accessible to all users by default; access is controlled by role-based permissions.

Question 39:

Correct Answers: A, B

Explanation:

A is correct because a storage integration manages permissions for secure S3 access.

B is correct because the S3 bucket URL must be specified in the external stage definition.

C is incorrect because setting up a private endpoint is not necessary for standard S3 access.

D is incorrect because encryption/decryption is typically managed by the cloud provider, not within Snowflake's configuration.

Question 40:

Correct Answers: A, B, D

Explanation:

A is correct because using multi-part file formats (smaller chunks) helps reduce load times by optimizing processing.

B is correct because parallel loading improves performance by utilizing multiple resources to load the data.

D is correct because limiting file sizes ensures better memory usage and efficient parsing during the load process.

C is incorrect because loading all data in a single transaction can negatively impact performance. It is better to break data into smaller chunks for better performance.

Question 41:

Which of the following commands is used to create a new stage in Snowflake?

Select 1 answer:

A) CREATE FILE FORMAT

B) CREATE STAGE

C) CREATE TABLE

D) CREATE DATABASE

Question 42:

What does the LIST command in Snowflake do?

Select 1 answer:

A) Lists all stages in the current schema

B) Lists files in a stage

C) Lists all tables in a schema

D) Lists the properties of a file format

Question 43:

Which command would you use to remove files from a stage in Snowflake?

Select 1 answer:

A) DROP FILE

B) REMOVE

C) DELETE FILE

D) DROP STAGE

Question 44:

How do you load data from a stage into a Snowflake table?

Select 1 answer:

A) INSERT INTO

B) COPY INTO

C) LOAD INTO

D) TRANSFER INTO

Question 45:

Which command gives information about the configuration of a Snowflake stage?

Select 1 answer:

A) DESCRIBE STAGE

B) SHOW STAGE

C) EXPLAIN STAGE

D) INFO STAGE

Answers and Explanations:

Question 41:

Correct Answers: B

Explanation:

- **B is correct** because the CREATE STAGE command is used to create a new stage in Snowflake for managing external data locations.

- **A is incorrect** because CREATE FILE FORMAT is used for creating file formats for loading or unloading data, not stages.

- **C is incorrect** because CREATE TABLE is used to create a new table, not a stage.

- **D is incorrect** because CREATE DATABASE creates a new database, not a stage.

Question 42:

Correct Answers: B

Explanation:

- **B is correct** because the LIST command is used to display files within a specified stage.

- **A is incorrect** because the LIST command does not list stages; SHOW STAGES lists stages.

- **C is incorrect** because the LIST command does not list tables in a schema; SHOW TABLES does that.

- **D is incorrect** because the LIST command does not display file format properties; SHOW FILE FORMATS does that.

Question 43:

Correct Answers: B

Explanation:

- **B is correct** because the REMOVE command is used to remove files from a Snowflake stage.

- **A is incorrect** because DROP FILE is not a valid Snowflake command for removing files from a stage.

- **C is incorrect** because DELETE FILE is not a valid Snowflake command.

- **D is incorrect** because DROP STAGE removes the entire stage, not the files within it.

Question 44:

Correct Answers: B

Explanation:

- **B is correct** because the COPY INTO command is used to load data from a stage into a Snowflake table.

- **A is incorrect** because INSERT INTO is used to insert data into a table, not from a stage.

- **C is incorrect** because LOAD INTO is not a valid Snowflake command.

- **D is incorrect** because TRANSFER INTO is not a valid Snowflake command.

Question 45:

Correct Answers: A

Explanation:

- **A is correct** because the DESCRIBE STAGE command provides information about the configuration and properties of a stage.

- **B is incorrect** because SHOW STAGE lists the stages but does not provide configuration details.

- **C is incorrect** because EXPLAIN STAGE is not a valid Snowflake command.

- **D is incorrect** because INFO STAGE is not a valid Snowflake command.

Question 46:

You are working with a Snowflake internal stage and want to upload a local file to the stage. Which of the following commands should you use?
Select 1 answer:
A) PUT
B) COPY INTO
C) UPLOAD FILE
D) ADD FILE

Question 47:

A user accidentally uploaded incorrect files to a Snowflake internal stage. Which of the following commands allows the user to replace those files during the upload process?
Select 1 answer:
A) PUT WITH FORCE=TRUE
B) REMOVE WITH REPLACE=TRUE
C) COPY INTO WITH FORCE=TRUE
D) UPDATE STAGE

Question 48:

You have a Snowflake internal stage named my_stage. You want to view all the files currently stored in the stage. Which of the following is the correct syntax?
Select 1 answer:
A) SHOW FILES IN my_stage;
B) LIST @my_stage;
C) DESCRIBE FILES IN my_stage;
D) SELECT FILES FROM @my_stage;

Question 49:

A user has deleted a file from a Snowflake internal stage using the REMOVE command. Which of the following is true about recovering the deleted file?
Select 1 answer:
A) Files can be recovered using the RESTORE FILE command.
B) Deleted files cannot be recovered from a Snowflake internal stage.
C) Files can be recovered from the Snowflake recycle bin.
D) Use the ROLLBACK FILE command to restore the file.

Question 50:

Which of the following storage locations are **automatically** provided with Snowflake internal stages?
Select 1 answer:
A) AWS S3
B) Snowflake-managed cloud storage
C) Google Cloud Storage
D) Azure Blob Storage

Answers and Explanations

Question 46:

Correct Answer: A
Explanation:

A is correct because the PUT command is used to upload local files to a Snowflake internal stage.

B is incorrect because COPY INTO is used to load data from a stage into a Snowflake table, not to upload files to a stage.

C is incorrect because UPLOAD FILE is not a valid Snowflake command.

D is incorrect because ADD FILE is not a valid Snowflake command.

Question 47:

Correct Answer: A
Explanation:

A is correct because PUT with the option FORCE=TRUE allows overwriting files that already exist in the internal stage.

B is incorrect because REMOVE deletes files but does not allow replacement during upload.

C is incorrect because COPY INTO loads data into a table but cannot replace files in the stage.

D is incorrect because UPDATE STAGE is not a valid Snowflake command.

Question 48:

Correct Answer: B
Explanation:

B is correct because the LIST command is used to display all files in a Snowflake internal or external stage, and the stage is referenced with @.

A is incorrect because SHOW FILES IN is not valid syntax in Snowflake.

C is incorrect because DESCRIBE FILES is not a valid Snowflake command.

D is incorrect because SELECT FILES FROM is invalid syntax for listing files in a stage.

Question 49:

Correct Answer: B
Explanation:

B is correct because files deleted from a Snowflake internal stage using the REMOVE command cannot be recovered. Once removed, they are permanently deleted.

A is incorrect because RESTORE FILE is not a valid Snowflake command.

C is incorrect because Snowflake does not have a recycle bin for staged files.

D is incorrect because ROLLBACK FILE is not a valid Snowflake command.

Question 50:

Correct Answer: B
Explanation:

B is correct because Snowflake internal stages use Snowflake-managed cloud storage automatically provided by Snowflake (backed by S3, Azure Blob, or GCS, depending on the Snowflake region).

A is incorrect because AWS S3 is external storage, not an internal stage.

C is incorrect because Google Cloud Storage is external storage.

D is incorrect because Azure Blob Storage is also external storage.

Question 51:

Which command shows all stages in the current schema?

Select 1 answer:

A) SHOW STAGES

B) DESCRIBE STAGES

C) LIST STAGES

D) DISPLAY STAGES

Question 52:

What does the CREATE STAGE command require when creating an external stage?

Select 1 answer:

A) The storage location URL

B) The file format type

C) Credentials for access

D) Both A and C

Question 53:

Which of the following options can you set when creating a file format for a stage?

Select 1 answer:

A) FIELD_OPTIONALLY_ENCLOSED_BY

B) STORAGE_INTEGRATION

C) STAGE_TYPE

D) COMPRESSION_TYPE

Question 54:

Which command would you use to unload data while applying a transformation in Snowflake?

Select 1 answer:

A) COPY INTO with a transformation

B) TRANSFER INTO with a condition

C) MOVE INTO with a transformation

D) EXTRACT INTO with a filter

Question 55:

Which of the following commands would you use to create a stage with specific file format options like compression?

Select 1 answer:

A) CREATE STAGE

B) CREATE STAGE with FILE_FORMAT options

C) CREATE FILE FORMAT

D) CREATE FILE OPTIONS

Answers and Explanations:

Question 51:

Correct Answers: A

Explanation:

A is correct because the SHOW STAGES command lists all stages in the current schema.

B is incorrect because DESCRIBE STAGES is not a valid Snowflake command for listing stages.

C is incorrect because LIST STAGES does not exist as a command.

D is incorrect because DISPLAY STAGES is not a valid Snowflake command.

Question 52:

Correct Answers: D

Explanation:

D is correct because when creating an external stage using the CREATE STAGE command, you must specify both the storage location URL and credentials for access.

A is incorrect because just specifying the storage location URL is insufficient; credentials for access are also required.

B is incorrect because the file format type is not required when creating an external stage.

C is incorrect because specifying credentials alone is not enough; the storage location URL is also necessary.

Question 53:

Correct Answers: A

Explanation:

A is correct because FIELD_OPTIONALLY_ENCLOSED_BY is a valid option for setting the field enclosure behavior when creating a file format.

B is incorrect because STORAGE_INTEGRATION is used for storage integration but not for creating a file format.

C is incorrect because STAGE_TYPE is related to stages, not file formats.

D is incorrect because COMPRESSION_TYPE is not a valid option for setting when creating a file format.

Question 54:

Correct Answers: A

Explanation:

A is correct because COPY INTO can be used to unload data while applying transformations during the process.

B is incorrect because TRANSFER INTO is not a valid Snowflake command for unloading data with a condition.

C is incorrect because MOVE INTO is not used for unloading data with a transformation.

D is incorrect because EXTRACT INTO is not a valid command for unloading data in Snowflake.

Question 55:

Correct Answers: B

Explanation:

B is correct because CREATE STAGE with FILE_FORMAT options is used when creating a stage and specifying file format options like compression.

A is incorrect because CREATE STAGE alone does not include file format options; you need to specify them as part of the stage creation.

C is incorrect because CREATE FILE FORMAT is used to define file formats, not stages.

D is incorrect because CREATE FILE OPTIONS is not a valid Snowflake command.

Question 56:

Which command is used to list the files in a Snowflake stage?

A) SHOW FILES IN STAGE

B) LIST FILES

C) LIST @stage_name

D) DESCRIBE FILES IN STAGE

Question 57:

Which of the following file formats is NOT directly supported by Snowflake when creating a stage?

A) CSV

B) JSON

C) ORC

D) XML

Question 58:

How do you specify a file format while creating an external stage in Snowflake?

A) FILE_FORMAT = (FORMAT_TYPE = 'CSV')

B) FILE_TYPE = 'CSV'

C) FORMAT = 'CSV'

D) EXTERNAL_FILE_FORMAT = 'CSV'

Question 59:

What does the REMOVE command do in relation to Snowflake stages?

A) Removes a stage from Snowflake

B) Deletes files from a stage

C) Deletes a file format from a stage

D) Removes data from a table

Question 60:

What is the default behavior of Snowflake when loading data from a stage without specifying a file format?

A) It automatically infers the format

B) It raises an error

C) It uses CSV by default

D) It uses JSON by default

Answers and Explanations:

Question 56:

Correct Answers: C

Explanation:

C is correct because LIST @stage_name is the correct command to list files in a specific stage in Snowflake.

A is incorrect because SHOW FILES IN STAGE is not a valid Snowflake command.

B is incorrect because LIST FILES is not a valid Snowflake command to list files in a stage.

D is incorrect because DESCRIBE FILES IN STAGE is not a valid Snowflake command for listing files.

Question 57:

Correct Answers: D

Explanation:

D is correct because Snowflake does not directly support the XML format when creating a stage.

A is incorrect because CSV is a supported file format in Snowflake.

B is incorrect because JSON is also a supported file format.

C is incorrect because ORC is a supported file format in Snowflake.

Question 58:

Correct Answers: A

Explanation:

A is correct because FILE_FORMAT = (FORMAT_TYPE = 'CSV') is the correct syntax to specify a file format while creating an external stage in Snowflake.

B is incorrect because FILE_TYPE = 'CSV' is not a valid option in Snowflake's stage creation.

C is incorrect because FORMAT = 'CSV' is not valid syntax for specifying file formats.

D is incorrect because EXTERNAL_FILE_FORMAT = 'CSV' is not a valid Snowflake syntax.

Question 59:

Correct Answers: B

Explanation:

B is correct because the REMOVE command in Snowflake is used to delete files from a stage.

A is incorrect because REMOVE does not delete a stage; it deletes files from the stage.

C is incorrect because the REMOVE command does not delete a file format from a stage.

D is incorrect because REMOVE is unrelated to removing data from a table.

Question 60:

Correct Answers: A

Explanation:

A is correct because Snowflake automatically infers the file format if none is specified when loading data from a stage.

B is incorrect because Snowflake does not raise an error in this case; it automatically infers the format.

C is incorrect because CSV is not used by default unless inferred by Snowflake.

D is incorrect because JSON is not the default; Snowflake attempts to infer the format first.

Question 61:

Which of the following options can you use to restrict file formats in a Snowflake stage?

A) FILE_FORMAT_TYPE

B) VALID_FILE_FORMATS

C) FILE_FORMAT

D) FORMAT_TYPE

Question 62:

Which Snowflake command is used to modify the properties of a stage?

A) ALTER STAGE

B) UPDATE STAGE

C) CHANGE STAGE

D) MODIFY STAGE

Question 63:

In the context of Snowflake, what is a named stage?

A) A stage with no file format

B) A stage that is created and stored in the database schema

C) A stage pointing to a specific S3 bucket

D) A stage that stores only compressed files

Question 64:

What is the purpose of the STAGE_TYPE property in a Snowflake stage?

A) To specify the file format of the stage

B) To define whether the stage is external or internal

C) To define the storage integration for the stage

D) To set the access permissions of the stage

Question 65:

Which of the following is a valid syntax to create an internal stage in Snowflake?

A) CREATE STAGE internal_stage

B) CREATE INTERNAL STAGE internal_stage

C) CREATE STAGE INTERNAL external_stage

D) CREATE STAGE STAGE_NAME LOCATION = 'path'

Answers and Explanations:

Question 61:

Correct Answers: C

Explanation:

C is correct because FILE_FORMAT is the correct option to specify and restrict file formats in a Snowflake stage.

A is incorrect because FILE_FORMAT_TYPE is not a valid option in Snowflake.

B is incorrect because VALID_FILE_FORMATS is not a valid Snowflake command for restricting file formats.

D is incorrect because FORMAT_TYPE does not restrict file formats in Snowflake.

Question 62:

Correct Answers: A

Explanation:

A is correct because ALTER STAGE is the Snowflake command used to modify the properties of an existing stage.

B is incorrect because UPDATE STAGE is not a valid Snowflake command for modifying stage properties.

C is incorrect because CHANGE STAGE is not a valid Snowflake command for modifying stage properties.

D is incorrect because MODIFY STAGE is not a valid Snowflake command for modifying stage properties.

Question 63:

Correct Answers: B

Explanation:

B is correct because a named stage in Snowflake is created and stored in the database schema, which can be referenced by name.

A is incorrect because a named stage in Snowflake typically has a file format.

C is incorrect because a named stage does not necessarily point to a specific S3 bucket.

D is incorrect because a named stage can store various file types, not just compressed files.

Question 64:

Correct Answers: B

Explanation:

B is correct because the STAGE_TYPE property in Snowflake stages is used to define whether the stage is external (e.g., linked to S3) or internal (e.g., located within Snowflake).

A is incorrect because STAGE_TYPE does not specify the file format; it specifies the type of stage (external or internal).

C is incorrect because STAGE_TYPE does not define storage integration; it is related to the stage's type.

D is incorrect because STAGE_TYPE does not set access permissions.

Question 65:

Correct Answers: B

Explanation:

B is correct because CREATE INTERNAL STAGE internal_stage is the valid syntax to create an internal stage in Snowflake.

A is incorrect because CREATE STAGE internal_stage is not valid without specifying the internal keyword.

C is incorrect because CREATE STAGE INTERNAL external_stage is incorrect syntax for internal stages.

D is incorrect because CREATE STAGE STAGE_NAME LOCATION = 'path' is not the correct syntax for creating an internal stage.

Question 61:

Which of the following options can you use to restrict file formats in a Snowflake stage?

Select 1 answer:

A) FILE_FORMAT_TYPE

B) VALID_FILE_FORMATS

C) FILE_FORMAT

D) FORMAT_TYPE

Question 62:

Which Snowflake command is used to modify the properties of a stage?

Select 1 answer:

A) ALTER STAGE

B) UPDATE STAGE

C) CHANGE STAGE

D) MODIFY STAGE

Question 63:

In the context of Snowflake, what is a named stage?

Select 1 answer:

A) A stage with no file format

B) A stage that is created and stored in the database schema

C) A stage pointing to a specific S3 bucket

D) A stage that stores only compressed files

Question 64:

What is the purpose of the STAGE_TYPE property in a Snowflake stage?

Select 1 answer:

A) To specify the file format of the stage

B) To define whether the stage is external or internal

C) To define the storage integration for the stage

D) To set the access permissions of the stage

Question 65:

Which of the following is a valid syntax to create an internal stage in Snowflake?

Select 1 answer:

A) CREATE STAGE internal_stage

B) CREATE INTERNAL STAGE internal_stage

C) CREATE STAGE INTERNAL external_stage

D) CREATE STAGE STAGE_NAME LOCATION = 'path'

Answers and Explanations:

Question 61:

Correct Answers: C

Explanation:

C is correct because FILE_FORMAT is the correct option to specify and restrict file formats in a Snowflake stage.

A is incorrect because FILE_FORMAT_TYPE is not a valid option in Snowflake.

B is incorrect because VALID_FILE_FORMATS is not a valid Snowflake command for restricting file formats.

D is incorrect because FORMAT_TYPE does not restrict file formats in Snowflake.

Question 62:

Correct Answers: A

Explanation:

A is correct because ALTER STAGE is the Snowflake command used to modify the properties of an existing stage.

B is incorrect because UPDATE STAGE is not a valid Snowflake command for modifying stage properties.

C is incorrect because CHANGE STAGE is not a valid Snowflake command for modifying stage properties.

D is incorrect because MODIFY STAGE is not a valid Snowflake command for modifying stage properties.

Question 63:

Correct Answers: B

Explanation:

B is correct because a named stage in Snowflake is created and stored in the database schema, which can be referenced by name.

A is incorrect because a named stage in Snowflake typically has a file format.

C is incorrect because a named stage does not necessarily point to a specific S3 bucket.

D is incorrect because a named stage can store various file types, not just compressed files.

Question 64:

Correct Answers: B

Explanation:

B is correct because the STAGE_TYPE property in Snowflake stages is used to define whether the stage is external (e.g., linked to S3) or internal (e.g., located within Snowflake).

A is incorrect because STAGE_TYPE does not specify the file format; it specifies the type of stage (external or internal).

C is incorrect because STAGE_TYPE does not define storage integration; it is related to the stage's type.

D is incorrect because STAGE_TYPE does not set access permissions.

Question 65:

Correct Answers: B

Explanation:

B is correct because CREATE INTERNAL STAGE internal_stage is the valid syntax to create an internal stage in Snowflake.

A is incorrect because CREATE STAGE internal_stage is not valid without specifying the internal keyword.

C is incorrect because CREATE STAGE INTERNAL external_stage is incorrect syntax for internal stages.

D is incorrect because CREATE STAGE STAGE_NAME LOCATION = 'path' is not the correct syntax for creating an internal stage.

WAREHOUSES

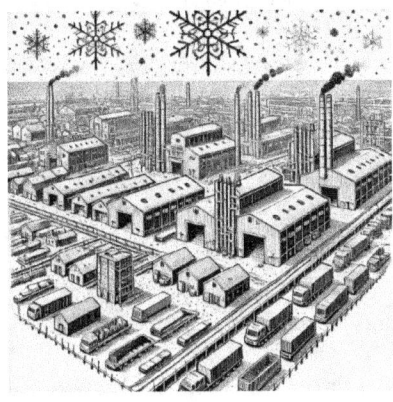

Question #1:
Which of the following SQL statements is used to resize a Snowflake virtual warehouse?
Options:
A. ALTER WAREHOUSE my_warehouse SET SIZE = 'XSMALL';
B. RESIZE WAREHOUSE my_warehouse TO 'XSMALL';
C. ALTER WAREHOUSE my_warehouse SET WAREHOUSE_SIZE = 'XSMALL';
D. CHANGE WAREHOUSE SIZE my_warehouse TO 'XSMALL';

Question #2:
What is the correct SQL syntax to suspend a Snowflake virtual warehouse?
Options:
A. SUSPEND WAREHOUSE my_warehouse;
B. ALTER WAREHOUSE my_warehouse SUSPEND;
C. STOP WAREHOUSE my_warehouse;
D. SUSPEND WAREHOUSE my_warehouse NOW;

Question #3.
What is the correct command to resume a suspended Snowflake virtual warehouse?
Options:
A. START WAREHOUSE my_warehouse;
B. RESUME WAREHOUSE my_warehouse;
C. ALTER WAREHOUSE my_warehouse RESUME;
D. UNSUSPEND WAREHOUSE my_warehouse;

Question #4.
Which of the following commands will show the status of a Snowflake warehouse?
Options:
A. SHOW WAREHOUSE my_warehouse STATUS;
B. SHOW WAREHOUSE STATUS FOR my_warehouse;
C. DESCRIBE WAREHOUSE my_warehouse;
D. SELECT STATUS FROM WAREHOUSES WHERE NAME = 'my_warehouse';

Question #5.

How would you modify the concurrency scaling policy of a Snowflake warehouse?

Options:

A. ALTER WAREHOUSE my_warehouse SET CONCURRENCY_SCALING = TRUE;
B. ALTER WAREHOUSE my_warehouse SET SCALING_POLICY = 'STANDARD';
C. SET WAREHOUSE my_warehouse SCALING_POLICY = 'ECONOMY';
D. MODIFY WAREHOUSE my_warehouse CONCURRENCY_SCALING = ON;

Question #1:
Correct Answer: A
Explanation:

A is Correct. The correct syntax for resizing a warehouse in Snowflake is using ALTER WAREHOUSE <name> SET SIZE = <size>
B is incorrect because RESIZE is not a valid Snowflake SQL keyword.
C is incorrect because WAREHOUSE_SIZE is not a valid parameter.
D is incorrect because CHANGE is not used to resize a warehouse.

Question #2:
Correct Answer: B
Explanation:

A is incorrect because SUSPEND WAREHOUSE is not a valid syntax.
B is correct. The correct syntax to suspend a warehouse is ALTER WAREHOUSE <name> SUSPEND;
C is incorrect because STOP is not a valid Snowflake SQL command for suspending a warehouse.
D is incorrect because NOW is not needed in the syntax.

Question #3:
Correct Answer: B
Explanation:

A is incorrect because START is not a valid Snowflake command to resume a warehouse.
B is correct. The correct syntax to resume a warehouse is RESUME WAREHOUSE <name>;
C is incorrect because ALTER WAREHOUSE is not required for the resume command.
D is incorrect because UNSUSPEND is not a valid command.

Question #4:
Correct Answer: A
Explanation:

A is correct. The correct syntax to show the status of a warehouse is SHOW WAREHOUSE <name> STATUS;.
B is incorrect because SHOW WAREHOUSE STATUS FOR is not valid syntax.
C is incorrect because DESCRIBE shows metadata, but not the status.
D is incorrect because SELECT is not used to query the warehouse status.

Question #5:
Correct Answer: A
Explanation:

A is correct. To enable concurrency scaling, use ALTER WAREHOUSE <name> SET CONCURRENCY_SCALING = TRUE;.

B is incorrect because SCALING_POLICY is not a valid parameter in the ALTER WAREHOUSE command.
C is incorrect because SET WAREHOUSE is not a valid command to modify concurrency scaling.
D is incorrect because MODIFY is not a valid Snowflake command.

Question #6.
What command is used to view the current usage of compute resources for a Snowflake warehouse?
Options:
A. SHOW WAREHOUSE USAGE my_warehouse;
B. SELECT USAGE FROM WAREHOUSE WHERE NAME = 'my_warehouse';
C. DESCRIBE WAREHOUSE my_warehouse USAGE;
D. SHOW WAREHOUSE my_warehouse USAGE;

Question #7.
Which SQL command is used to set the size of a Snowflake virtual warehouse?
Options:
A. ALTER WAREHOUSE my_warehouse SIZE = 'MEDIUM';
B. SET WAREHOUSE my_warehouse TO 'MEDIUM';
C. RESIZE WAREHOUSE my_warehouse TO 'MEDIUM';
D. ALTER WAREHOUSE my_warehouse SET SIZE = 'MEDIUM';

Question #8.
Which of the following statements is used to show the compute credits used by a Snowflake virtual warehouse?
Options:
A. SHOW WAREHOUSE CREDIT_USAGE my_warehouse;
B. SELECT CREDIT_USAGE FROM WAREHOUSE WHERE NAME = 'my_warehouse';
C. SHOW WAREHOUSE USAGE my_warehouse;
D. DESCRIBE WAREHOUSE USAGE my_warehouse;

Question #9.
How can you change the scaling policy for a Snowflake multi-cluster warehouse?
Options:
A. ALTER WAREHOUSE my_warehouse SET SCALING_POLICY = 'ECONOMY';
B. SET WAREHOUSE my_warehouse SCALING_POLICY = 'STANDARD';
C. CHANGE WAREHOUSE my_warehouse TO SCALING_POLICY 'ECONOMY';
D. MODIFY WAREHOUSE my_warehouse SET SCALING_POLICY = 'ECONOMY';

Question #6:
Correct Answer: D
Explanation:
A is incorrect because SHOW WAREHOUSE USAGE is valid but requires the warehouse name after SHOW.
B is incorrect because SELECT is not used to query warehouse usage.
C is incorrect because DESCRIBE does not show usage statistics.

D is correct. To view current warehouse usage, use SHOW WAREHOUSE <name> USAGE;.

Question #7:
Correct Answer: D
Explanation:
A is incorrect because SIZE = is not valid without SET.
B is incorrect because SET WAREHOUSE is not used for resizing.
C is incorrect because RESIZE WAREHOUSE is not valid syntax in Snowflake.
D is correct. The correct syntax to resize a warehouse is ALTER WAREHOUSE <name> SET SIZE = <size>.

Question #8:
Correct Answer: C
Explanation:
A is incorrect because SHOW WAREHOUSE CREDIT_USAGE is not a valid command.
B is incorrect because SELECT is not used to query warehouse usage or credits.
C is correct. To view compute usage and credit consumption, use SHOW WAREHOUSE <name> USAGE;.
D is incorrect because DESCRIBE does not show credit usage or compute resources.

Question #9:
Correct Answer: A
Explanation:
A is correct. Use ALTER WAREHOUSE <name> SET SCALING_POLICY = <policy>; to change the scaling policy.
B is incorrect because SET WAREHOUSE is not a valid command for changing scaling policy.
C is incorrect because CHANGE WAREHOUSE is not valid syntax.
D is incorrect because MODIFY is not a valid Snowflake SQL command.

Question #10.
What is the correct SQL syntax to enable auto-suspend on a Snowflake virtual warehouse?
Options:
A. ALTER WAREHOUSE my_warehouse SET AUTO_SUSPEND = 10;
B. ENABLE AUTO_SUSPEND FOR WAREHOUSE my_warehouse TO 10;
C. SET WAREHOUSE my_warehouse AUTO_SUSPEND = 10 MINUTES;
D. ALTER WAREHOUSE my_warehouse SET SUSPEND_AFTER 10 MINUTES;

Question #11.
You have a nightly ETL job that runs for a few hours. You need to ensure sufficient compute power for processing but avoid incurring idle costs after the ETL completes.
Options:
A. Create a large warehouse and set AUTO_SUSPEND to 1 minute.
B. Enable multi-cluster with "Economy" scaling policy.
C. Disable AUTO_SUSPEND to ensure continuous operation.
D. Set a small warehouse with AUTO_RESUME.

Question #12.
You have a reporting workload that requires high concurrency during business hours but

minimal usage outside. How would you configure it for optimal performance and cost?
Options:
A. Enable multi-cluster mode with MAX_CLUSTER_COUNT = 3.
B. Set the warehouse size to MEDIUM and enable AUTO_SUSPEND.
C. Use a single LARGE warehouse with AUTO_SUSPEND disabled.
D. Enable AUTO_RESUME and set the scaling policy to "Economy."

Question #13.
An analytics team needs ad-hoc access during the day. How can you keep costs low while ensuring the warehouse is available for these sporadic queries?
Options:
A. Set a short AUTO_SUSPEND timeout and enable AUTO_RESUME.
B. Use multi-cluster mode with a maximum of two clusters.
C. Increase the warehouse size to LARGE.
D. Disable AUTO_RESUME to control availability.

Question #14:
A data engineering team needs high compute power for an intensive workload running every morning. What configuration should you set to optimize for performance and efficiency?
Options:
A. Set the warehouse to LARGE and AUTO_SUSPEND after completion.
B. Use multi-cluster mode with "Standard" scaling.
C. Disable AUTO_SUSPEND to avoid interruptions.
D. Increase MIN_CLUSTER_COUNT to ensure minimum capacity.

Question #10:
Correct Answer: A
Explanation:
A is correct. The correct syntax to enable auto-suspend is ALTER WAREHOUSE <name> SET AUTO_SUSPEND = <time>.
B is incorrect because ENABLE AUTO_SUSPEND FOR is not valid syntax.
C is incorrect because SET WAREHOUSE is not used for auto-suspend configuration.
D is incorrect because SUSPEND_AFTER is not a valid parameter.

Question #11:
Correct Answer: A and D
Explanation:
A is correct because creating a large warehouse ensures sufficient compute power for the ETL job. Setting AUTO_SUSPEND to 1 minute helps minimize idle costs by suspending the warehouse shortly after the job completes.
D is correct because using a small warehouse with AUTO_RESUME minimizes costs when the warehouse is idle but ensures it automatically starts when the job begins. This setup is particularly cost-effective if the workload can tolerate a small warehouse.
B is incorrect because enabling multi-cluster with an "Economy" scaling policy is more suitable for unpredictable, high-concurrency workloads rather than a consistent nightly ETL job. This configuration may result in unnecessary costs due to provisioning multiple clusters.
C is incorrect because disabling AUTO_SUSPEND keeps the warehouse running continuously, which incurs idle costs even when no ETL jobs are running. This goes against the goal of minimizing costs after the ETL completes.

Question #12:
Correct Answer: A and B
Explanation:
A is correct because enabling multi-cluster mode with MAX_CLUSTER_COUNT = 3 ensures high concurrency during peak business hours by provisioning additional clusters as needed. This configuration optimizes performance for concurrent queries while limiting the number of clusters to control costs.
B is correct because setting the warehouse size to MEDIUM and enabling AUTO_SUSPEND ensures moderate compute power for reporting workloads while minimizing costs during periods of inactivity.
C is incorrect because using a single LARGE warehouse with AUTO_SUSPEND disabled leads to unnecessary costs during idle periods outside business hours.
D is incorrect because setting the scaling policy to "Economy" is not ideal for workloads requiring high concurrency, as this policy prioritizes cost over performance and might not handle peak workloads efficiently.

Question #13:
Correct Answer: A and B
Explanation:
A is correct because setting a short AUTO_SUSPEND timeout and enabling AUTO_RESUME ensures the warehouse is suspended quickly when idle, minimizing costs, and automatically resumes when a query is executed, ensuring availability during sporadic use.
B is correct because using multi-cluster mode with a maximum of two clusters ensures that the warehouse scales for high concurrency during busy periods while controlling costs by limiting the number of clusters.
C is incorrect because increasing the warehouse size to LARGE would result in unnecessary costs for sporadic queries. A smaller warehouse would be more cost-effective.
D is incorrect because disabling AUTO_RESUME would require manual intervention to start the warehouse, leading to delays and reducing availability for the analytics team.

Question #14:
Correct Answer: A and D
Explanation:
A is correct because setting the warehouse size to LARGE ensures sufficient compute power for the workload, while setting AUTO_SUSPEND ensures the warehouse is suspended when not in use, minimizing idle costs.
D is correct because increasing the MIN_CLUSTER_COUNT ensures that a minimum number of clusters are always available for performance, which is essential for high compute tasks that need reliability.
B is incorrect because using multi-cluster mode with "Standard" scaling is not as efficient for daily intensive workloads, which might not require multiple clusters.
C is incorrect because disabling AUTO_SUSPEND will result in continuous running of the warehouse, incurring higher costs.

Question #15
Your company has unpredictable spikes in traffic, and you want to handle them without continuously running the warehouse. What setup is ideal?
Options:
A. Enable multi-cluster mode with MAX_CLUSTER_COUNT = 5.

B. Increase the warehouse size to XLARGE.
C. Use AUTO_RESUME and set AUTO_SUSPEND to a short timeout.
D. Set the scaling policy to "Economy."

Question #16
A small team runs frequent but lightweight queries. You want to ensure low costs with adequate performance.
Options:
A. Use a SMALL warehouse with AUTO_SUSPEND.
B. Increase the warehouse size to LARGE.
C. Enable AUTO_RESUME and set a short AUTO_SUSPEND timeout.
D. Enable multi-cluster mode with "Standard" scaling policy.

Question #17
A data processing job requires high compute capacity but only runs once a day. Which configuration ensures the job runs efficiently without idle costs?
Options:
A. Use a LARGE warehouse with AUTO_SUSPEND.
B. Enable AUTO_RESUME with a short timeout.
C. Use multi-cluster mode for scalability.
D. Set AUTO_SUSPEND to "Never."

Question #18
A high-concurrency workload requires immediate availability and performance scaling. How would you configure the warehouse?
Options:
A. Enable multi-cluster with "Standard" scaling policy.
B. Set a LARGE warehouse with AUTO_RESUME.
C. Disable AUTO_SUSPEND to avoid startup delays.
D. Set MIN_CLUSTER_COUNT to 2.

Question #19
Your team requires short bursts of compute power during business hours but not outside of it. What configuration would ensure the warehouse is available only when needed?
Options:
A. Enable AUTO_RESUME and set AUTO_SUSPEND to a short timeout.
B. Disable AUTO_SUSPEND during business hours.
C. Use multi-cluster mode with MAX_CLUSTER_COUNT = 3.
D. Set a small warehouse with "Economy" scaling.

Question #15:
Correct Answer: A and C
Explanation:
A is correct because enabling multi-cluster mode with a MAX_CLUSTER_COUNT of 5 allows the warehouse to scale dynamically to handle traffic spikes while controlling costs by limiting the maximum number of clusters.
C is correct because using AUTO_RESUME and setting a short AUTO_SUSPEND timeout ensures that the warehouse only runs when needed, minimizing idle costs.

B is incorrect because increasing the warehouse size to XLARGE is excessive for handling spikes and would result in higher ongoing costs, even when not needed.
D is incorrect because the "Economy" scaling policy is more suitable for minimizing costs during off-peak times, but multi-cluster mode with proper scaling controls is better for handling unpredictable traffic.

Question #16:
Correct Answer: A and C
Explanation:
A is correct because using a SMALL warehouse minimizes costs while providing sufficient performance for lightweight queries. The AUTO_SUSPEND setting ensures the warehouse is suspended when not in use.
C is correct because enabling AUTO_RESUME and setting a short AUTO_SUSPEND timeout helps ensure the warehouse is available when needed, while minimizing idle time and costs.
B is incorrect because increasing the warehouse size to LARGE is unnecessary and would result in higher costs, which is not ideal for a small team running lightweight queries.
D is incorrect because enabling multi-cluster mode with "Standard" scaling is overkill for a small team with lightweight queries, as it introduces unnecessary complexity and cost.

Question #17:
Correct Answer: A and B
Explanation:
A is correct because using a LARGE warehouse ensures that the job has sufficient compute power while the AUTO_SUSPEND setting ensures that the warehouse is suspended when the job is not running, avoiding idle costs.
B is correct because enabling AUTO_RESUME ensures that the warehouse automatically resumes when the job starts and suspends when done, minimizing idle time and costs.
C is incorrect because multi-cluster mode is unnecessary for a job that runs only once a day and does not require scalability for concurrency.
D is incorrect because setting AUTO_SUSPEND to "Never" would mean the warehouse stays active indefinitely, leading to higher costs.

Question #18:
Correct Answer: A and D
Explanation:
A is correct because enabling multi-cluster mode with "Standard" scaling allows the warehouse to scale up immediately based on high concurrency demands, providing the necessary resources when needed.
D is correct because setting MIN_CLUSTER_COUNT to 2 ensures that at least two clusters are always available, which is necessary for high concurrency workloads.
B is incorrect because setting a LARGE warehouse alone may not be sufficient to handle high concurrency efficiently, and it would lead to higher costs.
C is incorrect because disabling AUTO_SUSPEND would result in continuous running of the warehouse, incurring unnecessary costs.

Question #19:
Correct Answer: A and C
Explanation:
A is correct because enabling AUTO_RESUME with a short AUTO_SUSPEND timeout ensures that the warehouse only runs during business hours, minimizing idle costs.
C is correct because using multi-cluster mode with MAX_CLUSTER_COUNT set to 3 ensures the warehouse can scale during business hours, while also controlling costs by limiting the number of clusters.

B is incorrect because disabling AUTO_SUSPEND would result in continuous operation during business hours, which could lead to higher costs.
D is incorrect because using a small warehouse with "Economy" scaling might not provide the necessary compute power for bursts during business hours.

Question #20
A scheduled task requires continuous availability for multiple queries over a short duration each day. How would you configure the warehouse for efficiency?
Options:
A. Use a LARGE warehouse and disable AUTO_SUSPEND.
B. Enable AUTO_RESUME and set AUTO_SUSPEND for minimal idle time.
C. Set up multi-cluster mode with "Economy" scaling.
D. Use a small warehouse and set AUTO_SUSPEND to "Never."

Question #21.
Which of the following statements are true about Snowflake's virtual warehouses?
Options:
A. Warehouses can automatically suspend and resume based on activity.
B. Warehouses are billed based on the amount of data stored.
C. A warehouse can have multiple concurrent clusters in multi-cluster mode.
D. Virtual warehouses process queries but do not store data.

Question #22.
What determines the scaling of virtual warehouses in Snowflake's multi-cluster mode?
Options:
A. User-defined query concurrency thresholds.
B. Storage capacity within the warehouse.
C. Load balancing on warehouse clusters.
D. Total number of users accessing the warehouse.

Question #23.
Which Snowflake feature allows a virtual warehouse to start automatically when a query is submitted?
Options:
A. Auto-Resume
B. Scaling Policy
C. Multi-cluster Mode
D. Query Acceleration

Question #24.
In Snowflake, what is the primary purpose of a virtual warehouse?
Options:
A. To store tables and databases.
B. To execute data processing tasks.
C. To manage user authentication.
D. To optimize disk storage.

Question #20:
Correct Answer: B and C
Explanation:
B is correct because enabling AUTO_RESUME ensures the warehouse is available when the task starts, and setting a short AUTO_SUSPEND timeout minimizes idle time, ensuring efficient cost management.
C is correct because multi-cluster mode with the "Economy" scaling policy allows the warehouse to scale efficiently for multiple queries without excessive costs during off-peak times.
A is incorrect because disabling AUTO_SUSPEND would keep the warehouse running continuously, leading to unnecessary costs.
D is incorrect because setting AUTO_SUSPEND to "Never" would also result in continuous operation, incurring higher costs.

Question #21:
Correct Answer: A, C, D
Explanation:
A is correct. Snowflake's virtual warehouses can be configured to automatically suspend when idle and resume when activity is detected. This feature helps optimize compute costs.
B is incorrect. Warehouses are billed based on compute usage, not on the amount of data stored. Data storage costs are separate and billed based on the storage consumed in Snowflake.
C is correct. In multi-cluster mode, a warehouse can scale out to multiple concurrent clusters to handle varying query workloads. This ensures better performance for concurrent user queries.
D is correct. Virtual warehouses in Snowflake are compute resources designed to execute queries and do not store data. Data is stored in Snowflake's centralized storage layer, separate from the compute layer.

Question #22:
Correct Answer: A
Explanation:
A is correct. Multi-cluster mode in Snowflake scales warehouses based on user-defined concurrency thresholds. These thresholds specify when additional clusters should be added to manage higher workloads and ensure consistent performance.
B is incorrect. Storage capacity is not a factor in scaling virtual warehouses. Snowflake separates compute and storage, and scaling in multi-cluster mode is tied to query concurrency, not storage limits.
C is incorrect. While Snowflake uses load balancing across clusters, this is a result of scaling, not the determinant for scaling. The actual scaling decision is based on query concurrency thresholds.
D is incorrect. The total number of users does not directly trigger scaling. Scaling occurs when the workload or query concurrency exceeds the specified thresholds, not just because of the number of users accessing the warehouse.

Question #23:
Correct Answer: A
Explanation:

A is correct. The Auto-Resume feature enables a suspended warehouse to start automatically when a query is submitted, ensuring no manual intervention is needed to activate the warehouse.
B is incorrect. Scaling Policy governs how a warehouse scales in multi-cluster mode, not its ability to resume automatically.
C is incorrect. Multi-cluster mode deals with scaling clusters to handle workloads, but it does not control whether a warehouse starts automatically.
D is incorrect. Query Acceleration is a different feature designed to enhance query performance, not to manage warehouse suspension or resumption.

Question #24:
Correct Answer: B
Explanation:
A is incorrect. Tables and databases are stored in Snowflake's storage layer, separate from the compute resources provided by virtual warehouses.
B is correct. Virtual warehouses are designed to execute queries and perform data processing tasks, acting as the compute layer in Snowflake's architecture.
C is incorrect. User authentication is managed by Snowflake's centralized authentication and authorization systems, not by virtual warehouses.
D is incorrect. Disk storage optimization is part of Snowflake's storage architecture and not related to the functionality of virtual warehouses.

Question #25.
When a virtual warehouse is in auto-suspend mode, how does it affect billing?
Options:
A. Charges are incurred only while queries are running.
B. Billing continues even when there are no queries.
C. Charges are based solely on storage.
D. It reduces storage cost but not compute cost.

Question #26.
How does Snowflake's multi-cluster warehouse mode handle query concurrency?
Options:
A. By adding additional nodes to the warehouse.
B. By distributing queries across multiple clusters.
C. By increasing storage allocation.
D. By pausing unused clusters.

Question #27.
Which setting can be configured to specify how long a Snowflake warehouse should remain active without queries before it suspends?
Options:
A. Auto-Suspend Time
B. Query Timeout
C. Warehouse Scaling Policy
D. Cluster Concurrency Limit

Question #28.
Which of the following does not impact the compute cost of a Snowflake virtual warehouse?

Options:
A. The number of clusters in use.
B. The amount of storage in use.
C. The size of the warehouse (e.g., Small, Medium).
D. The duration the warehouse is running.

Question #29.
Which Snowflake feature allows for a warehouse to scale dynamically based on user concurrency needs?
Options:
A. Auto-Resume
B. Elastic Data Pool
C. Multi-cluster Warehouse
D. Storage Compression

Question #25:
Correct Answer: A
Explanation:
A is correct. When in auto-suspend mode, compute charges are incurred only when the warehouse is active and processing queries. This helps optimize costs during idle times.
B is incorrect. Billing does not continue when the warehouse is suspended.
C is incorrect. Compute costs are separate from storage costs; storage is billed independently regardless of warehouse activity.
D is incorrect. Auto-suspend affects compute costs, not storage costs.

Question #26:
Correct Answer: B
Explanation:
A is incorrect. Additional nodes are not added to a single cluster; instead, new clusters are spun up to handle load.
B is correct. Multi-cluster mode distributes queries across multiple clusters to efficiently handle high concurrency.
C is incorrect. Storage allocation does not directly impact query concurrency.
D is incorrect. Unused clusters are paused to optimize costs, but this does not explain how concurrency is handled.

Question #27:
Correct Answer: A
Explanation:
A is correct. Auto-suspend time is the configurable setting that determines the duration a warehouse remains active without queries before suspending.
B is incorrect. Query timeout refers to how long a query can run before it is automatically terminated.
C is incorrect. Warehouse scaling policy governs scaling behavior, not suspension.
D is incorrect. Cluster concurrency limit defines the maximum concurrency, unrelated to suspension behavior.

Question #28:
Correct Answer: B
Explanation:
A is incorrect. The number of clusters directly impacts compute costs in multi-cluster mode.
B is correct. Storage costs are billed separately and do not affect compute costs.
C is incorrect. The size of the warehouse determines compute costs based on the resources allocated.
D is incorrect. Compute costs are also influenced by the duration the warehouse is active.

Question #29:
Correct Answer: C
Explanation:
A is incorrect. Auto-Resume allows a warehouse to start automatically when a query is submitted but does not handle scaling.
B is incorrect. Elastic Data Pool is not a Snowflake feature related to scaling concurrency.
C is correct. Multi-cluster warehouses dynamically scale by adding or removing clusters to handle user concurrency demands.
D is incorrect. Storage Compression reduces data storage size but has no impact on warehouse scaling.

Question #30.
In Snowflake, what effect does choosing an "Economy" scaling policy for a multi-cluster warehouse have?
Options:
A. Reduces warehouse size during peak load times.
B. Prioritizes cost savings over immediate scaling.
C. Distributes compute resources equally among users.
D. Suspends unused clusters immediately to save storage.

Question #31.
What happens if you try to resume a Snowflake warehouse that is already running?
Options:
A. The warehouse will create a duplicate and start both.
B. Snowflake will throw an error.
C. The request will be ignored.
D. The warehouse will restart and reset its compute metrics.

Question #32.
When should you consider using a multi-cluster warehouse in Snowflake?
Options:
A. When you need more storage.
B. When you need higher query concurrency.
C. When you want data to be backed up automatically.
D. When you need additional network bandwidth.

Question #33.
Which of the following is the most cost-effective way to manage an infrequently used warehouse?
Options:

A. Set the warehouse to never suspend.
B. Set a short auto-suspend period.
C. Set up a multi-cluster warehouse.
D. Increase the warehouse size to reduce processing time.

Question #34.
Which statement best describes Snowflake's scaling policy in multi-cluster warehouses?
Options:
A. Only one cluster will be active at any time.
B. Clusters are added and removed based on query load.
C. Clusters are duplicated for each query to ensure performance.
D. Clusters only scale down but do not scale up.

Question #30:
Correct Answer: B
Explanation:
A is incorrect. "Economy" scaling does not reduce warehouse size; it adjusts the number of clusters more gradually during scaling.
B is correct. The "Economy" scaling policy is designed to prioritize cost savings by scaling more conservatively, potentially delaying additional cluster allocation.
C is incorrect. Distributing resources among users relates to query execution within a cluster, not the scaling policy.
D is incorrect. The "Economy" policy does not immediately suspend unused clusters; it focuses on gradual scaling behavior

Question #31.
Correct Answer: C
Explanation:
A is incorrect. Snowflake does not duplicate warehouses; only one instance of a warehouse is active at any time.
B is incorrect. Snowflake does not throw an error when attempting to resume an already running warehouse.
C is correct. When a warehouse is already running, a resume request is ignored since the warehouse is active.
D is incorrect. Snowflake does not reset or restart compute metrics for an active warehouse.

Question #32
Correct Answer: B
Explanation:
A is incorrect. Multi-cluster warehouses are designed to handle query concurrency, not to provide additional storage.
B is correct. Multi-cluster warehouses allow Snowflake to handle a high number of concurrent queries by activating multiple clusters dynamically.
C is incorrect. Data backups are managed by Snowflake's Time Travel and Fail-safe features, not by warehouses.
D is incorrect. Network bandwidth is not managed by the multi-cluster warehouse feature.

Question #33.
Correct Answer: B
Explanation:
A is incorrect. Leaving the warehouse running continuously for infrequent use results in unnecessary compute costs.
B is correct. Configuring a short auto-suspend period ensures the warehouse suspends quickly when idle, minimizing costs.
C is incorrect. Multi-cluster warehouses are for handling high concurrency, not for cost optimization of infrequent usage.
D is incorrect. Increasing warehouse size increases costs and is unnecessary for infrequent queries.

Question #34.
Correct Answer: B
Explanation:
A is incorrect. Multi-cluster warehouses can activate multiple clusters as needed for load balancing.
B is correct. Clusters are dynamically scaled up or down based on query load, ensuring performance efficiency.
C is incorrect. Queries are distributed across clusters rather than being duplicated.
D is incorrect. Clusters scale both up and down based on query demand.

Question #35.
What happens if all clusters of a multi-cluster warehouse are busy, and additional queries are submitted?
Options:
A. The queries will fail.
B. Additional clusters will be activated if scaling is enabled.
C. Queries will be queued until a cluster is free.
D. The warehouse will automatically increase its storage.

Question #36.
If a Snowflake warehouse is set to auto-suspend after 10 minutes, what is the best practice for a high-frequency query workload?
Options:
A. Keep the auto-suspend at 10 minutes.
B. Set the auto-suspend to a lower value.
C. Disable auto-suspend.
D. Set the warehouse to multi-cluster mode.

Question #37.
Which of the following configurations will help control costs if a warehouse is used infrequently during off-peak hours?
Options:
A. Use a large warehouse size and keep it running.
B. Enable auto-suspend with a short idle time.
C. Set the warehouse to "Economy" scaling policy.
D. Enable auto-resume only during peak hours.

Question #38.
Which scaling policy should be used for predictable workloads with moderate concurrency requirements in Snowflake?
Options:
A. Economy
B. Standard
C. Unlimited
D. High Performance

Question #39.
What happens to active queries if a Snowflake warehouse is suspended during their execution?
Options:
A. They are paused and continue once the warehouse resumes.
B. The queries fail and must be re-submitted.
C. They finish processing before the suspension.
D. They are transferred to another active warehouse.

Question #35.
Correct Answer: B and C
Explanation:
A is incorrect. Queries will not fail due to busy clusters; they are either queued or handled by scaling up.
B is correct. If scaling is enabled, new clusters are activated to handle the additional queries.
C is correct. If no scaling capacity is available, queries will be queued until resources become free.
D is incorrect. Storage capacity is unrelated to compute resources and does not affect query handling.

Question #36
Correct Answer: C
Explanation:
A and B are incorrect. Frequent queries will keep the warehouse active, causing unnecessary suspensions and resumptions, increasing costs and latency.
C is correct. Disabling auto-suspend ensures the warehouse remains active, reducing delays caused by repeated resumptions.
D is incorrect. Multi-cluster mode is designed to handle query concurrency, not frequent suspensions.

Question #37.
Correct Answer: B
Explanation:
A is incorrect. Keeping a large warehouse running unnecessarily increases compute costs.
B is correct. Setting auto-suspend with a short idle time minimizes compute costs by suspending the warehouse quickly during inactivity.
C is incorrect. The "Economy" scaling policy applies to multi-cluster warehouses, not infrequent use of single clusters.
D is incorrect. Auto-resume ensures the warehouse starts automatically for any workload, not just peak hours

Question #38.
Correct Answer: B
Explanation:
A is incorrect. The "Economy" scaling policy prioritizes cost savings and is more suitable for variable concurrency requirements.
B is correct. The "Standard" scaling policy balances performance and cost for predictable workloads with moderate concurrency.
C and D are incorrect. These are not valid scaling policies in Snowflake.

Question #39.
Correct Answer: C
Explanation:
A is incorrect. Queries do not pause during suspension; they complete if already started.
B is incorrect. Snowflake ensures that all active queries complete before the warehouse is suspended.
C is correct. Snowflake guarantees active queries finish processing before suspending the warehouse.
D is incorrect. Queries are not transferred to another warehouse.

Question #40.
Which action will most directly impact warehouse query performance in Snowflake?
Options:
A. Adjusting auto-resume settings.
B. Increasing the warehouse size.
C. Enabling multi-cluster mode with a "Standard" scaling policy.
D. Configuring Time Travel to a longer period.

Question #41.
Your company has a small warehouse configured for daily reporting tasks, but query performance is inconsistent during high-traffic periods. What configuration change would most likely improve performance while controlling costs?
A. Increase the warehouse size to Medium.
B. Enable multi-cluster mode with a maximum of two clusters.
C. Increase the auto-suspend period to reduce frequent suspending.
D. Configure warehouse scaling policy to "Economy."

Question #42.
You manage a Snowflake warehouse with an unpredictable workload, ranging from low to high concurrency. What setup would ensure cost-effective scaling while handling variable query demand?
A. Use a single large warehouse with no multi-cluster option.
B. Set up a small warehouse with auto-suspend and auto-resume enabled.
C. Use multi-cluster mode with "Economy" scaling policy.
D. Disable auto-suspend to ensure the warehouse is always available.

Question #43.

A virtual warehouse processes ad-hoc queries for analysts who work in different time zones. Which configuration would minimize costs while ensuring availability when queries are submitted?
A. Enable auto-suspend with a short idle timeout.
B. Increase the warehouse size to handle all users.
C. Set up a multi-cluster warehouse with unlimited scaling.
D. Disable auto-resume to control access times.

Question #44.

You need to run a resource-intensive ETL process every night at midnight. Which of the following configurations would ensure efficient processing without incurring high costs during idle hours?
A. Use a large warehouse with auto-suspend set to a long period.
B. Use a large warehouse with auto-suspend enabled immediately after queries complete.
C. Use a multi-cluster warehouse to ensure scalability.
D. Use a small warehouse and increase the auto-resume delay.

Question #45.

Your team frequently runs analytical queries on a large dataset, causing concurrency issues. Which configuration change would likely improve performance?
A. Increase the warehouse size to maximize compute resources.
B. Enable multi-cluster mode and set a maximum of 3 clusters.
C. Use a single extra-large warehouse.
D. Disable auto-suspend to prevent interruptions.

Question #40.
Correct Answer: B and C
Explanation:
A is incorrect. Auto-resume ensures the warehouse is available but does not affect query performance.
B is correct. Increasing the warehouse size provides more compute power, which improves query execution speed.
C is correct. Enabling multi-cluster mode with a "Standard" scaling policy ensures better performance by distributing queries across clusters.
D is incorrect. Time Travel is a data retention feature and does not directly impact query performance.

Question #41.
Correct Answer: B
Explanation:
A could improve performance but may increase costs without optimizing for traffic spikes.
C is incorrect as adjusting auto-suspend does not impact performance.
D prioritizes cost savings and may not improve query performance during high-traffic times.

Question #42.
Correct Answer: C
Explanation:

A lacks flexibility for variable demand and may lead to higher costs.
B will not handle high concurrency effectively due to the small warehouse size.
D would incur costs unnecessarily during low activity.

Question #43.
Correct Answer: A
Explanation:
B could increase costs without benefiting intermittent usage.
C may lead to higher costs since unlimited scaling isn't necessary for ad-hoc, low-frequency use.
D could prevent users from accessing the warehouse when needed.

Question #44.
Correct Answer: B
Explanation:
A may result in unnecessary costs if the warehouse remains active after the ETL finishes.
C would not be cost-effective for a fixed ETL schedule with low concurrency needs.
D may not provide the needed capacity for resource-intensive ETL processes.

Question #45:
Correct Answer: B
Explanation:
B is correct. Enabling multi-cluster mode with a maximum of 3 clusters allows Snowflake to handle high concurrency by scaling out compute resources when needed.
A is incorrect because increasing the warehouse size improves individual query performance but does not address concurrency issues effectively.
C is incorrect because a single extra-large warehouse may be expensive and still won't handle concurrency as efficiently as multiple clusters.
D is incorrect because disabling auto-suspend does not resolve concurrency issues and may result in unnecessary costs.

Question #46.

During peak business hours, your warehouse frequently reaches capacity, delaying queries. What approach would help handle high traffic while managing costs during off-peak times?
A. Use a single large warehouse and keep it running.
B. Enable multi-cluster mode with "Standard" scaling policy.
C. Increase the auto-suspend period.
D. Set the scaling policy to "Economy" and disable multi-cluster mode.

Question #47.

A business unit requires immediate response times for critical reports at the start of every hour. What is the best way to minimize startup delays?
A. Enable auto-resume and set auto-suspend to 1 minute.
B. Disable auto-suspend for the warehouse.
C. Increase warehouse size to ensure resources are always available.
D. Enable multi-cluster mode with "Economy" policy.

Question #48.

You have an irregular query load with low usage during weekends. How can you minimize costs while ensuring the warehouse is available during the week?
A. Set the warehouse to auto-suspend with a longer period over the weekend.
B. Manually suspend the warehouse on weekends.
C. Use a small warehouse with no auto-suspend.
D. Enable multi-cluster mode for peak performance on weekends.

Question #49.

Your organization runs a scheduled job every weekday that requires high compute power for a short duration. What configuration ensures efficiency without incurring high idle costs?
A. Use a large warehouse and keep it running during weekdays.
B. Enable auto-suspend with a short timeout and auto-resume.
C. Use a small warehouse and schedule a daily manual start and stop.
D. Set the warehouse scaling policy to "Economy."

Question #50.

You need to handle a variable workload that scales up significantly at random times. What is the best warehouse configuration for managing this without manual intervention?
A. Use a large warehouse and keep it active all day.
B. Use multi-cluster mode with a short auto-suspend setting.
C. Enable multi-cluster mode with an "Economy" scaling policy.
D. Use a small warehouse and rely on auto-resume only.

Question #46:
Correct Answer: B
Explanation:
B is correct. Enabling multi-cluster mode with the "Standard" scaling policy allows Snowflake to scale out during peak traffic and scale in during off-peak times, effectively managing both performance and costs.
A is incorrect because keeping a single large warehouse running continuously can be costly and does not dynamically adjust to traffic variations.
C is incorrect because increasing the auto-suspend period does not address the issue of capacity during peak hours.
D is incorrect because disabling multi-cluster mode limits scalability, making it less effective for handling high traffic during peak times.

Question #47:
Correct Answer: B
Explanation:
B is correct. Disabling auto-suspend ensures the warehouse remains active, eliminating startup delays and providing immediate response times for critical reports.
A is incorrect because frequent suspends could still cause delays when resuming the warehouse.

C is incorrect because increasing warehouse size does not address startup delays; it primarily improves compute capacity.
D is incorrect because the "Economy" policy prioritizes cost savings and may not prevent startup delays

Question #48:
Correct Answer: B
Explanation:
B is correct. Manually suspending the warehouse on weekends ensures no unnecessary costs when query load is low while keeping it ready for weekday use.
A is incorrect because setting a longer auto-suspend period could still lead to idle costs over the weekend.
C is incorrect as keeping a small warehouse active without auto-suspend incurs costs even during low activity.
D is incorrect because enabling multi-cluster mode is unnecessary given the low usage on weekends.

Question #49:
Correct Answer: B
Explanation:
B is correct. Enabling auto-suspend with a short timeout and auto-resume ensures that the warehouse is only running when needed, efficiently handling the high compute job while minimizing idle costs.
A is incorrect because keeping a large warehouse running all day, even during idle periods, incurs unnecessary costs.
C is incorrect because manually starting and stopping the warehouse every day is inefficient and adds overhead.
D is incorrect because the "Economy" scaling policy prioritizes cost savings over performance, which may not be suitable for high compute tasks.

Question #50:
Correct Answer: B
Explanation:
B is correct. Using multi-cluster mode with a short auto-suspend setting ensures that the warehouse can dynamically scale up during workload spikes and scale down during idle times, effectively managing variable workloads without manual intervention.
A is incorrect because keeping a large warehouse active all day would incur unnecessary costs during low activity periods.
C is incorrect because the "Economy" scaling policy prioritizes cost savings and may not scale up quickly enough to handle sudden spikes in workload.
D is incorrect because relying on a small warehouse with auto-resume might cause delays or resource constraints during high-demand periods.

SNOWFLAKE STREAMS

Question #1:

You are using Snowflake Streams to track changes to a table. Which of the following are correct regarding how Streams capture data changes?
Select 2 answers:
A. Streams capture all changes, including both data insertions and deletions.
B. Streams capture only data insertions and modifications to rows.
C. Streams automatically track historical versions of each row in the base table.
D. Streams do not capture deleted rows, but will capture data insertions and updates.

Question #2:
You want to ensure that your stream captures every change in real-time, without any delays. Which of the following methods should you use to ensure the Stream reflects changes immediately?
Select 2 answers:
A. Use STREAMS with AUTOMATIC mode to update after every commit.
B. Use a continuous MERGE process to apply changes as soon as they happen.
C. Use TASKS to schedule the processing of changes every minute.
D. Use TASKS to trigger the processing immediately after a change is detected in the stream.

Question #3:
Which of the following are valid reasons to use a Snowflake Stream instead of using a query-based approach to track changes in a table?
Select 3 answers:
A. Streams automatically handle incremental data processing without needing to write complex SQL.
B. Streams can capture data changes across multiple tables with a single Stream object.
C. Streams allow for tracking of changes on a row-by-row basis, making them more granular than query-based approaches.
D. Streams track changes even when the data is deleted, ensuring no changes are missed.

E. Streams improve performance by reducing the need for large full table scans to detect changes.

Question #4:
You are using Snowflake Streams to track changes in a large table. You notice that some updates and deletions are missing from the stream. What could be the reason for this?
Select 2 answers:
A. The stream was created on a table that is missing a primary key.
B. The stream was created on a view instead of a base table.
C. The stream's retention period has expired, and older changes are no longer available.
D. The table does not use clustering keys, causing changes to be missed during large data modifications.

Question #5:
You need to capture all changes to a Snowflake table and then replicate those changes to another system for analytics purposes. Which of the following are the best practices for using Streams in this scenario?
Select 3 answers:
A. Use a MERGE statement to continuously apply changes to the destination table.
B. Use a TASK to automate the processing of changes in the stream.
C. Use SEQUENCING to manually process changes in a specific order.
D. Ensure that the stream is only applied to the target system once the changes are committed.
E. Use a QUERY to fetch changes from the stream at periodic intervals.

Answers and Explanations
Question #1:
Correct Answers: A,D
Explanations:
A: Correct because Streams capture changes to both inserted and deleted rows.
D: Correct because Streams track insertions and updates to rows but do not capture deleted rows.
B: Incorrect because Streams track insertions, updates, and deletions (in certain configurations).
C: Incorrect because Streams do not store historical versions of rows; that's handled by Time Travel.

Question #2:
Correct Answers: B,D
Explanations:
B: Correct because a continuous MERGE operation applies changes immediately.
D: Correct because TASKS can trigger processing as soon as changes are detected.
A: Incorrect because AUTOMATIC mode does not exist for Streams.
C: Incorrect because scheduling every minute introduces unnecessary delays.

Question #3:

Correct Answers: A,C,E
Explanations:
A: Correct because Streams simplify incremental data tracking.
C: Correct because Streams track changes at the row level.
E: Correct because Streams eliminate full-table scans, improving performance.
B: Incorrect because a Stream tracks changes for only one table.
D: Incorrect because Streams do not track deleted data by default.

Question #4:
Correct Answers: C,D
Explanations:
C: Correct because the retention period expiry can result in missed changes.
D: Correct because clustering keys improve performance and ensure changes are accurately captured.
A: Incorrect because Streams do not require a primary key to track changes.
B: Incorrect because Streams can be created on a view.

Question #5:
Correct Answers: A,B,E
Explanations:
A: Correct because MERGE is ideal for applying changes continuously.
B: Correct because TASKS automate processing of stream changes.
E: Correct because periodic querying ensures no changes are missed.
C: Incorrect because Streams inherently capture changes in order.
D: Incorrect because Streams process changes immediately without needing committed transactions.

Question #6:
Which of the following are true regarding the behavior of Streams when used with a Snowflake table?
Select 2 answers:
A. Streams only track changes when the underlying table has a unique constraint.
B. Streams can be created on a table without any clustering keys or primary keys.
C. Streams automatically handle insertions but need manual intervention to track updates and deletes.
D. Streams automatically reset and capture changes whenever a full table reload occurs.

Question #7:
You want to use a Snowflake Stream to track changes to a large dataset and replicate these changes to an external system. What is the most efficient way to handle the captured changes from the Stream?
Select 3 answers:
A. Use MERGE operations to process changes directly in the target system, applying them as they occur.
B. Use a COPY INTO command to batch load changes from the stream into the target system.
C. Use TASKS to schedule the regular processing of changes from the stream.
D. Use SEQUENCING to ensure the order of change processing from the stream.

E. Use a third-party data integration tool to pull changes from the Stream at regular intervals.

Question #8:
You want to create a Stream on a table in Snowflake to capture data changes and periodically move those changes to another table for auditing purposes. Which of the following approaches are best suited for capturing and moving these changes?
Select 2 answers:
A. Use a TABLE STREAM on the source table and use a MERGE operation to apply changes to the audit table.
B. Create a TASK that executes a MERGE statement to move Stream data to the audit table.
C. Create a MATERIALIZED VIEW on top of the Stream to capture changes in real-time.
D. Use a VIEW based on the Stream to capture changes in real-time.

Question #9:
A developer wants to use Streams to capture the exact sequence of changes to a table for an audit trail. Which of the following are true about Snowflake Streams' ability to track the sequence of changes?
Select 3 answers:
A. Streams record the type of operation (INSERT, UPDATE, DELETE) for each row.
B. Streams provide the exact timestamp for each change, allowing precise ordering.
C. Streams track changes with a specific offset, ensuring order within a transaction.
D. Streams can be combined with TASKS to process changes in order of occurrence.

Question #10:
Which of the following statements about Snowflake Streams retention policy are true?
Select 2 answers:
A. Streams have a fixed retention period of 7 days.
B. Streams' retention period can be configured up to a maximum of 90 days.
C. The retention period for Streams is linked to the TIME TRAVEL period of the underlying table.
D. A Stream's retention period is reset each time changes are consumed.

Answers and Explanations:

Question #6:
Correct Answers: B, D
B: Correct because a Stream can be created on a table regardless of whether it has clustering keys or primary keys.
D: Correct because when a full table reload occurs (e.g., using COPY INTO), the Stream resets, and the changes are captured from the point of the reload.
Wrong Answers:
A: Incorrect because Streams can track changes regardless of the presence of unique constraints on the underlying table.
C: Incorrect because Streams automatically track insertions, updates, and deletes; no manual intervention is required.

Question #7:

Correct Answers: A, B, C

A: Correct because MERGE operations allow for continuous and efficient processing of changes, applying them in real-time to the destination system.

B: Correct because COPY INTO can be used to batch load the changes from the stream, ensuring efficient bulk processing.

C: Correct because TASKS automate the processing, ensuring that changes are handled on a timely basis without manual intervention.

Wrong Answers:

D: Incorrect because sequencing is generally unnecessary for managing Stream changes as Snowflake ensures they are processed in the order they occur.

E: Incorrect because relying on third-party tools might introduce unnecessary complexity and delays.

Question #8:

Correct Answers: A, B

A: Correct because a Stream can be used in conjunction with a MERGE operation to apply incremental changes to the audit table.

B: Correct because a TASK can automate this process, periodically running the MERGE statement to ensure that changes are captured and moved efficiently.

Wrong Answers:

C: Incorrect because MATERIALIZED VIEWS do not work directly with Streams for capturing changes in real-time.

D: Incorrect because a regular VIEW cannot capture and persist changes on its own; it only reflects the current state of the data.

Question #9:

Correct Answers: A, C, D

A: Correct because Streams record the type of data operation, essential for building an audit trail.

C: Correct because Streams track changes with an offset, which helps in ensuring order within a single transaction.

D: Correct because TASKS can be scheduled to process changes in sequence, maintaining the intended order of operations.

Wrong Answers:

B: Incorrect because Streams do not track the precise timestamp of each change. Instead, they rely on a transactional offset to determine order within a transaction.

Question #10:

Correct Answers: C, D

C: Correct because Streams rely on the TIME TRAVEL capability of Snowflake, meaning their retention period is directly tied to the TIME TRAVEL settings of the source table.

D: Correct because each time changes are consumed from a Stream, the retention period is effectively reset, allowing for a new interval of data tracking.

Wrong Answers:

A: Incorrect because the retention period is not fixed to 7 days; it depends on the TIME TRAVEL configuration.

B: Incorrect because Snowflake's Stream retention is generally limited by the TIME TRAVEL settings, not an arbitrary maximum of 90 days.

Question 11:
When using Streams on Snowflake tables, which of the following are limitations to be aware of?
Select 3 answers:
A. A Stream cannot be created on tables using TRANSIENT storage.
B. A Stream cannot capture changes from tables with more than 10 million rows.
C. A Stream may need to be re-created if a full data reload on the source table occurs.
D. A Stream cannot be created directly on external tables.
E. Streams are not supported for data inserted using COPY INTO commands.

Question 12:
Which of the following are benefits of using Snowflake Streams in ETL pipelines?
Select 3 answers:
A. Streams capture data changes in real-time without requiring full-table scans.
B. Streams allow you to capture DDL changes, making it easier to track schema modifications.
C. Streams reduce ETL pipeline complexity by simplifying incremental data capture.
D. Streams enable efficient snapshot-based data replication.
E. Streams allow easy integration with TASKS for scheduling and automation.

Question 13:
You are using a Stream to track changes on a Snowflake table that receives large volumes of data throughout the day. You want to ensure that you do not miss any changes when querying the Stream. Which of the following approaches should you consider?
Select 3 answers:
A. Query the Stream frequently and process changes in smaller batches.
B. Increase the TIME TRAVEL retention period of the table to extend the Stream's retention.
C. Ensure the Stream is queried at least once within its retention period.
D. Use a TASK with a specific frequency to automate the processing of changes from the Stream.
E. Manually reset the Stream's retention period by truncating the table.

Question 14:
Which of the following are valid use cases for Snowflake Streams in an analytics pipeline?
Select 3 answers:
A. Real-time data auditing for compliance.
B. Automatically capturing schema changes on external tables.
C. Performing incremental loads into downstream systems.
D. Tracking data changes from Snowflake Views.
E. Applying only the latest data changes to data warehouse tables.

Question 15:
A Snowflake Stream is used to capture changes on a table that is frequently updated. The stream needs to be continuously monitored and changes applied to a target table every hour. Which of the following methods would best help manage and automate this?
Select 2 answers:
A. Use a MATERIALIZED VIEW on top of the Stream.
B. Create a TASK to execute every hour to move Stream data to the target table.

C. Set up a continuous query to read directly from the Stream.
D. Use a MERGE statement to apply the Stream data to the target table.
E. Increase the TIME TRAVEL setting to minimize data loss.

Answers and Explanations:

Question 11:
Correct Answers: C,D,E
Explanations:
C is correct because a full data reload (e.g., COPY INTO) can reset the Stream, requiring it to be re-created to track new changes.
D is correct because Streams cannot directly track changes on external tables.
E is correct because COPY INTO commands bypass Snowflake's change-tracking mechanisms.
A is incorrect because Streams can be created on TRANSIENT tables.
B is incorrect because there is no row limit for Streams to track changes.

Question 12:
Correct Answers: A,C,E
Explanations:
A is correct because Streams track incremental changes without full-table scans.
C is correct because Streams make incremental data capture simple, reducing ETL complexity.
E is correct because Streams integrate with TASKS for scheduled and automated operations.
B is incorrect because Streams do not capture schema (DDL) changes.
D is incorrect because Streams are row-based and not for snapshot-based replication.

Question 13:
Correct Answers: A,B,D
Explanations:
A is correct because querying frequently reduces the risk of missing data.
B is correct because TIME TRAVEL retention extends the Stream's retention.
D is correct because TASKS automate data processing and reduce manual effort.
C is incorrect because querying frequently is more reliable than just relying on retention period compliance.
E is incorrect because truncating the table does not reset or extend Stream retention.

Question 14:
Correct Answers: A,C,E
Explanations:
A is correct because Streams track changes useful for compliance.
C is correct because Streams simplify incremental loads for ETL.
E is correct because Streams apply only the latest changes, reducing redundant processing.
B is incorrect because Streams do not capture schema (DDL) changes and are not supported on external tables.
D is incorrect because Streams do not track changes on Views.

Question 15:
Correct Answers: B,D

Explanations:
B is correct because TASKS automate hourly processing of Stream data.
D is correct because MERGE applies changes efficiently to the target table.
A is incorrect because MATERIALIZED VIEWS are not compatible with Streams.
C is incorrect because continuous queries on Streams are not supported.
E is incorrect because TIME TRAVEL helps with retention but does not automate hourly processing.

Question #16:
When using Snowflake Streams for capturing changes in a source table, which of the following characteristics apply to Streams?
Select 3 answers:
A. Streams allow querying only the latest changes since the last query.
B. Streams support real-time change data capture with external tables.
C. Streams reset each time changes are queried and consumed.
D. Streams are automatically updated when the source table is modified.
E. Streams provide the exact order of changes as they occur.

Question #17:
You are tasked with building an ETL pipeline in Snowflake where Streams will be used to track changes in a table and load those changes to an external system. What factors should you consider to ensure no data loss?
Select 3 answers:
A. Schedule TASKS to process Stream data frequently enough to stay within the retention period.
B. Set a longer TIME TRAVEL retention period on the source table to extend Stream retention.
C. Create multiple Streams on the table for redundancy.
D. Ensure Stream queries are written to handle duplicate entries.
E. Use a VIEW on top of the Stream to directly query the changes.

Question #18:
A data engineer is setting up a Stream to capture changes on a Snowflake table. What must they ensure to prevent data from being missed due to Stream retention limits?
Select 1 answer:
A. Query the Stream at least once before the retention period expires.
B. Create a MATERIALIZED VIEW on top of the Stream for real-time updates.
C. Configure a Stream retention period longer than 7 days.
D. Set up the Stream on an external table to avoid retention limits.

Question #19:
Which of the following statements is true regarding Snowflake Streams?
Select 1 answer:
A. A Stream on a table can track DDL (schema) changes.
B. A Stream's retention period can be manually configured for each Stream.
C. Streams can be used directly on a VIEW to track changes.
D. A Stream tracks only data modifications (inserts, updates, deletes) on the table.

Question #20:
A team wants to use a Stream to capture incremental data changes and load them into a downstream table daily. Which of the following actions best accomplishes this goal?
Select 1 answer:
A. Use a TASK scheduled daily to query and process data from the Stream.
B. Create a MATERIALIZED VIEW on top of the Stream and load data incrementally.
C. Query the Stream only at the end of the month to capture all monthly changes.
D. Set up a Stream on an external table to capture the data.

Answers and Explanations

Question #16
Correct Answers: A,C,D
Explanations:
A: Correct because Streams only track the latest changes since the last query, making them efficient for incremental data capture.
C: Correct because Streams reset after each query, capturing only new changes in subsequent queries.
D: Correct because Streams automatically capture any modifications to the source table, ensuring they remain up-to-date.
B: Incorrect because Streams do not support external tables.
E: Incorrect because Streams do not guarantee the exact order of changes.

Question #17
Correct Answers: A,B,D
Explanations:
A: Correct because processing Stream data frequently prevents changes from expiring.
B: Correct because a longer TIME TRAVEL retention extends the period during which Stream changes are available.
D: Correct because handling duplicates in queries ensures data integrity.
C: Incorrect because creating multiple Streams on the same table does not provide redundancy for data retention.
E: Incorrect because VIEWs cannot be directly used on Streams.

Question #18
Correct Answer: A
Explanations:
A: Correct because querying the Stream within the retention period ensures changes are not missed.
B: Incorrect because MATERIALIZED VIEWS cannot be created on Streams.
C: Incorrect because the Stream retention period is tied to TIME TRAVEL settings, which have a maximum of 90 days.
D: Incorrect because Streams cannot be created on external tables.

Question #19
Correct Answer: D

Explanations:
D: Correct because Streams track only data modifications such as inserts, updates, and deletes.
A: Incorrect because Streams do not track DDL changes.
B: Incorrect because the Stream retention period is governed by TIME TRAVEL settings and cannot be manually configured.
C: Incorrect because Streams cannot be created directly on VIEWs.

Question #20
Correct Answer: A
Explanations:
A: Correct because TASKs allow automated scheduling to query and process Stream data daily.
B: Incorrect because MATERIALIZED VIEWS cannot directly use Streams for incremental data capture.
C: Incorrect because querying only monthly risks missing data due to retention limits.
D: Incorrect because Streams cannot be created on external tables.

Question #21:
What is a primary use case for Snowflake Streams in data engineering?
A. Capturing schema changes in a Snowflake table.
B. Automating data replication for disaster recovery.
C. Tracking only the current state of data in a table.
D. Capturing and tracking row-level changes for ETL processing.

Question #22:
Which of the following would cause a Snowflake Stream to be automatically reset?
A. The Stream's retention period is exceeded.
B. A new Stream is created on the same table.
C. The source table's TIME TRAVEL setting is disabled.
D. A TRUNCATE operation is performed on the source table.

Question #23:
You are creating a Stream on a table to track all updates. After some time, you notice that some updates are missing in the Stream output. What is a likely cause?
A. The table's TIME TRAVEL period was set to 0.
B. The Stream was queried and then re-queried within the retention period.
C. The Stream was created on a VIEW instead of a table.
D. The Stream's retention period is shorter than the frequency of queries

Question #24:
Which operation on a Snowflake table would invalidate a Stream created on it?
A. Deleting a single row in the table.
B. Updating a column value in the table.
C. Running a COPY INTO command to bulk load data.
D. Adding a new column to the table.

Question #25:
How does Snowflake handle Streams if the source table's TIME TRAVEL is altered to a shorter retention period?
A. The Stream's retention period will automatically shorten.
B. The Stream will continue to retain data for the previous retention period.
C. The Stream becomes invalid and stops tracking changes.
D. Streams are unaffected by changes in TIME TRAVEL.

Answers and Explanations

Question #21:
Correct Answer: D
Explanations:
D is correct because Streams are designed to capture row-level changes, making them ideal for ETL processes.
A is incorrect because Streams do not capture schema (DDL) changes.
B is incorrect because Streams are not used for data replication; they are designed for incremental change tracking.
C is incorrect because Streams track data changes, not just the current state.

Question #22:
Correct Answer: D
Explanations:
D is correct because a TRUNCATE operation resets the Stream by removing all rows, effectively clearing the change tracking.
A is incorrect because when the retention period is exceeded, only the oldest changes are removed, not the entire Stream.
B is incorrect because creating another Stream does not reset existing Streams.
C is incorrect because disabling TIME TRAVEL affects retention but does not automatically reset Streams.

Question #23:
Correct Answer: D
Explanations:
D is correct because if the retention period is shorter than the query interval, changes can be lost between queries.
A is incorrect because TIME TRAVEL must be enabled for Streams, but a period of 0 would prevent creating a Stream initially.
B is incorrect because querying within the retention period should not affect the Stream's functionality.
C is incorrect because Streams cannot be created on VIEWs, so this setup would not be possible.

Question #24:
Correct Answer: C
Explanations:

C is correct because COPY INTO for bulk loading bypasses Streams, meaning the operation won't be captured.
A and B are incorrect because row-level deletions and updates are tracked by Streams.
D is incorrect because adding columns (a DDL operation) does not impact Streams, which focus on data changes.

Question #25:
Correct Answer: A
Explanations:
A is correct because the Stream's retention period is directly tied to the TIME TRAVEL period of the source table.
B is incorrect because Streams cannot retain data longer than the current TIME TRAVEL setting.
C is incorrect because the Stream does not stop tracking; it simply adjusts to the new retention.
D is incorrect because Streams are indeed affected by TIME TRAVEL changes.

Question #26:
You want to query all rows inserted into a table named sales_data and captured by a Stream named sales_data_stream. Which SQL command will retrieve the data from the Stream?
Select 1 answer:
A. SELECT * FROM sales_data_stream;
B. SELECT * FROM sales_data WHERE metadata$action = 'INSERT';
C. SELECT * FROM sales_data_stream WHERE action = 'INSERT';
D. SELECT * FROM sales_data_stream WHERE metadata$action = 'INSERT';

Question #27:
You need to retrieve only the rows deleted from a table using a Stream named customer_stream. What query should you use?
Select 1 answer:
A. SELECT * FROM customer_stream WHERE metadata$action = 'DELETE';
B. SELECT * FROM customer_stream WHERE action = 'DELETE';
C. SELECT * FROM customer_stream WHERE metadata$action = 'REMOVE';
D. SELECT * FROM customer_stream WHERE metadata_action = 'DELETE';

Question #28:
You want to identify updated rows in a table using a Stream named product_stream. Which query will correctly filter for rows where values were modified?
Select 1 answer:
A. SELECT * FROM product_stream WHERE metadata$action = 'MODIFY';
B. SELECT * FROM product_stream WHERE metadata$action = 'UPDATE';
C. SELECT * FROM product_stream WHERE metadata$action = 'CHANGE';
D. SELECT * FROM product_stream WHERE action = 'UPDATE';

Question #29:

You want to retrieve rows from a Stream that were either inserted or updated. You have a Stream on a table called orders named orders_stream. Which query will retrieve these changes?
Select 1 answer:
A. SELECT * FROM orders_stream WHERE metadata$action IN ('INSERT', 'UPDATE');
B. SELECT * FROM orders_stream WHERE metadata$action = 'INSERT' OR action = 'UPDATE';
C. SELECT * FROM orders_stream WHERE action IN ('INSERT', 'UPDATE');
D. SELECT * FROM orders_stream WHERE metadata$action = 'ADD' OR metadata$action = 'MODIFY';

Question #30:
You want to merge changes from a Stream named inventory_stream into a target table named inventory. Which command will ensure that the changes are applied correctly?
Select 1 answer:

A.
MERGE INTO inventory USING inventory_stream ON inventory.id = inventory_stream.id WHEN MATCHED AND inventory_stream.metadata$action = 'UPDATE' THEN UPDATE SET inventory.quantity = inventory_stream.quantity WHEN MATCHED AND inventory_stream.metadata$action = 'DELETE' THEN DELETE WHEN NOT MATCHED THEN INSERT (id, quantity) VALUES (inventory_stream.id, inventory_stream.quantity);

B.
MERGE INTO inventory ON inventory.id = inventory_stream.id WHEN MATCHED THEN UPDATE SET inventory.quantity = inventory_stream.quantity WHEN NOT MATCHED THEN INSERT (id, quantity) VALUES (inventory_stream.id, inventory_stream.quantity);

C.
MERGE INTO inventory USING inventory_stream WHEN MATCHED THEN UPDATE SET inventory.quantity = inventory_stream.quantity WHEN NOT MATCHED THEN INSERT (id, quantity) VALUES (inventory_stream.id, inventory_stream.quantity);

D.
MERGE INTO inventory USING inventory_stream ON inventory.id = inventory_stream.id WHEN MATCHED THEN UPDATE SET inventory.quantity = inventory_stream.quantity WHEN NOT MATCHED AND inventory_stream.metadata$action = 'INSERT' THEN INSERT (id, quantity) VALUES (inventory_stream.id, inventory_stream.quantity);

Answers and Explanations

Question #26:
Correct Answer: A
Explanation:
A is correct because querying the Stream itself (sales_data_stream) will return all rows captured by the Stream, with metadata columns automatically provided to indicate actions like INSERT, UPDATE, or DELETE.
B, C, and D are incorrect because they involve metadata column names or filtering conditions that are either unnecessary or invalid.

Question #27:
Correct Answer: A

Explanation:
A is correct because metadata$action in Streams can be used to filter for specific types of changes, such as DELETE.
B is incorrect because the column name action is invalid; it should be metadata$action.
C is incorrect because REMOVE is not a recognized action in Streams; the correct term for deletions is DELETE.
D is incorrect due to the incorrect syntax (should be metadata$action).

Question #28:
Correct Answer: B
Explanation:
B is correct because the correct metadata action for updates is UPDATE, and metadata$action is the appropriate column for filtering changes.
A is incorrect because MODIFY is not a valid metadata$action value in Streams.
C is incorrect because CHANGE is not a recognized action in Snowflake Streams.
D is incorrect because the column name action is invalid.

Question #29:
Correct Answer: A
Explanation:
A is correct because metadata$action allows filtering for multiple change types in Streams, and IN ('INSERT', 'UPDATE') accurately filters both inserted and updated rows.
B and C are incorrect because action is not a valid column; the correct column is metadata$action.
D is incorrect because ADD and MODIFY are not valid actions in Snowflake Streams.

Question #30:
Correct Answer: A
Explanation:
A is correct because it checks metadata$action to apply updates, deletions, and insertions accordingly, ensuring all changes are correctly applied.
B is incorrect because it does not differentiate actions and will not handle deletions from the Stream.
C is incorrect because it lacks the USING clause and does not check metadata$action.
D is incorrect because it only explicitly handles insertions and misses update and delete logic.

Question #31:
A developer wants to track only the rows that have been inserted or deleted from a users table in Snowflake. A Stream named users_stream has been created on the users table. Which query should be used to capture only these specific changes?
A.
SELECT * FROM users_stream WHERE metadata$action = 'INSERT';
B.
SELECT * FROM users_stream WHERE metadata$action = 'DELETE';
C.
SELECT * FROM users_stream WHERE metadata$action IN ('INSERT', 'DELETE');
D.

SELECT * FROM users_stream WHERE metadata$action = 'UPDATE';

Question #32:
You need to query a Stream named orders_stream on an orders table to find only the updated rows. Which query will correctly retrieve these rows?

A.
SELECT * FROM orders_stream WHERE metadata$action = 'UPDATE';
B.
SELECT * FROM orders_stream WHERE action = 'UPDATE';
C.
SELECT * FROM orders_stream WHERE metadata$update = TRUE;
D.
SELECT * FROM orders_stream WHERE metadata$action = 'MODIFY';

Question #33:
To merge changes from a Stream named products_stream into the products table, you want to apply insertions and updates but ignore deletions. Which merge command will achieve this?

A.
MERGE INTO products USING products_stream ON products.id = products_stream.id WHEN MATCHED AND products_stream.metadata$action = 'UPDATE' THEN UPDATE SET products.price = products_stream.price WHEN NOT MATCHED THEN INSERT (id, price) VALUES (products_stream.id, products_stream.price);
B.
MERGE INTO products USING products_stream ON products.id = products_stream.id WHEN MATCHED THEN UPDATE SET products.price = products_stream.price WHEN NOT MATCHED THEN INSERT (id, price) VALUES (products_stream.id, products_stream.price);
C.
MERGE INTO products USING products_stream ON products.id = products_stream.id WHEN MATCHED AND products_stream.metadata$action IN ('INSERT', 'UPDATE') THEN INSERT (id, price) VALUES (products_stream.id, products_stream.price);

Question #34:
A data engineer needs to monitor rows in a Stream named inventory_stream for records that were either inserted or updated. Which query should they use?

A.
SELECT * FROM inventory_stream WHERE metadata$action = 'INSERT' OR metadata$action = 'UPDATE';
B.
SELECT * FROM inventory_stream WHERE metadata$action = 'INSERT';
C.
SELECT * FROM inventory_stream WHERE metadata$action = 'UPDATE';
D.
SELECT * FROM inventory_stream WHERE metadata$action IN ('INSERT', 'UPDATE');

Question #35:
A Stream named sales_stream on the sales table is set up to capture changes. Which query allows viewing all rows where records were deleted?

A.

SELECT * FROM sales_stream WHERE metadata$action = 'DELETE';
B.
SELECT * FROM sales_stream WHERE metadata$action IN ('DELETE');
C.
SELECT * FROM sales_stream WHERE metadata$action = 'REMOVE';
D.
SELECT * FROM sales_stream WHERE action = 'DELETE';

Answers and Explanations

Question #31:
Correct Answers: A,B
Explanation:
A and B are correct because they filter rows where metadata$action indicates an INSERT or DELETE, which captures only new rows and deletions, respectively.
C is incorrect because it captures both actions together without distinguishing them.
D is incorrect because UPDATE tracks only modified rows, not insertions or deletions.

Question #32:
Correct Answer: A
Explanation:
A is correct because metadata$action = 'UPDATE' accurately filters updated rows.
B is incorrect because action is not a valid column name; it should be metadata$action.
C is incorrect because metadata$update is not a valid field in Streams.
D is incorrect because MODIFY is not a valid value for metadata$action; the correct value is UPDATE.

Question #33:
Correct Answer: A
Explanation:
A is correct because it filters updates and includes unmatched rows for insertions, ignoring deletions.
B is incorrect because it does not specify conditions for metadata$action, potentially mishandling deletes.
C is incorrect because it misuses INSERT in a WHEN MATCHED clause, which is invalid.

Question #34:
Correct Answer: D
Explanation:
D is correct because the IN clause efficiently captures both inserted and updated rows.
A is correct but less efficient as it uses multiple conditions instead of a concise IN clause.
B is incorrect because it filters only inserted rows.
C is incorrect because it filters only updated rows.

Question #35:
Correct Answer: A
Explanation:

A is correct because metadata$action = 'DELETE' is the proper syntax for filtering deleted records.
B is redundant for a single condition.
C is incorrect because REMOVE is not a valid value for metadata$action.
D is incorrect because action is not a recognized column in Streams

---

Question #36:
A data engineer needs to share data changes from a table in real-time with a different Snowflake account. The changes are tracked using a Stream, and Time Travel is enabled. Which approach will allow sharing these continuous changes most effectively?
A. Share the base table directly with the other account and use a Stream in the recipient account to track changes.
B. Use Secure Data Sharing to share the Stream directly with the other account.
C. Enable Time Travel for the Stream and share Time Travel data with the other account.
D. Share the base table and rely on Time Travel for the recipient to access past data.

Question #37:
Your organization uses a Stream on a table that captures changes, and a Stored Procedure processes these changes every hour. Recently, some rows processed by the Stored Procedure were reprocessed, leading to duplicate records in the target table. What is the most likely reason for this issue?
A. The Stored Procedure is not configured to handle incremental loads from the Stream.
B. The Stream was created without enabling Time Travel.
C. The Stream's offset was reset before each run of the Stored Procedure.
D. Time Travel was not enabled on the target table.

Question #38:
An analyst needs to review changes to a table captured by a Stream from two days ago. However, the Stream has already processed newer changes. Which feature can they use to access the version of the Stream's data from two days prior?
A. Use Time Travel to access the historical version of the Stream.
B. Rewind the Stream to the previous day's offset.
C. Use the base table's Time Travel to retrieve changes as they were two days ago.
D. Create a new Stream on the table and specify an offset date.

Question #39:
A data engineer wants to create a Stored Procedure that processes data from a Stream and then clears out the Stream's processed records to avoid reprocessing. What should they include in the Stored Procedure to handle this correctly?
A. Explicitly reset the Stream offset after processing.
B. Process the Stream data and let Snowflake automatically clear the processed records.
C. Manually mark records as processed by updating the Stream's metadata.
D. Include a condition to skip already-processed records on subsequent runs.

Question #40:
You have a Time Travel feature enabled on a table and a Stream tracking changes. If you accidentally delete some rows in the table, how can you restore the table to its state before deletion while ensuring the Stream continues to track further changes?

A. Use Time Travel to restore the table to the previous state, and then recreate the Stream.
B. Use Time Travel to restore the table, and the Stream will continue tracking changes without any additional steps.
C. Recreate both the table and Stream from a historical snapshot.
D. Use Time Travel to retrieve the deleted data and manually insert it into the table.

Answers and Explanations

Question #36:
Correct Answer: D
Explanation:
A: Incorrect because only base tables—not Streams—can be shared with other accounts.
B: Incorrect because Streams cannot be directly shared with other accounts through Secure Data Sharing.
C: Incorrect because Time Travel data is only accessible within the original account and is not part of Secure Data Sharing.
D: Correct because sharing the base table with Time Travel allows the recipient to access prior states of the table without using a Stream.

Question #37:
Correct Answer: A
Explanation:
A: Correct because if the Stored Procedure does not properly mark or process rows incrementally, it can re-read changes, leading to duplicates.
B: Incorrect because Time Travel is independent of how the Stream captures changes.
C: Incorrect because resetting the Stream's offset is not typically automatic and would require manual intervention.
D: Incorrect because Time Travel on the target table does not influence the behavior of the Stream on the source table.

Question #38:
Correct Answer: C
Explanation:
A: Incorrect because Time Travel on Streams is not available; only the base table's data can be accessed via Time Travel.
B: Incorrect as Snowflake Streams do not support manual rewinding to previous offsets.
C: Correct because Time Travel can be used on the base table to access the state of data from two days ago.

D: Incorrect because a new Stream would only start capturing changes from the point of creation.

Question #39:
Correct Answers: B,D
Explanation:
A: Incorrect because Streams in Snowflake automatically advance their offsets, and manual resets are not typical.
B: Correct because Snowflake manages the Stream's offset automatically after each query, avoiding the need for explicit clearing.
C: Incorrect because updating Stream metadata is not supported in Snowflake; Streams are read-only structures.
D: Correct as including a condition to avoid reprocessing already-read records ensures that duplicates are not processed.

Question #40:
Correct Answer: B
Explanation:
A: Incorrect because there's no need to recreate the Stream when using Time Travel.
B: Correct as Snowflake Streams will continue capturing new changes even after restoring the table using Time Travel.
C: Incorrect because restoring the table through Time Travel does not require recreating the Stream.
D: Incorrect because manually reinserting data is unnecessary if Time Travel is enabled.

SNOWFLAKE TASKS

Question 01:

A data pipeline in Snowflake is implemented using a task that processes new data from a table. The task is set up with a schedule but does not seem to execute. What could be the reason for this behavior?
A. The task has been created without specifying a SQL statement to execute.
B. The task requires a parent task to be completed before it can execute.
C. The task is not enabled.
D. The warehouse associated with the task is suspended.

Question 02:

You have a task in Snowflake that executes a stored procedure to process new data in a staging table. The task is enabled and has a schedule, but you notice that the stored procedure is not executing. What could be the issue?
A. The task is blocked because a dependent task failed.
B. The stored procedure requires elevated privileges that the task does not have.
C. The task has exceeded the maximum execution time allowed by Snowflake.
D. The SQL statement in the task definition is invalid.

Question 03:

A Snowflake administrator has created a task that triggers daily to process data from multiple tables. The task occasionally fails due to a transient error in the data source. How can the task be configured to handle such failures?
A. Use a retry policy in the task to automatically rerun on failure.
B. Configure the task to execute manually after fixing the error.
C. Adjust the schedule of the task to run less frequently.
D. Create a parent task that verifies data integrity before the task executes.

Question 04:

You are managing a series of tasks in Snowflake, where Task B depends on Task A to complete successfully. However, Task B runs before Task A has finished. What could resolve this issue?
A. Set Task A as the parent task for Task B.
B. Increase the priority of Task A in the task queue.

C. Enable error notifications for Task A and Task B.
D. Modify the schedule of Task B to ensure it runs after Task A.

Question 05:

A task in Snowflake that aggregates data is running slower than expected, causing delays in downstream processes. What could you do to optimize the task's performance?
A. Increase the size of the virtual warehouse used by the task.
B. Cluster the data in the base table used by the task.
C. Enable caching for the task.
D. Reduce the task's execution frequency to minimize load.

Answers and Explanations:

Question 01:

Correct Answer: C, D
Explanation:

- C is correct because tasks in Snowflake do not execute unless they are explicitly enabled.

- D is correct because if the associated warehouse is suspended, the task cannot execute as it requires compute resources.

- A is incorrect because a task cannot be created without a SQL statement; it would fail at creation.

- B is incorrect because not all tasks require a parent task; this depends on how the task chain is configured.

Question 02:

Correct Answer: A, B
Explanation:

- A is correct because a task can be blocked if a dependent (parent) task fails.

- B is correct because stored procedures may require specific privileges that are not granted to the task's role.

- C is incorrect because Snowflake tasks do not have a defined maximum execution time, although performance issues may arise.

- D is incorrect because a task with an invalid SQL statement cannot be created successfully.

Question 03:

Correct Answer: A, D
Explanation:

- A is correct because implementing a retry policy helps handle transient errors and ensures the task retries automatically.

- D is correct because a parent task can check for data integrity, reducing the risk of task failure due to bad data.

- B is incorrect because manual execution defeats the purpose of automation in Snowflake tasks.

- C is incorrect because adjusting the schedule does not address the root cause of the transient errors.

Question 04:

Correct Answer: A, D
Explanation:

- A is correct because setting a parent task ensures that Task B executes only after Task A completes successfully.

- D is correct because modifying the schedule to align with Task A's completion can also ensure Task B executes at the correct time.

- B is incorrect because task priority is not a feature that determines execution sequence in Snowflake tasks.

- C is incorrect because enabling notifications does not address execution sequencing.

Question 05:

Correct Answer: A, B
Explanation:

- A is correct because increasing the warehouse size provides more compute resources, which can improve task execution time.

- B is correct because clustering data optimizes query performance by reducing the data scanned during task execution.

- C is incorrect because caching is not a feature available for tasks in Snowflake.

- D is incorrect because reducing execution frequency does not improve task performance; it only reduces system load.

Question 06:

You have set up a Snowflake task to process data from a stream capturing changes in a table. The task is scheduled to run every hour, but the data changes are not being captured. What could be the issue?

A. The stream was created on a non-clustered table.

B. The task is not properly configured to use the stream.

C. The stream has reached its maximum number of captured changes.

D. The task execution interval is too long and misses changes.

Question 07:

A Snowflake task reads from a stream and processes changes captured in a source table. You notice that some data changes are skipped during task execution. What could be the reason?

A. The stream is configured with a RETENTION_TIME that is too short.

B. The task is not consuming the stream in a timely manner, causing changes to be missed.

C. The task is configured with an incorrect schema to access the stream.

D. The task is executing on a schedule that conflicts with when data changes are captured.

Question 08:

You are using Snowflake streams and tasks to process change data capture (CDC) for an ETL pipeline. After running the task, you notice the processed data does not match the expected output. Which of the following could be a likely cause?

A. The task is reading from an inactive stream.

B. The stream captures too many changes for the task to process.

C. The task is running on an insufficiently sized warehouse.

D. The stream does not capture delete operations from the source table.

Question 09:

You have a Snowflake task that is configured to process data changes from a stream every 15 minutes. However, the task is frequently missing data updates that occur between executions. What could be the reason?

A. The task execution frequency is too short to capture all changes.

B. The stream does not retain changes between task executions.

C. The stream is not properly configured to track all changes.

D. The task is being throttled due to high data volume.

Question 10:

A Snowflake task is set up to process data captured by a stream. You notice that the task's execution time is increasing due to large volumes of changes in the stream. Which action will most effectively improve the task's performance?

A. Increase the size of the warehouse for the task.

B. Optimize the task to process smaller batches of data from the stream.

C. Increase the frequency of the task's execution to reduce data load.

D. Disable stream retention to reduce the data volume.

Answers and Explanations:

Question 06:

Correct Answer: B, D

Explanation:

- B is correct because the task must be properly configured to read from and use the stream for change data capture.

- D is correct because a longer task execution interval may miss data changes, especially if the changes occur more frequently than the task's schedule.

- A is incorrect because stream functionality is not impacted by table clustering.

- C is incorrect because the stream does not have a maximum change capture limit; it tracks changes continuously as long as data is available.

Question 07:

Correct Answer: B, A

Explanation:

- B is correct because the task must process data in a timely manner to avoid missing changes. If the task is not fast enough, some changes may be skipped.

- A is correct because if the stream's retention time is too short, data changes may be purged before the task can process them.

- C is incorrect because schema configuration is not typically the cause of skipped changes unless there is a specific permission issue.

- D is incorrect because task scheduling conflicts generally do not affect data capture unless the stream has not been correctly processed.

Question 08:

Correct Answer: A, C

Explanation:

- **A** is correct because if the stream is inactive or has been consumed already, the task will not be able to read the changes from it.

- **C** is correct because if the stream schema or configuration is incorrect, it could prevent the task from processing the captured changes.

- **B** is incorrect because a properly configured stream will handle large volumes of changes without issue.

- **D** is incorrect because Snowflake streams can capture all DML operations, including deletes, as long as the stream is configured appropriately.

Question 09:

Correct Answer: B, D

Explanation:

- **B** is correct because streams track changes within a specific retention window; if the task's execution frequency is too low, changes that occur outside of the retention window may be missed.

- **D** is correct because high data volume can cause the task to be throttled, potentially skipping changes in the stream.

- **A** is incorrect because the task's frequency is likely fine if the execution time is properly optimized.

- **C** is incorrect because streams are designed to track all changes once configured properly.

Question 10:

Correct Answer: B, A

Explanation:

- **B** is correct because optimizing the task to process smaller data batches will reduce its processing time and improve performance.

- **A** is correct because increasing the warehouse size can improve task execution performance by providing more compute resources.

- **C** is incorrect because increasing the task frequency will not necessarily improve performance; it might even exacerbate processing times.

- **D** is incorrect because stream retention has nothing to do with task performance; it affects change capture availability.

Question 11:

You are using Snowflake Tasks, which are serverless, and you notice that the task execution time is inconsistent. What could be the most likely reason for this behavior?

A. The task is overloading the serverless compute resources.

B. Snowflake automatically adjusts the compute resources allocated to the task, leading to variability.

C. The task is configured with a fixed compute size, which limits resources.

D. The serverless execution model is designed to allocate compute only when needed, causing delays.

Question 12:

A Snowflake task is running with serverless execution. You observe that the task occasionally experiences significant delays in execution. Which of the following is most likely the cause of this delay?

A. The serverless compute resources are being throttled due to high concurrency.

B. The task is not using enough compute resources to handle the data volume.

C. The task has been configured with an incorrect execution interval.

D. Serverless execution does not provide sufficient resources for complex queries.

Question 13:

You are using Snowflake's serverless execution for tasks, and you are seeing a delay in processing. How can you improve the task's performance without manually allocating compute resources?

A. Optimize the SQL query used in the task to reduce compute load.

B. Increase the task execution frequency to trigger more compute usage.

C. Manually allocate more compute resources to the task.

D. Adjust the warehouse size to improve performance.

Question 14:

A Snowflake task is serverless, and you observe that task failures are occurring intermittently. Which of the following is the most likely cause of the issue?

A. Snowflake's serverless execution model is temporarily unavailable.

B. The task is failing because it exceeds the allocated compute resources.

C. Task failures are typically caused by network issues unrelated to serverless execution.

D. Serverless execution does not support tasks requiring high concurrency.

Question 15:

You are using a Snowflake task with serverless execution to process large datasets. The task is running slower than expected. What could be the best way to address the performance issue?

A. Reconfigure the task to run on a larger dedicated warehouse.

B. Investigate query optimization to reduce resource consumption.

C. Increase the task execution interval to allow more time for processing.

D. Increase the size of the task's serverless execution resources manually.

Answers and Explanations:

Question 11:

Correct Answer: B

Explanation:

- B is correct because Snowflake automatically adjusts compute resources for serverless tasks, which can cause variability in execution time depending on workload and resource availability.

- A is incorrect because serverless execution does not require users to manage compute resources.

- C is incorrect because serverless tasks do not have fixed compute sizes; they scale automatically.

- D is incorrect because serverless execution allocates compute resources dynamically as needed, without explicit allocation from the user.

Question 12:

Correct Answer: A

Explanation:

- A is correct because serverless tasks may experience delays if the compute resources are throttled due to high concurrency.

- B is incorrect because serverless tasks automatically scale compute resources based on workload, meaning there is no manual allocation issue.

- C is incorrect because the execution interval does not directly impact resource allocation in serverless execution.

- D is incorrect because serverless execution is designed to handle varying workloads without needing specific resources.

Question 13:

Correct Answer: A

Explanation:

- A is correct because optimizing SQL queries can reduce resource consumption, improving task performance under Snowflake's serverless execution.

- B is incorrect because increasing execution frequency doesn't solve performance issues related to serverless task execution.

- C is incorrect because manual allocation of compute resources is not needed in serverless execution.

- D is incorrect because task performance issues are typically related to query optimization, not warehouse size.

Question 14:

Correct Answer: B

Explanation:

- B is correct because the most likely cause of task failures in serverless execution is exceeding available compute resources, leading to task failures.

- A is incorrect because Snowflake's serverless execution model is highly available and is unlikely to experience outages.

- C is incorrect because network issues are not typically tied to Snowflake's serverless execution.

- D is incorrect because serverless tasks can handle a high level of concurrency by dynamically allocating resources.

Question 15:

Correct Answer: B

Explanation:

- B is correct because optimizing queries can reduce resource consumption and improve the performance of serverless tasks without manual intervention.

- A is incorrect because serverless execution does not involve configuring dedicated warehouses for tasks.

- **C is incorrect** because increasing execution intervals may delay processing but will not address the root cause of performance issues.

- **D is incorrect** because manual size adjustments are not applicable in a serverless model, where Snowflake handles resource allocation automatically.

Question 16:

You have multiple tasks in Snowflake, and you want to create a dependency such that one task triggers another once it completes. Which feature would you use to achieve this?

A. Task Tree

B. Task Chaining

C. Snowflake Streams

D. Materialized View Triggers

Question 17:

In a Snowflake Task Tree, you want Task A to trigger Task B, which in turn triggers Task C. How should Task B be configured?

A. Task B should be set with a TRIGGERS clause to directly trigger Task C.

B. Task B should depend on Task A's successful completion before triggering Task C.

C. Task B should be scheduled independently of Task A to trigger Task C.

D. Task B should be executed manually after Task A completes.

Question 18:

You have a Snowflake task chain where Task A triggers Task B, and Task B triggers Task C. What happens if Task B fails?

A. Task A will automatically rerun Task B to ensure completion.

B. Task C will be triggered, but Task B's failure will prevent it from completing.

C. Task C will not be triggered until Task B successfully completes.

D. Task A will not run again until Task C completes.

Question 19:

In Snowflake Task Trees, which of the following is a correct way to ensure a task is only triggered when a preceding task has successfully completed?

A. Set the AFTER dependency clause for the task.

B. Configure the task to run immediately upon task failure.

C. Use ON FAILURE for task dependencies.

D. Define the task with START AFTER for successful completion only.

Question 20:

You have a task chain in Snowflake where Task A triggers Task B, and Task B triggers Task C. If Task A runs successfully but Task B fails, what is the expected behavior for Task C?

A. Task C will be triggered as soon as Task A completes.

B. Task C will not be triggered unless Task B completes successfully.

C. Task C will be triggered even if Task B fails, as long as Task A completes.

D. Task C will automatically attempt to rerun if Task B fails.

Answers and Explanations:

Question 16:

Correct Answer: B

Explanation:

- **B** is correct because **Task Chaining** allows tasks to be linked, where the completion of one task triggers the next in the chain.

- **A** is incorrect because "Task Tree" is a general concept, not a specific feature in Snowflake.

- **C** is incorrect because Snowflake Streams are used for change data capture and do not directly manage task dependencies.

- **D** is incorrect because materialized views do not control task triggering.

Question 17:

Correct Answer: B

Explanation:

- **B** is correct because **Task B** should depend on Task A's successful completion before it can trigger Task C.

- **A** is incorrect because the TRIGGERS clause doesn't work this way in task chaining.

- **C** is incorrect because Task B must depend on Task A for proper sequencing.

- **D** is incorrect because manual execution would defeat the purpose of automating the task chain.

Question 18:

Correct Answer: C

Explanation:

- **C** is correct because Task C will not be triggered unless Task B completes successfully in a task chain.

- **A** is incorrect because Task A does not rerun Task B on failure; it moves forward in the chain.

- **B** is incorrect because Task C would not trigger on failure; it only triggers after Task B succeeds.

- **D** is incorrect because the failure of Task B prevents Task C from running, regardless of Task A's status.

Question 19:

Correct Answer: A

Explanation:

- **A** is correct because the AFTER clause in Snowflake task dependencies ensures a task is triggered only after a preceding task successfully completes.

- **B** is incorrect because failure does not automatically trigger subsequent tasks.

- **C** is incorrect because ON FAILURE is used for tasks to handle failure cases, not successful completion dependencies.

- **D** is incorrect because START AFTER does not guarantee that the task will only run upon success, which is what the AFTER clause handles.

Question 20:

Correct Answer: B

Explanation:

- **B** is correct because Task C will not be triggered unless Task B completes successfully in the chain.

- A is incorrect because Task C will only be triggered if Task B is successful, not immediately after Task A.

- C is incorrect because Task C should not run unless Task B succeeds.

- D is incorrect because Task C will not automatically retry on Task B's failure; the task chain halts.

Answers and Explanations:

Question 21:

You need a Snowflake task to run every day at midnight to process new data. Which of the following cron expressions should you use to schedule this task?

A. 0 0 * * *

B. 0 12 * * *

C. 0 0 1 * *

D. 0 12 1 * *

Question 22:

You have a Snowflake task that processes incoming data and triggers subsequent tasks. You want this task to run automatically when new data is ingested into a table. What would be the most effective method for triggering this task?

A. Use a cron-based schedule to run the task every hour.

B. Use an event-based trigger linked to a Snowflake Stream.

C. Manually execute the task whenever new data is ingested.

D. Configure the task to run on a fixed schedule, regardless of new data.

Question 23:

You have a scheduled Snowflake task that runs every night at 2:00 AM. If the task fails to run at its scheduled time, what happens next?

A. Snowflake will automatically rerun the task at the next available time slot.

B. Snowflake will not retry the task and it will need to be manually triggered.

C. The task will automatically reschedule itself for the next day.

D. Snowflake will notify the administrator, but the task will not be retried.

Question 24:

Which of the following is a correct way to create a Snowflake task that runs every 5 minutes and is triggered by a table insert event?

A. Use a cron schedule */5 * * * * and link the task to a stream on the table.

B. Use a fixed cron schedule */5 * * * * and manually execute the task after each insert.

C. Create a Snowflake Task with a RUN ON EVENT trigger based on a table insert.

D. Use AFTER INSERT clause in the task definition to trigger the task automatically.

Question 25:

You have a Snowflake task that is scheduled to run every hour. The task depends on the successful completion of another task. If the dependent task fails, what happens to the scheduled task?

A. The scheduled task will automatically execute regardless of the dependent task's status.

B. The scheduled task will not run until the dependent task completes successfully.

C. The scheduled task will trigger and attempt to execute, even if the dependent task fails.

D. The scheduled task will fail silently without any notification.

Answers and Explanations:

Question 21:

Correct Answer: A

Explanation:

- A is correct because 0 0 * * * is a valid cron expression for scheduling the task to run at midnight every day.

- B is incorrect because 0 12 * * * runs the task at 12 PM, not midnight.

- C is incorrect because 0 0 1 * * schedules the task to run on the first day of every month, not daily.

- D is incorrect because 0 12 1 * * runs the task on the first day of every month at 12 PM, not daily.

Question 22:

Correct Answer: B

Explanation:

- B is correct because an event-based trigger linked to a **Snowflake Stream** can automatically trigger a task when new data is ingested.

- A is incorrect because running the task on a cron schedule every hour is not event-driven; it is a fixed interval approach.

126

- C is incorrect because manually executing tasks does not take advantage of automation and event-driven processing.

- D is incorrect because scheduling the task without checking for new data results in unnecessary runs and inefficiency.

Question 23:

Correct Answer: B

Explanation:

- B is correct because if the scheduled task fails, Snowflake will not automatically retry it; it must be manually triggered.

- A is incorrect because Snowflake does not automatically rerun failed tasks.

- C is incorrect because Snowflake does not automatically reschedule a failed task for the next day.

- D is incorrect because while Snowflake may notify the administrator, the task will not automatically retry on failure.

Question 24:

Correct Answer: A

Explanation:

- A is correct because */5 * * * * is a valid cron expression for scheduling the task to run every 5 minutes, and linking it to a **Stream** ensures the task is triggered by table inserts.

- B is incorrect because manually executing the task after each insert goes against the goal of automation and event-driven execution.

- C is incorrect because there is no RUN ON EVENT clause in Snowflake task definitions.

- D is incorrect because there is no AFTER INSERT clause in Snowflake task definitions; task triggers are configured via streams or cron expressions.

Question 25:

Correct Answer: B

Explanation:

- B is correct because Snowflake tasks that depend on other tasks will not run until the dependent task completes successfully.

- A is incorrect because the scheduled task will respect the dependency and only run if the dependent task is successful.

127

- **C** is incorrect because if the dependent task fails, the scheduled task will not run.
- **D** is incorrect because the task will not fail silently; Snowflake will notify administrators if the task fails.

SNOWPIPE

Question #1:
Which of the following best describes the purpose of SnowPipe in Snowflake?
Options:
A. SnowPipe is used for automated, continuous data ingestion from external stages into Snowflake tables.
B. SnowPipe handles batch data loading at scheduled intervals.
C. SnowPipe is designed for archiving historical data in Snowflake.
D. SnowPipe supports real-time analytics by pre-computing results.

Question #2:
Which of the following components are required to set up a data loading pipeline with SnowPipe?
Options:
A. External stage, notification integration, and pipe definition
B. External stage, database replication, and table indexes
C. Data pipeline services, external storage, and table partitioning
D. Snowflake Task Scheduler, data mart, and automated SQL queries

Question #3:
When using SnowPipe, how is the data ingestion triggered from an external stage?
Options:
A. By running a manual COPY INTO command.
B. Through notifications such as S3 events, Azure Event Grid, or Google Pub/Sub messages.
C. By enabling auto-ingest in Snowflake's user interface.
D. By scheduling Snowflake Tasks.

Question #4:
A data engineer is setting up SnowPipe to ingest data from an AWS S3 bucket. Which permissions must be granted to ensure Snowflake can access and load the data?
Options:
A. Permissions on the S3 bucket for Snowflake's IAM role
B. Full access to Snowflake's SQL warehouse
C. Read access to all databases in Snowflake
D. Read and write access to the SnowPipe object in Snowflake

Question #5:
A team wants to load JSON files into Snowflake using SnowPipe. Which of the following are

necessary to ensure that data from JSON files is correctly parsed and loaded?
Options:
A. Define a schema with JSON-specific parsing settings.
B. Create a file format for JSON with TYPE = JSON.
C. Use column names that match JSON key names.
D. Run the data ingestion manually using COPY INTO.

Answers and Explanations

Question #1:
Correct Answer: A
Explanation:
A is correct because SnowPipe allows for automated, continuous data ingestion from external stages into Snowflake tables, enabling near real-time loading.
B is incorrect because SnowPipe does not handle batch data loading at scheduled intervals.
C is incorrect because SnowPipe is not designed for archiving historical data.
D is incorrect because SnowPipe does not support real-time analytics by pre-computing results.

Question #2:
Correct Answer: A
Explanation:
A is correct because setting up SnowPipe requires an external stage (e.g., S3 bucket), a notification integration (e.g., S3 events or Azure Event Grid), and a pipe definition to automate data ingestion.
B is incorrect because database replication and table indexes are unrelated to SnowPipe.
C is incorrect because data pipeline services, external storage, and table partitioning are not necessary for SnowPipe.
D is incorrect because Snowflake Task Scheduler, data marts, and automated SQL queries are unrelated to SnowPipe setup.

Question #3:
Correct Answer: B
Explanation:
A is incorrect because manual COPY INTO commands are not part of SnowPipe's automated data ingestion process.
B is correct because SnowPipe is triggered by notifications such as S3 events, Azure Event Grid, or Google Pub/Sub messages to automate data ingestion.
C is incorrect because enabling auto-ingest through Snowflake's UI is not a supported feature for SnowPipe.
D is incorrect because Snowflake Tasks are used for scheduling SQL queries, not triggering SnowPipe ingestion.

Question #4:
Correct Answer: A
Explanation:
A is correct because Snowflake requires read permissions on the S3 bucket for the IAM role used in the external stage to access files for ingestion.
B is incorrect because SnowPipe does not require access to Snowflake's SQL warehouse.
C is incorrect because read access to all databases in Snowflake is unrelated to SnowPipe's data ingestion process.

D is incorrect because SnowPipe does not require specific read/write access to the SnowPipe object itself in Snowflake.

Question #5:
Correct Answer: B
Explanation:
A is incorrect because defining a schema with JSON-specific parsing settings is unnecessary for SnowPipe.
B is correct because SnowPipe requires a file format defined with TYPE = JSON to parse JSON files correctly.
C is incorrect because SnowPipe does not rely on column names matching JSON keys; the file format settings handle parsing.
D is incorrect because running COPY INTO manually is not part of SnowPipe's automated ingestion process.

Question #6:
How is SnowPipe billed in Snowflake?
Options:
A. Based on the storage used for ingested data
B. By the amount of data processed for ingestion
C. Based on the number of queries executed in SnowPipe
D. By the compute resources used during ingestion

Question #7:
If SnowPipe is configured to ingest files with auto-ingest notifications, what happens if a file fails to load due to an error?
Options:
A. SnowPipe retries automatically until successful.
B. The failed file is skipped and noted in the load history with error details.
C. The ingestion stops until the error is resolved.
D. SnowPipe archives the file in an error directory in the S3 bucket.

Question #8:
You are configuring SnowPipe to load data from an external S3 stage. Which of the following steps must be completed to set up SnowPipe correctly for automated loading? (Select all that apply)
Options:
A. Create an external stage pointing to the S3 bucket.
B. Define a SnowPipe with a COPY INTO command referencing the target table and external stage.
C. Configure an S3 bucket notification to trigger SnowPipe on new files.
D. Assign a Snowflake role with write access to the S3 bucket.
E. Run a REFRESH STAGE command to initialize SnowPipe on the stage.

Question #9:
A Snowflake administrator is troubleshooting an issue where files are not loading automatically into Snowflake from an Azure Blob storage stage configured with SnowPipe. Which of the following are likely causes? (Select all that apply)
Options:
A. Missing notification integration with Azure Event Grid.
B. Insufficient read permissions on the storage account for Snowflake's external integration.
C. Incorrect COPY INTO command syntax in the pipe definition.
D. Expired SnowPipe token for accessing the Blob storage.
E. Lack of a virtual warehouse assigned to SnowPipe.

Question #10:
When setting up SnowPipe for data ingestion, you need to minimize costs while ensuring high reliability of data loading. Which of the following approaches should you take? (Select all that apply)
Options:
A. Set up notification-based SnowPipe to load data continuously.
B. Use manual COPY INTO commands instead of SnowPipe to control data loading frequency.
C. Configure SnowPipe to ingest only necessary file types using a pattern filter in the stage.
D. Use a higher compute warehouse to process SnowPipe jobs faster.
E. Optimize file sizes for efficient SnowPipe ingestion.

Answers and Explanations

Question #6
Correct Answer: B
Explanation:
B is correct because SnowPipe is billed based on the amount of data processed during ingestion, not storage or compute resources.
A is incorrect because storage costs are separate from ingestion billing.
C is incorrect because SnowPipe billing does not depend on the number of queries executed.
D is incorrect because SnowPipe does not use dedicated compute resources for ingestion.

Question #7
Correct Answer: B
Explanation:
B is correct because when a file fails to load, SnowPipe skips the file and logs the error details in the load history for review and troubleshooting.
A is incorrect because SnowPipe does not automatically retry failed file loads.
C is incorrect because ingestion does not stop entirely due to a single file error.
D is incorrect because SnowPipe does not archive failed files in the source bucket.

Question #8
Correct Answers: A, B, and C
Explanation:
A: Correct. SnowPipe requires an external stage to locate and access files in S3.
B: Correct. A pipe must be created with a COPY INTO command that specifies the target table and external stage.
C: Correct. An S3 bucket notification triggers SnowPipe to begin data ingestion automatically.
D: Incorrect. Snowflake needs read access to the S3 bucket, not write access.
E: Incorrect. REFRESH STAGE is not used for SnowPipe. It relies on event-based triggering for continuous data ingestion.

Question #9
Correct Answers: A, B, and C
Explanation:
A: Correct. Notification integration with Azure Event Grid is required to automatically trigger SnowPipe on new file arrivals.
B: Correct. Snowflake needs read permissions on the storage account; insufficient permissions prevent data access.
C: Correct. An incorrect COPY INTO syntax in the pipe definition can prevent files from loading if the pipe fails to process.
D: Incorrect. SnowPipe does not use an "access token" to connect to Azure Blob storage; it relies on the external integration and assigned permissions.
E: Incorrect. SnowPipe does not require a virtual warehouse to process data ingestion, as it operates independently of Snowflake compute resources for loading.

Question #10
Correct Answers: A, C, and E
Explanation:
A: Correct. Notification-based SnowPipe ensures automatic, event-driven ingestion, which reduces manual intervention and provides high reliability.
C: Correct. Configuring pattern filters ensures only relevant files are loaded, reducing unnecessary ingestion and associated costs.
E: Correct. Using optimized file sizes for ingestion improves efficiency and reduces costs by ensuring smoother data processing.
B: Incorrect. Manual COPY INTO commands are more labor-intensive and could lead to higher operational overhead compared to SnowPipe's automation.
D: Incorrect. SnowPipe does not use Snowflake compute warehouses for ingestion, as it's billed based on data processed.

Question #11:
A team needs to monitor SnowPipe to ensure data is ingested correctly from Google Cloud Storage. Which of the following monitoring and troubleshooting steps should they implement? (Select all that apply)
A. Check the SnowPipe history for successful and failed file loads.
B. Enable logging in Google Cloud Storage to verify that Snowflake has read each file.
C. Use the SHOW PIPES command to verify SnowPipe configuration and status.
D. Adjust the SnowPipe batch size to optimize for smaller files.
E. Review Snowflake's FAILED_LOADS view for detailed error messages.

Question #12:
Which of the following statements about SnowPipe's load latency is correct?
A. SnowPipe offers zero-latency data loading for all file sizes.
B. SnowPipe aims for near real-time data loading with a typical latency of a few minutes.
C. SnowPipe load latency is determined by the size of the virtual warehouse assigned to it.
D. SnowPipe has a fixed 10-minute delay before beginning ingestion.

Question #13:
In a SnowPipe configuration, where would you find detailed information about failed data loads?
A. In the COPY_HISTORY table in Snowflake.
B. In the FAILED_LOADS view associated with SnowPipe.
C. By running the SHOW LOAD ERRORS command in Snowflake.
D. By checking the Snowflake Warehouse monitoring dashboard.

Question #14:
A team wants to load only CSV files from an Amazon S3 bucket using SnowPipe. Which configuration step would ensure that only CSV files are ingested?
A. Define a file format with TYPE = CSV in SnowPipe.
B. Specify a file extension pattern filter in the external stage configuration.
C. Use a virtual warehouse to validate file formats before ingestion.
D. Configure SnowPipe to discard non-CSV files automatically.

Question #15:
Which command would you use to view the configuration and status of a specific SnowPipe in Snowflake?
A. SHOW PIPES

B. DESCRIBE PIPE
C. LIST PIPE STATUS
D. VIEW PIPE CONFIG

Answers and Explanations

Question #11:
Correct Answers: A, B, C, and E
Explanation:
A: Correct. Checking SnowPipe history shows the status of file loads, including successful and failed ones.
B: Correct. Enabling Google Cloud Storage logging helps verify Snowflake's access to files, which is crucial for troubleshooting access issues.
C: Correct. The SHOW PIPES command helps verify the SnowPipe configuration and status.
E: Correct. The FAILED_LOADS view provides detailed error messages for troubleshooting failed loads.
D: Incorrect. SnowPipe processes files individually upon trigger and does not use batch size adjustments.

Question #12:
Correct Answer: B
Explanation:
SnowPipe is designed for near real-time data ingestion with typical latency of a few minutes.
A: Incorrect. SnowPipe does not provide zero-latency loading.
C: Incorrect. SnowPipe operates independently of a virtual warehouse.
D: Incorrect. SnowPipe does not impose a fixed 10-minute delay for ingestion.

Question #13:
Correct Answer: B
Explanation:
The FAILED_LOADS view contains detailed information about files that failed to load, including error messages.
A: Incorrect. The COPY_HISTORY table provides load history but does not include detailed error messages.
C: Incorrect. SHOW LOAD ERRORS is not a valid command for SnowPipe.
D: Incorrect. The Snowflake Warehouse monitoring dashboard does not display file load errors for SnowPipe.

Question #14:
Correct Answer: B
Explanation:
Specifying a file extension pattern filter in the external stage configuration ensures that only CSV files are ingested by SnowPipe.
A: Incorrect. Defining a file format as CSV does not restrict ingestion to only CSV files.
C: Incorrect. A virtual warehouse does not validate file formats for ingestion.
D: Incorrect. SnowPipe does not discard non-CSV files; filtering must be configured in the stage.

Question #15:
Correct Answer: A
Explanation:

The SHOW PIPES command provides configuration and status information for SnowPipes in Snowflake.
B: Incorrect. DESCRIBE PIPE is not a valid command.
C: Incorrect. LIST PIPE STATUS is not a valid command.
D: Incorrect. VIEW PIPE CONFIG is not a valid command.

Question #16:
Which of the following could cause SnowPipe to fail in loading a file from Azure Blob Storage?
A. Incorrect storage account region
B. Incorrect file format specified in the SnowPipe definition
C. Unassigned virtual warehouse
D. Incorrect timestamp format in the source data

Question #17:
What is the primary difference between SnowPipe and a standard COPY INTO command for data ingestion in Snowflake?
A. SnowPipe is triggered manually, while COPY INTO is automated.
B. SnowPipe offers continuous, event-driven ingestion, while COPY INTO is typically run as a batch operation.
C. SnowPipe can ingest only structured data, while COPY INTO can handle any data format.
D. SnowPipe requires a virtual warehouse, while COPY INTO does not.

Question #18:
A Snowflake user notices that SnowPipe ingestion has stopped. Which of the following should be checked first?
A. Whether the external stage URL is accessible
B. The virtual warehouse is running
C. The notification integration with the storage provider
D. The size of the files being ingested

Question #19:
Which two Snowflake features are required to set up automated data ingestion using SnowPipe with an Amazon S3 bucket?
A. An external stage pointing to the S3 bucket
B. A Snowflake virtual warehouse for compute
C. An S3 bucket notification integration
D. A Snowflake Task that schedules data loads

Question #20:
When configuring SnowPipe for continuous data ingestion, which two components should you verify if data isn't loading as expected?
A. Permissions on the external storage location
B. The status of Snowflake's virtual warehouse
C. The SnowPipe definition and its SQL syntax
D. The availability of compute nodes in Snowflake

Question #16:
Correct Answer: B
Explanation:

B: Correct. An incorrect file format specified in the SnowPipe definition can cause files to fail loading because SnowPipe must parse files based on the configured format (e.g., CSV, JSON).
A: Incorrect. The storage account region mismatch would prevent access but is not specific to SnowPipe failures.
C: Incorrect. SnowPipe does not rely on a virtual warehouse for its operations.
D: Incorrect. Timestamp format issues in the source data do not directly prevent SnowPipe from initiating file ingestion.

Question #17:
Correct Answer: B
Explanation:
B: Correct. SnowPipe supports continuous, event-driven ingestion, making it suitable for near real-time data ingestion, while COPY INTO is typically run as a manual or scheduled batch process.
A: Incorrect. SnowPipe is event-driven, not manually triggered.
C: Incorrect. Both SnowPipe and COPY INTO can handle structured and semi-structured data formats.
D: Incorrect. SnowPipe does not require a virtual warehouse for its ingestion operations.

Question #18:
Correct Answer: C
Explanation:
C: Correct. Notification integrations with the storage provider are crucial for SnowPipe's event-driven ingestion, and any misconfiguration or disconnection could halt ingestion.
A: Incorrect. The external stage URL must be accessible, but this is less likely to be the primary issue if ingestion has worked previously.
B: Incorrect. SnowPipe does not use a virtual warehouse for ingestion.
D: Incorrect. File size issues alone would not directly stop SnowPipe ingestion.

Question #19:
Correct Answers: A and C
Explanation:
A: Correct. An external stage pointing to the S3 bucket is necessary for Snowflake to locate and access the files for ingestion.
C: Correct. An S3 bucket notification integration ensures that SnowPipe is triggered automatically when new files are added.
B: Incorrect. SnowPipe does not require a virtual warehouse to perform its ingestion.
D: Incorrect. Snowflake Tasks are not required for SnowPipe as it operates through event triggers, not scheduled processes.

Question #20:
Correct Answers: A and C
Explanation:
A: Correct. Proper permissions on the external storage location (e.g., S3, Azure Blob) are essential for SnowPipe to access and load files.
C: Correct. Errors in the SnowPipe definition, such as incorrect SQL syntax in the COPY INTO command, can prevent files from loading.
B: Incorrect. SnowPipe does not rely on a virtual warehouse for ingestion tasks.
D: Incorrect. SnowPipe ingestion does not depend on the availability of compute nodes in Snowflake.

Question #21:

Which two of the following methods can help reduce costs associated with SnowPipe?
A. Using file filters to ingest only necessary files
B. Increasing SnowPipe's data retention period
C. Reducing the number of notification events sent to SnowPipe
D. Assigning a smaller virtual warehouse to SnowPipe

Question #22:
A data engineer needs to verify successful file ingestion into Snowflake using SnowPipe. Which two methods can be used to monitor and troubleshoot SnowPipe load activity?
A. Checking the LOAD_HISTORY view for SnowPipe status
B. Using the SHOW PIPES command to verify pipe configuration
C. Reviewing the Snowflake Warehouse activity log
D. Checking the Snowflake user access log

Question #23:
In order to use SnowPipe for loading JSON data from Google Cloud Storage, which two components must be configured?
A. A Google Cloud notification integration
B. A virtual warehouse with high compute capacity
C. A JSON file format for the SnowPipe configuration
D. A Snowflake Task to manage ingestion frequency

Question #24:
Which Snowflake command provides a list of all defined pipes and their current status in the account?
- A. DESCRIBE PIPE
- B. SHOW PIPES
- C. LIST PIPES
- D. VIEW PIPES

Question #25:
When using SnowPipe to load data from S3, which service or feature notifies Snowflake of new files ready for ingestion?
- A. AWS Lambda
- B. S3 bucket notification
- C. AWS EventBridge
- D. Snowflake Task

Answers and Explanations

Question #21: Correct Answers: A and C
Explanation:
A: Using file filters ensures that only the necessary files are ingested, reducing data processing costs.
C: Reducing the number of notification events sent to SnowPipe reduces the frequency of ingestion, which helps manage costs.
B: Incorrect. Increasing data retention does not directly impact SnowPipe costs.
D: Incorrect. SnowPipe does not use a virtual warehouse, so this option is not applicable.

Question #22: Correct Answers: A and B
Explanation:

A: Checking the LOAD_HISTORY view is essential for monitoring file ingestion statuses, showing both successes and failures.
B: Using the SHOW PIPES command provides details about the pipe's configuration and status, which can help identify issues.
C: Incorrect. SnowPipe does not rely on a virtual warehouse for ingestion, so the warehouse activity log is not helpful.
D: Incorrect. The user access log does not track SnowPipe ingestion activities.

Question #23: Correct Answers: A and C
Explanation:
A: A Google Cloud notification integration is required to trigger SnowPipe when files are added to Google Cloud Storage.
C: Specifying a JSON file format is necessary to correctly parse and load JSON data from Google Cloud Storage.
B: Incorrect. SnowPipe does not require a virtual warehouse for ingestion.
D: Incorrect. Snowflake Tasks are not necessary for SnowPipe, as it operates with event-based triggers.

Question #24: Correct Answer: B
Explanation:
B: The SHOW PIPES command displays all defined pipes and their current status, helping users monitor and manage SnowPipe configurations.
A: Incorrect. DESCRIBE PIPE provides details about a specific pipe but not a list of all pipes.
C: Incorrect. LIST PIPES is not a valid Snowflake command.
D: Incorrect. VIEW PIPES is not a valid Snowflake command either.

Question #25: Correct Answer: B
Explanation:
B: S3 bucket notifications are used to trigger SnowPipe when new files are uploaded to an S3 bucket.
A: Incorrect. AWS Lambda is not required to notify Snowflake of new files; S3 notifications serve this purpose.
C: Incorrect. AWS EventBridge is not used for this task.
D: Incorrect. Snowflake Tasks are not involved in notifying SnowPipe of new files.

Question #26:
Which of the following best describes the purpose of the FAILED_LOADS view in Snowflake when using SnowPipe?
 A. It lists all files that have successfully loaded into Snowflake.
 B. It shows details about files that failed to load, including error messages.
 C. It contains configuration details for each SnowPipe.
 D. It displays the history of user access to SnowPipe.

Question #27:
A data engineer needs to load data from Google Cloud Storage into Snowflake continuously. Which type of notification must be set up to automate this process with SnowPipe?
A. Google Cloud Pub/Sub
B. Google Cloud Function
C. Google Cloud Scheduler
D. Google Cloud EventBridge

Question #28:

Which Snowflake command provides information on the history of files loaded by SnowPipe, including details like file names and load times?
A. COPY_HISTORY
B. SHOW HISTORY
C. LIST LOADS
D. LOAD_HISTORY

Question #29:
If a file is successfully ingested by SnowPipe, where can a data engineer find information on that ingestion event?
A. COPY_HISTORY
B. FAILED_LOADS
C. SHOW PIPES
D. FILE_LOG

Question #30:
Which statement is true regarding SnowPipe's requirement for compute resources?
A. SnowPipe requires a virtual warehouse to process each data load.
B. SnowPipe is billed based on data processed and does not require a virtual warehouse.
C. SnowPipe requires compute clusters to process JSON data specifically.
D. SnowPipe requires both a virtual warehouse and compute clusters to process data.

Answers and Explanations

Question #26:
Correct Answer: B
Explanation:
B: The FAILED_LOADS view provides details about files that failed to load, including error messages, which helps with troubleshooting issues.
A: Incorrect. The view that lists files that have successfully loaded would not be the FAILED_LOADS view.
C: Incorrect. The FAILED_LOADS view does not contain configuration details for SnowPipe.
D: Incorrect. The FAILED_LOADS view does not track user access history to SnowPipe.

Question #27:
Correct Answer: A
Explanation:
A: Google Cloud Pub/Sub is used to send notifications to Snowflake when new files are added to Google Cloud Storage, which triggers SnowPipe to load the data.
B: Incorrect. Google Cloud Function is not used to trigger SnowPipe ingestion directly.
C: Incorrect. Google Cloud Scheduler does not send event-based notifications to SnowPipe.
D: Incorrect. Google Cloud EventBridge is not a service used for triggering SnowPipe.

Question #28:
Correct Answer: A
Explanation:
A: The COPY_HISTORY command provides the history of files loaded by SnowPipe, including file names, timestamps, and load statuses.
B: Incorrect. SHOW HISTORY is not a valid Snowflake command.
C: Incorrect. LIST LOADS is not a valid Snowflake command to check file load history.

D: Incorrect. LOAD_HISTORY does not exist for checking file ingestion details. COPY_HISTORY is the correct command.

Question #29:
Correct Answer: A
Explanation:
A: The COPY_HISTORY view contains details about successfully loaded files, including their names, timestamps, and load statuses.
B: Incorrect. FAILED_LOADS tracks only failed file ingestion events, not successful ones.
C: Incorrect. SHOW PIPES provides information about pipes, but not about specific file ingestion events.
D: Incorrect. FILE_LOG is not a valid view for tracking file ingestion details.

Question #30:
Correct Answer: B
Explanation:
B: SnowPipe is billed based on data processed and does not require a virtual warehouse for its operations. It is an event-driven service independent of compute resources.
A: Incorrect. SnowPipe does not require a virtual warehouse for processing data; it functions independently of virtual warehouses.
C: Incorrect. SnowPipe does not rely on compute clusters for processing JSON data specifically.
D: Incorrect. SnowPipe operates independently of compute resources like virtual warehouses and compute clusters.

Question #31:
When loading data into Snowflake using SnowPipe, which two factors can impact the speed of data ingestion?
A. The file size and format of the data being ingested
B. The compute capacity of the virtual warehouse used by SnowPipe
C. The latency of the external storage service
D. The Snowflake account region

Question #32:
In SnowPipe, where can you review error messages for any files that failed to load?
A. COPY_HISTORY
B. FAILED_LOADS
C. LOAD_ERRORS
D. PIPE_LOG

Question #33:
A data engineer is trying to monitor SnowPipe's ingestion progress. Which two Snowflake objects provide information about the status and history of ingestions?
A. COPY_HISTORY
B. SNOWPIPE_HISTORY
C. FAILED_LOADS
D. LOADED_FILES

Question #34:
Which statement is true about the COPY INTO command in SnowPipe?

- A. It must be run manually each time new data arrives.
- B. It is triggered automatically when new files arrive in the external stage.
- C. It requires a virtual warehouse for each load.
- D. It requires Snowflake Tasks to trigger ingestion.

Question #35:
To automate data ingestion with SnowPipe from an Azure Blob Storage container, which two configurations are essential?
- A. A virtual warehouse assigned to SnowPipe
- B. An Azure event grid notification integration
- C. An external stage configured with the container's URL
- D. A Snowflake Task to schedule ingestion

Answers and Explanations

Question #31:
Correct Answer: A and C
Explanation:
A: The file size and format impact ingestion speed, as larger files or more complex formats (like JSON) can require more time to process.
C: The latency of the external storage (e.g., S3 or GCS) can impact how quickly SnowPipe accesses files for ingestion.
Incorrect Answers Explanation:
B: Incorrect. SnowPipe does not rely on a virtual warehouse for data ingestion, so its speed isn't influenced by virtual warehouse size.
D: Incorrect. The region of the Snowflake account itself doesn't directly affect SnowPipe ingestion speed, though regions should ideally align for efficiency.

Question #32:
Correct Answer: B
Explanation:
B: FAILED_LOADS contains specific details and error messages for files that failed to load, which is crucial for troubleshooting.
Incorrect Answers Explanation:
A: Incorrect. COPY_HISTORY lists successfully loaded files but doesn't provide error messages for failures.
C: Incorrect. LOAD_ERRORS is not a valid Snowflake system view or table.
D: Incorrect. PIPE_LOG is not a Snowflake system table; the correct table for reviewing failed ingestions is FAILED_LOADS.

Question #33:
Correct Answer: A and C
Explanation:
A: COPY_HISTORY provides a history of files that SnowPipe has successfully loaded.
C: FAILED_LOADS gives details on any files that failed to load, making it useful for monitoring ingestion issues.
Incorrect Answers Explanation:
B: Incorrect. SNOWPIPE_HISTORY does not exist; COPY_HISTORY and FAILED_LOADS serve these roles.
D: Incorrect. LOADED_FILES is not a valid system table for tracking ingestion status; COPY_HISTORY is the correct view.

Question #34:
Correct Answer: B
Explanation:
B: SnowPipe automatically triggers the COPY INTO command when new files are detected in the external stage, allowing for continuous data ingestion.
Incorrect Answers Explanation:
A: Incorrect. The COPY INTO command is automated in SnowPipe and does not require manual execution.
C: Incorrect. SnowPipe does not require a virtual warehouse to operate.
D: Incorrect. SnowPipe is event-driven and doesn't need Snowflake Tasks to initiate ingestion.

Question #35:
Correct Answer: B and C
Explanation:
B: Azure event grid notification integration is required to notify SnowPipe when new files are available in Blob Storage.
C: An external stage configured with the URL of the container allows SnowPipe to access files in Azure Blob Storage.
Incorrect Answers Explanation:
A: Incorrect. SnowPipe does not use a virtual warehouse for its operation.
D: Incorrect. Snowflake Tasks are unnecessary since SnowPipe uses event-driven notifications for ingestion.

Question #36:
In which situation would you check the FAILED_LOADS view in Snowflake?
- A. To verify the current configuration of a SnowPipe
- B. To troubleshoot files that failed during ingestion
- C. To monitor Snowflake Task failures
- D. To view the history of successful file loads

Question #37:
Which Snowflake view would you query to see detailed information about files that SnowPipe has successfully loaded into a table?
- A. LOAD_HISTORY
- B. COPY_HISTORY
- C. PIPE_HISTORY
- D. DATA_LOADS

Question #38:
When setting up SnowPipe for continuous data ingestion from Amazon S3, which two configurations are required to initiate the data loading process?
- A. An S3 event notification
- B. A Snowflake Task for scheduling
- C. An external stage pointing to the S3 bucket
- D. A virtual warehouse with auto-suspend

Question #39:
If data ingestion using SnowPipe is slow, which two strategies can help improve performance?
- A. Increasing the size of the virtual warehouse used by SnowPipe
- B. Ensuring files are smaller and split into multiple parts
- C. Configuring Snowflake Tasks to check for new files more frequently
- D. Reducing latency with the external storage location

Question #40:
What is a primary benefit of using SnowPipe over a scheduled batch load in Snowflake?
- A. SnowPipe only requires a one-time configuration
- B. SnowPipe does not use compute resources in Snowflake
- C. SnowPipe allows for near-real-time data ingestion
- D. SnowPipe can be configured with a virtual warehouse for speed

---

Answers and Explanations

Question #36: Correct Answer: B
Explanation:
B: The FAILED_LOADS view is specifically designed to provide error details for files that could not be ingested by SnowPipe.
A: Incorrect. The SHOW PIPES command or pipe configuration commands are used to check SnowPipe configuration, not FAILED_LOADS.
C: Incorrect. Snowflake Tasks are unrelated to SnowPipe ingestion and are tracked separately.
D: Incorrect. Successful ingestions are found in COPY_HISTORY, not FAILED_LOADS.

Question #37: Correct Answer: B
Explanation:
B: COPY_HISTORY is the correct view to check for details on files that were successfully ingested by SnowPipe, including timestamps and file names.
A: Incorrect. LOAD_HISTORY does not exist in Snowflake; the correct view for successful loads is COPY_HISTORY.
C: Incorrect. PIPE_HISTORY is not a valid view in Snowflake.
D: Incorrect. DATA_LOADS is not a recognized view for tracking file loads in SnowPipe.

Question #38: Correct Answer: A and C
Explanation:
A: Correct. S3 event notifications are needed to automatically trigger SnowPipe when new files arrive in the S3 bucket.
C: Correct. An external stage pointing to the S3 bucket must be configured to allow SnowPipe to locate and access files.
B: Incorrect. Snowflake Tasks are not required since SnowPipe is triggered by event notifications.
D: Incorrect. SnowPipe does not require a virtual warehouse; it operates independently of warehouse resources.

Question #39: Correct Answer: B and D
Explanation:
B: Correct. Smaller files that are split into multiple parts can improve ingestion performance, as SnowPipe can process files faster and in parallel.
D: Correct. Reducing latency from the external storage (e.g., ensuring the storage location is in the same region as Snowflake) can improve data transfer speed.
A: Incorrect. SnowPipe does not use a virtual warehouse, so increasing warehouse size does not affect ingestion speed.
C: Incorrect. Snowflake Tasks are irrelevant to SnowPipe ingestion, which is triggered by external storage notifications.

Question #40: Correct Answer: C
Explanation:

C: SnowPipe's main advantage over batch loading is its ability to provide near-real-time data ingestion, which is especially useful for time-sensitive data processing.
A: Incorrect. Although SnowPipe is typically a one-time setup, this is not its primary benefit compared to batch loading.
B: Incorrect. SnowPipe does incur Snowflake costs based on data volume processed, even though it doesn't use a virtual warehouse.
D: Incorrect. SnowPipe doesn't use a virtual warehouse for ingestion; it's event-driven and handles data as soon as it arrives.

DATA CLONING

Question #01:
You need to create a clone of a database in Snowflake for testing purposes, ensuring no data duplication occurs and that the cloning process is fast. Which Snowflake feature should you use to achieve this?
Options:
A. Zero-Copy Cloning
B. Time Travel
C. Data Sharing
D. Materialized Views

Question #02:
What is the main benefit of using **zero-copy cloning** in Snowflake for creating a new schema?
Options:
A. It reduces the cost of storing data by creating a full duplicate of the original data.
B. It enables fast cloning of the schema without using additional storage for the initial copy.
C. It automatically performs a full refresh of the cloned schema every 24 hours.
D. It ensures data is always available in the clone, even if the original data is deleted.

Question #03:
Which of the following statements is true about **zero-copy cloning** in Snowflake?
Options:
A. Clones only store metadata and no actual data initially, which saves storage space.
B. Cloning a table creates an exact copy of the data, with a separate set of physical storage.
C. Clones are always a snapshot of the original data at the time of cloning.
D. You can perform DML operations on a clone, and these changes will be reflected in the original object.

Question #04:
When performing a **zero-copy clone** of a database in Snowflake, which of the following is true about the relationship between the original and the cloned objects?
Options:
A. The cloned object behaves as a fully independent copy, and changes in the clone do not affect the original.

B. The cloned object is physically separate from the original and contains its own storage, so no changes are reflected in the original object.
C. The cloned object shares data storage with the original until any changes are made to the clone.
D. The cloned object can only be accessed by users with the same privileges as those granted on the original object.

Question #05:
You are performing a **zero-copy clone** of a table in Snowflake, and you want to make changes to the cloned table without impacting the original table. What happens when you modify data in the cloned table?
Options:
A. The changes will automatically be reflected in the original table as well.
B. The clone will take up additional storage once changes are made, as only modified data will be stored separately.
C. The cloned table becomes a permanent duplicate of the original, requiring manual synchronization for further updates.
D. Changes to the clone will not consume extra storage or affect the original data, as clones initially share the same underlying storage.

Answers and Explanations

Question #01:
Correct Answer: A
Explanation:
A is correct because zero-copy cloning allows Snowflake to create clones of databases, schemas, tables, or other objects without physically duplicating the data, which aligns with the requirement for fast and minimal storage overhead cloning.
B is incorrect because Time Travel refers to querying data as it existed at a specific point in time, not cloning.
C is incorrect because Data Sharing is used for sharing data between Snowflake accounts, not cloning objects.
D is incorrect because Materialized Views store the results of a query in a persistent table-like structure, not for cloning.

Question #02:
Correct Answer: B
Explanation:
B is correct because zero-copy cloning allows for fast cloning without the need for additional storage for the data initially. It only stores metadata and uses pointers to the original data.
A is incorrect because zero-copy cloning does not duplicate the data; it only references it.
C is incorrect because zero-copy cloning does not automatically refresh a cloned object; it only provides a snapshot at the time of cloning.
D is incorrect because zero-copy cloning allows access to the cloned data, but it doesn't protect the clone from being impacted if the original data is deleted.

Question #03:

Correct Answer: A
Explanation:
A is correct because zero-copy cloning uses a pointer-based approach, meaning that initially, only metadata is stored, with no actual data copied. This minimizes storage usage.
B is incorrect because cloning does not create a physical copy of the data; it uses pointers to reference the original data until modifications occur.
C is incorrect because zero-copy cloning is not a snapshot but a reference to the data at the time of cloning.
D is incorrect because changes in the clone do not affect the original data, as clones are independent once changes are made.

Question #04:
Correct Answer: C
Explanation:
C is correct because in zero-copy cloning, the cloned object shares the underlying data storage with the original until changes are made in the clone.
A is incorrect because while the clone behaves independently once changes are made, initially, it shares the underlying data.
B is incorrect because zero-copy cloning does not physically separate the cloned object; it relies on shared storage until modifications are made.
D is incorrect because while access to the clone can be controlled with permissions, this is not unique to clones in Snowflake; it applies to all objects.

Question #05:
Correct Answer: B, D
Explanation:
B is correct because once changes are made to the cloned table, Snowflake will use additional storage for the modified data, separating it from the original data.
D is correct because zero-copy cloning ensures that changes to the clone do not impact the original data, and no additional storage is used for unchanged data.
A is incorrect because changes made to the clone will not affect the original table unless explicitly copied or synchronized.
C is incorrect because changes to the clone are stored separately, and it doesn't require manual synchronization for further updates.

Question #06:
A user wants to clone a large table in Snowflake. They are concerned about the time it will take to clone the data, as the table contains millions of rows. What is the key benefit of Snowflake's cloning feature in this scenario?
Options:
A. Cloning the table in Snowflake will take several minutes, depending on the size of the data.
B. Cloning in Snowflake is instantaneous, regardless of the size of the data.
C. The data will be duplicated during the cloning process, which may affect performance.
D. Cloning will require the data to be manually copied from the original location to a new location.

Question #07:

You want to create a snapshot of a table in Snowflake to use as a backup. Which of the following statements is true regarding Snowflake's cloning feature?
Options:
A. Cloning creates an independent copy of the data that is physically duplicated in Snowflake.
B. Cloning creates a logical copy of the data without duplicating the underlying storage, making it more efficient.
C. Cloned tables are always read-only and cannot be modified.
D. Cloning a table will result in a permanent duplication of the data and increase storage costs.

Question #08:
A user clones a schema in Snowflake, and later updates some data in the original schema. What happens to the data in the cloned schema?
Options:
A. The data in the cloned schema is immediately updated to reflect the changes in the original schema.
B. The cloned schema remains static and unaffected by changes made to the original schema after the clone.
C. The cloned schema automatically updates every 24 hours to match the original schema.
D. The changes to the original schema are ignored, and the cloned schema must be manually refreshed.

Question #09:
You are cloning a large table in Snowflake for testing purposes. Which of the following best describes the behavior of the cloned table?
Options:
A. The cloned table uses the same data as the original table but is independent, meaning changes to the original table do not affect the clone.
B. The cloned table and the original table are tightly linked, and changes to the clone automatically update the original table.
C. The cloned table is not accessible for querying until the cloning process is completed, which could take a significant amount of time.
D. The cloned table is an exact physical copy of the original table, including its structure and data.

Question #10:
A team wants to test changes to a table in Snowflake without affecting the original table. They decide to clone the table. Which of the following is true regarding Snowflake's cloning behavior?
Options:
A. The cloned table is independent of the original table, and any changes made to the original table will not affect the clone.
B. The cloned table still shares storage with the original table and any changes made to the original table will be reflected in the clone.
C. Cloning is not possible with Snowflake's database; the table must be manually replicated.
D. Once the table is cloned, it becomes read-only, and no changes can be made to it.

Answers and Explanations

Question #06:
Correct Answer: B
Explanation:
B is correct because Snowflake's cloning feature is instantaneous, regardless of the size of the data, as it only creates a logical copy, not duplicating the actual data.
A is incorrect because cloning in Snowflake does not depend on the size of the data and is instantaneous.
C is incorrect because the cloning process does not involve data duplication, and there is no performance hit.
D is incorrect because Snowflake handles cloning in a way that does not require manual data copying.

Question #07:
Correct Answer: B
Explanation:
B is correct because Snowflake uses a schema-on-read approach for cloning, meaning it creates a logical copy without duplicating the underlying storage.
A is incorrect because cloning does not physically duplicate the data in Snowflake.
C is incorrect because cloned tables are not read-only and can be modified.
D is incorrect because cloning does not permanently duplicate data; it uses minimal additional storage as it is a logical copy.

Question #08:
Correct Answer: B
Explanation:
B is correct because Snowflake's cloning creates a snapshot of the data at the time of cloning. Changes to the original table after cloning will not affect the cloned schema.
A is incorrect because the data in the cloned schema does not automatically update when the original schema is modified.
C is incorrect because Snowflake does not update the clone automatically every 24 hours.
D is incorrect because cloning in Snowflake creates a snapshot, and there is no need to manually refresh the clone after the original schema is changed.

Question #09:
Correct Answer: A
Explanation:
A is correct because the cloned table in Snowflake uses the same data as the original table, but it is independent in terms of changes—modifications to the original table do not affect the clone.
B is incorrect because the cloned table is independent and does not automatically update when the original table is modified.
C is incorrect because the cloned table is immediately accessible for querying, and there is no significant delay involved.
D is incorrect because the cloned table is a logical copy, and its data is not physically duplicated.

Question #10:
Correct Answer: A
Explanation:
A is correct because the cloned table is independent, and any changes made to the original table will not affect the clone.
B is incorrect because the cloned table does not share storage with the original table in a way that would make changes to the original automatically reflected in the clone.
C is incorrect because cloning is a core feature in Snowflake, and tables can be cloned for testing.
D is incorrect because the cloned table can be modified independently of the original table.

Question #11:
A user wants to clone a table in Snowflake at a specific point in time, using Time Travel. Which of the following statements is true regarding the cloning process?
Options:
A. Cloning a table using Time Travel allows you to revert to a previous state of the table, but the clone will not include any historical data.
B. When cloning a table with Time Travel, the cloned table will include the data as it was at the specified point in time, including any historical changes.
C. Time Travel compatibility with cloning is only available for tables in the current database, not across databases.
D. The cloned table will always reference the most recent version of the data, ignoring the Time Travel specification.

Question #12:
A team wants to use Snowflake's Time Travel feature to clone a database at a specific point in the past for recovery purposes. Which of the following is true?
Options:
A. Time Travel can only be used to clone tables, not entire databases.
B. Time Travel allows cloning a database, and the clone will include all objects (tables, schemas, etc.) as they were at the specified point in time.
C. When cloning a database using Time Travel, only the schema of the database is restored, and tables must be manually cloned.
D. Time Travel cannot be used for database cloning; it is only applicable for tables.

Question #13:
A user successfully clones a table in Snowflake using Time Travel, but notices that the clone does not contain any historical changes after the specified point in time. What could be the issue?
Options:
A. Time Travel has a limitation that prevents historical changes from being cloned.
B. The clone was created using the wrong timestamp for the Time Travel period.
C. The cloned table is read-only, so historical data changes cannot be applied.
D. The Time Travel retention period for the table has expired, and the historical data is no longer available.

Question #14:

A Snowflake user needs to clone a table at a specific point in time, using Time Travel, and make changes to the cloned table without affecting the original table. What will happen if the user updates the cloned table after cloning?

Options:

A. The clone will remain unaffected by the changes made to the original table, as Snowflake cloning creates an independent copy.

B. The changes made to the cloned table will automatically reflect in the original table, as cloning creates a link between the two.

C. The clone will update in real time as changes are made to the original table, even though the cloning process occurred at a specific point in time.

D. Time Travel will prevent any modifications to the cloned table, making it a permanent snapshot.

Question #15:

A Snowflake administrator wants to clone a table from an earlier date and use it for audit purposes. Which statement correctly describes the behavior of the cloned table with Time Travel?

Options:

A. The cloned table will include all changes made after the specified point in time, including any modifications from the current period.

B. The cloned table will only contain data as it was at the specified time and will not include any changes made after that point.

C. Time Travel does not work with cloned tables, so the audit process must rely on manual snapshots.

D. Cloning using Time Travel will create a new table with the same name as the original table, replacing the current table in the database.

Answers and Explanations

Question #11:
Correct Answer: B
Explanation:
B is correct because when cloning a table with Time Travel, the clone will include the data exactly as it was at the specified point in time, including historical changes.
A is incorrect because cloning with Time Travel will include the historical data up to the specified timestamp.
C is incorrect because Time Travel can be used for cloning across databases.
D is incorrect because the clone will reflect the state of the data as of the specified point in time, not the most recent version.

Question #12:
Correct Answer: B
Explanation:
B is correct because Time Travel allows you to clone an entire database, and the clone will include all objects (tables, schemas, etc.) at the specified point in time.
A is incorrect because Time Travel does allow cloning of databases, not just tables.

C is incorrect because cloning a database with Time Travel will include all objects, not just the schema.
D is incorrect because Time Travel can be used for database cloning.

Question #13:
Correct Answer: B, D
Explanation:
B is correct because the clone could be created using the wrong timestamp, causing it to not reflect the correct historical data.
D is correct because if the Time Travel retention period has expired, historical data will no longer be available for cloning.
A is incorrect because Time Travel allows historical changes to be cloned, as long as the retention period is not expired.
C is incorrect because the cloned table is not read-only and can be modified after cloning.

Question #14:
Correct Answer: A
Explanation:
A is correct because once the clone is created using Time Travel, it becomes an independent table. Changes made to the original table will not affect the cloned table.
B is incorrect because cloning creates an independent copy, and changes to one do not affect the other.
C is incorrect because the cloned table remains static at the point in time it was cloned and does not reflect real-time updates.
D is incorrect because Time Travel allows modifications to the cloned table after it has been created.

Question #15:
Correct Answer: B
Explanation:
B is correct because cloning with Time Travel captures the state of the data at the specified time, and the cloned table will not include any changes made after that point.
A is incorrect because the cloned table does not include any changes after the specified time.
C is incorrect because Time Travel is fully compatible with cloning and does not require manual snapshots.
D is incorrect because Time Travel will not replace the original table; the clone is a separate table created at the point in time.

Question #16:
You cloned a table in Snowflake for a development environment to test new features. After testing, you decide to update the original table. What happens to the cloned table?
Options:
A. The cloned table is automatically updated to reflect changes in the original table.

B. The cloned table remains unchanged, and the updates to the original table will not affect it.
C. The cloned table will automatically revert to its original state when the original table is updated.
D. The cloned table becomes inaccessible once changes are made to the original table.

Question #17:
You want to make changes to a dataset without altering the original dataset in Snowflake. Which of the following methods would you use?
Options:
A. Perform the changes directly on the original dataset.
B. Clone the dataset, then make changes to the clone.
C. Create a backup of the original dataset and then modify the backup.
D. Create a temporary table and modify it as needed.

Question #18:
You clone a large schema in Snowflake to experiment with new data modeling techniques. While experimenting, you make several modifications to the cloned schema. What happens to the original schema?
Options:
A. The original schema is updated automatically to reflect changes made in the cloned schema.
B. The original schema remains unchanged as the cloned schema is independent.
C. The original schema becomes read-only once the clone is created.
D. The cloned schema will automatically discard changes made to it and reset to the original state.

Question #19:
A data scientist creates a clone of a production table in Snowflake to run some experiments on data transformations. What is the impact on the original production table?
Options:
A. The original production table is unaffected by any changes made to the clone.
B. Any changes to the clone will also affect the original production table, as they share the same data.
C. The clone will not be able to access data from the original table and will require a data import.
D. The clone will automatically update when the original production table is updated.

Question #20:
You are tasked with testing new features on a dataset in Snowflake without impacting the production data. What would be the best approach?
Options:
A. Clone the dataset and apply the new features to the clone without affecting the production data.
B. Apply the changes directly to the production dataset and test the features.
C. Export the data to a different database for testing purposes.
D. Create a new schema and manually copy the data into the schema for testing.

Answers and Explanations

Question #16:
Correct Answer: B
Explanation:
B is correct because once the clone is created, it is independent of the original table. Changes made to the original table do not affect the clone.
A is incorrect because the cloned table does not automatically update with changes from the original.
C is incorrect because the clone does not revert to its original state after changes to the original table.
D is incorrect because the clone remains accessible regardless of changes to the original table.

Question #17:
Correct Answer: B
Explanation:
B is correct because cloning allows you to create an independent copy of the dataset, and you can modify the clone without affecting the original dataset.
A is incorrect because performing changes directly on the original dataset will alter the data for all users.
C is incorrect because backing up and modifying the backup is unnecessary when cloning is available, offering a more efficient solution.
D is incorrect because creating a temporary table is not the most efficient way to experiment without altering the original dataset, especially for larger datasets.

Question #18:
Correct Answer: B
Explanation:
B is correct because the cloned schema is independent of the original schema. Changes made to the clone will not affect the original schema.
A is incorrect because the original schema will not update automatically with changes made to the cloned schema.
C is incorrect because cloning does not make the original schema read-only; it remains modifiable.
D is incorrect because the cloned schema retains its changes and does not reset automatically to the original state.

Question #19:
Correct Answer: A
Explanation:
A is correct because changes made to the clone do not affect the original production table. The clone is independent and can be modified without impacting the original.
B is incorrect because the clone and the original table are independent; changes to the clone do not affect the original.
C is incorrect because the clone retains access to the original data without needing to import it.

D is incorrect because the clone does not automatically update with changes to the original table; it remains static at the time of cloning.

Question #20:
Correct Answer: A
Explanation:
A is correct because cloning the dataset allows you to work on an independent copy, ensuring that any changes made during testing will not affect the production data.
B is incorrect because modifying the production dataset directly will affect the data and potentially disrupt production processes.
C is incorrect because exporting the data to another database for testing is inefficient and complicates the workflow compared to using a clone.
D is incorrect because manually copying data into a new schema is cumbersome and less efficient than cloning for testing purposes.

Question #21:
A Snowflake user wants to clone a large table to test changes without impacting the performance of the original table. Which of the following statements is correct about the impact of cloning on the original table?
Options:
A. Cloning a table in Snowflake requires a significant amount of compute resources, affecting the performance of the original table.
B. The original table's performance is unaffected by the cloning process since only metadata and pointers are created.
C. The cloning process degrades the performance of the original table by consuming additional storage space.
D. The cloning process in Snowflake slows down queries on the original table due to the copying of data.
E. Snowflake cloning creates a duplicate of the original table, which will consume additional compute resources during the cloning process.

Question #22:
You are cloning a table in Snowflake that is being used for frequent queries. How will the cloning process impact the performance of the original table during this operation?
Options:
A. The cloning process will have no impact on the performance of the original table, as Snowflake only creates metadata and pointers for the clone.
B. The original table will experience a temporary performance drop while cloning is taking place, as data is copied over.
C. Cloning the table will cause Snowflake to replicate the entire table, which could slow down query performance on the original table.
D. Cloning in Snowflake requires no resources and does not affect the performance of the original table or its queries.
E. The cloning process will result in additional compute load on the original table, which may slow down operations on the source table.

Question #23:

A data analyst wants to create a clone of a table in Snowflake to test a new data model without affecting performance. Which of the following statements is true about the cloning process and its impact on the original table?

Options:

A. Cloning creates a logical copy of the table using metadata, which does not require additional compute resources, ensuring no performance impact on the original table.
B. Cloning duplicates the data and creates an independent copy, which can lead to performance degradation in the original table due to increased compute consumption.
C. The cloning process copies all of the original data into the clone, which results in a performance hit for the original table.
D. Cloning can only be done if the original table is not being queried, as this operation affects performance.
E. The clone will have a performance impact on the original table during the creation process, especially with larger datasets.

Question #24:

A team is concerned about the potential performance impact when cloning large tables in Snowflake. How does Snowflake's cloning mechanism ensure that there is no performance degradation?

Options:

A. Snowflake uses metadata pointers to create the clone, meaning no additional data is physically copied, and the original table's performance is unaffected.
B. Cloning duplicates all the data and this will cause significant compute load, which affects performance.
C. Snowflake requires significant additional resources to clone large tables, which will impact performance.
D. The original table will undergo a resource-heavy copy process during cloning, which slows down the performance of any queries running on it.
E. Cloning in Snowflake only works if the original table is not being actively queried to avoid performance impacts.

Question #25:

You are performing a test by cloning a table that contains millions of rows in Snowflake. How will this cloning operation affect the performance of your system?

Options:

A. The cloning operation will affect performance because the large dataset will require Snowflake to duplicate the data, using significant compute resources.
B. Snowflake's cloning mechanism will not impact performance, as the clone is created instantly using metadata pointers rather than duplicating the data.
C. The original table's performance will be negatively impacted because Snowflake uses compute resources to clone the large dataset.
D. The cloning process will slow down performance for any queries on the original table, especially with large datasets.
E. Cloning a large dataset in Snowflake will cause a performance hit on the entire system since all data must be physically replicated.

Answers and Explanations

Question #21:
Correct Answer: B
Explanation:
B is correct because Snowflake's cloning process is instantaneous and does not involve duplicating data. It only uses metadata and pointers, meaning the original table's performance is not impacted.
A is incorrect because cloning does not require compute resources to copy data, and therefore does not impact performance.
C is incorrect because cloning does not consume significant additional storage or degrade performance.
D is incorrect because there is no performance slowdown during the cloning process in Snowflake.
E is incorrect because the cloning process does not require additional compute resources to duplicate the data.

Question #22:
Correct Answer: A, D
Explanation:
A is correct because Snowflake's cloning mechanism does not affect the original table's performance. It only creates a logical copy using metadata.
D is correct because Snowflake cloning is very efficient, requiring no additional resources and causing no impact on the performance of the original table or queries.
B is incorrect because cloning does not cause a performance drop, as no data is copied during the cloning process.
C is incorrect because cloning does not physically copy the data, so it cannot cause performance degradation.
E is incorrect because cloning does not consume additional compute resources.

Question #23:
Correct Answer: A
Explanation:
A is correct because Snowflake cloning works by using metadata pointers, meaning the original data is not duplicated. Thus, no additional resources are used, and performance is not impacted.
B is incorrect because cloning does not require duplicating the data.
C is incorrect because no data is physically copied, so there is no performance degradation in the original table.
D is incorrect because Snowflake allows cloning even while the original table is being queried, with no performance impact.
E is incorrect because Snowflake's cloning mechanism does not cause performance impact during its creation, even with large datasets.

Question #24:
Correct Answer: A
Explanation:
A is correct because Snowflake uses metadata pointers to create the clone, so no physical data is copied, ensuring there is no impact on performance.
B is incorrect because no data duplication occurs in the cloning process.

C is incorrect because Snowflake cloning does not consume significant resources that would degrade performance.
D is incorrect because cloning does not require copying resources, so it does not affect performance.
E is incorrect because cloning in Snowflake has no impact on performance even if the original table is queried during the cloning process.

Question #25:
Correct Answer: B
Explanation:
B is correct because Snowflake's cloning mechanism uses metadata pointers, so no physical data duplication occurs, and thus there is no impact on performance, even with large datasets.
A is incorrect because Snowflake does not duplicate the data during cloning, so there is no compute load associated with the process.
C is incorrect because cloning does not require significant resources to copy data.
D is incorrect because the cloning process does not cause a slowdown in the original table's performance.
E is incorrect because the cloning process does not replicate data and thus does not cause a performance hit.

RESULTS CACHING

Question #1:

You have a highly transactional table that is frequently updated. Users often run reports on this table. Despite result caching being enabled, the queries do not benefit from cached results. What is the most likely cause?
A. Result caching is not enabled for highly transactional tables.
B. Result caching is invalidated due to frequent data changes.
C. The size of the warehouse is too small to utilize caching.
D. Using a CTE prevents the use of result caching.

Question #2:

A large set of queries is executed in parallel, but some queries are significantly slower than others, even when the queries are identical. What could be the cause of the slow queries?
A. Result caching does not work for complex queries.
B. Parallel execution inherently slows down queries.
C. Session variables or settings differ across queries, causing cache misses.
D. Snowflake limits cache usage based on concurrent query numbers.

Question #3:

Your organization runs a series of analytical queries every day. The data involved doesn't change often, and users expect rapid query responses. However, the queries are running slowly despite result caching being enabled. What configuration should you verify to ensure caching is used effectively?
A. Dynamic session-specific parameters are being used, invalidating the cache.
B. Clustering keys need to be defined for better performance.
C. Query types are incompatible with result caching.
D. The warehouse size needs to be increased for effective caching.

Question #4:

You want to reduce query execution time for a frequently run report but don't want to recompute the results every time. How can you use result caching or an alternative feature in Snowflake to achieve this?
A. Rely solely on result caching for faster query performance.
B. Use CTEs to precompute results and reduce query execution time.

159

C. Increase the warehouse size for better performance.
D. Create a materialized view to precompute and store query results.

Question #5:

You notice that your result cache is not being utilized for queries that run with different session variables. What could be causing this issue, and how can you ensure that the result cache is used?
A. Result caching does not work for queries involving user-specific data.
B. Session-specific variables or dynamic parameters are invalidating the cache.
C. The role used for queries is preventing cache utilization.
D. Query concurrency is too high to allow effective caching.

Answers and Explanations:

Question #1:
Correct Answer: B
Explanation:
B is correct. Result caching is bypassed when the underlying data changes, as Snowflake detects that the cached result would no longer be valid. This often happens with highly transactional tables where frequent updates, inserts, or deletes occur.
A is incorrect because result caching can be enabled on any table, but it's impacted by data changes.
C is incorrect because the warehouse size does not directly influence whether caching is used; it's more related to the availability of cached results.
D is incorrect because a CTE does not inherently prevent result caching; it's the data change that causes cache invalidation.

Question #2:
Correct Answer: C
Explanation:
C is correct. Query results may be slower when queries run in parallel if there is a cache miss, which can happen if session variables or user-specific settings are different across parallel queries. This prevents the queries from benefiting from the result cache, even though the queries themselves are identical.
A is incorrect because result caching works for complex queries, as long as the conditions for cache validity are met.
B is incorrect because parallel execution doesn't necessarily lead to slower queries unless cache miss conditions exist.
D is incorrect because Snowflake does not limit cache use based on the number of queries running concurrently.

Question #3:
Correct Answer: A
Explanation:
A is correct. To ensure that result caching is effective, you must verify that no session-specific

parameters (like CURRENT_DATE, USER() function, or other dynamic session variables) are used in the queries. These can invalidate the cache.
B is incorrect because clustering keys improve performance but do not directly affect result caching.
C is incorrect because the type of queries does not impact whether result caching will be used as long as the query structure is consistent across runs.
D is incorrect because increasing warehouse size doesn't impact result caching directly. It only affects compute resources and query execution speed.

Question #4:
Correct Answer: D
Explanation:
D is correct. To reduce query execution time for frequently run reports, you can use a **materialized view**, which stores precomputed query results. This reduces the need to recompute the results each time the query runs. Materialized views benefit from result caching when they are queried.
A is incorrect because result caching alone may not be sufficient for consistent performance on complex queries.
B is incorrect because result caching does not store intermediate results of CTEs or dynamic query structures.
C is incorrect because using a larger warehouse only speeds up the computation but does not guarantee that the results will be cached.

Question #5:
Correct Answer: B
Explanation:
B is correct. Result caching is session-specific. If the session variables are different (such as a user-specific session or a date parameter like CURRENT_DATE), the cache will not be used because the results are considered different for each session. To ensure caching is used, you must ensure consistency in session settings.
A is incorrect because query results are not cached based on user-specific data. It's the session variables or dynamic content that invalidates caching.
C is incorrect because Snowflake caches the results of queries regardless of user role, but session variables or dynamic functions are what invalidate the cache.
D is incorrect because result caching is not affected by query concurrency but by the conditions mentioned above.

Question #6:
You have a query that is executed multiple times throughout the day with the same dataset. However, you notice that result caching is not being used even though the underlying data hasn't changed. What could be the reason?

Question #7:
A user reports that their queries are consistently returning slower than expected, despite

having sufficient compute resources. Upon investigation, you find that the queries are not leveraging result caching. Which of the following is the most likely cause?

Question #8:
A customer is querying a table that gets updated frequently. They are asking how they can improve query performance for repeated queries without having to rebuild the results each time. What Snowflake feature can help in this case?

Question #9:
You are running a large set of identical queries in a highly parallelized workload, but the result cache is not being utilized. What is the most likely reason for this?

Question #10:
Your team has noticed that result caching is not being used for queries that run at different times of the day but against the same data. What could be the most likely reason, and how can you resolve it?

Answers and Explanations:

Question #6:
Correct Answer: A
Explanation:
A is correct. Result caching in Snowflake depends on the exact query and underlying data consistency. If a session variable or dynamic value (like CURRENT_DATE) is used, even if the underlying data hasn't changed, the query results won't be cached because the session context is considered different.
B is incorrect because clustering keys or indexing do not affect result caching directly; they may improve query performance but not caching itself.
C is incorrect because larger warehouses do not affect whether result caching is utilized, but they can speed up query execution when the cache is not used.
D is incorrect because data changes trigger cache invalidation, but in this case, the data hasn't changed.

Question #7:
Correct Answer: D
Explanation:
D is correct. Queries in Snowflake are not cached when session-specific variables are used. This could include USER() or CURRENT_TIMESTAMP, which causes Snowflake to treat each query as distinct, even if the data and structure are identical.
A is incorrect because result caching is not impacted by warehouse size directly; it's the query structure and session variables that matter.
B is incorrect because although Snowflake can handle complex queries, it still caches results when the queries and context are the same.
C is incorrect because this issue is related to session variables, not the query structure.

Question #8:
Correct Answer: C
Explanation:
C is correct. A **materialized view** is a precomputed view of data that is stored and can be queried like a regular table. This helps improve performance for repeated queries on the same data without requiring them to be recomputed every time.
A is incorrect because result caching stores results for a query run only in the current session, not across different sessions.
B is incorrect because a CTE is only computed at runtime and does not benefit from result caching across executions.
D is incorrect because a larger warehouse only impacts execution speed, not caching of results.

Question #9:
Correct Answer: A
Explanation:
A is correct. Result caching in Snowflake is session-specific, so when running identical queries across multiple sessions or in parallel, caching won't be used if session variables differ (such as USER() or CURRENT_TIMESTAMP). To ensure caching, queries must have the same session context.
B is incorrect because even parallel queries with identical data will not utilize the cache if there are session-specific variables.
C is incorrect because query concurrency doesn't directly impact result caching—it's the consistency of session context and query structure that matters.
D is incorrect because Snowflake's result cache is not bypassed due to the volume of parallel queries; it is dependent on query similarity and session state.

Question #10:
Correct Answer: B
Explanation:
B is correct. The result cache in Snowflake is invalidated by session-specific variables, such as CURRENT_TIMESTAMP or other dynamic values, causing queries to treat the same data as distinct. To ensure result caching is used, remove such variables or make the session context consistent.
A is incorrect because increasing warehouse size doesn't affect whether result caching will be used—it's about query consistency and session context.
C is incorrect because the time of day doesn't impact whether result caching is utilized unless the query or session context changes.
D is incorrect because result caching is dependent on the query structure and session variables, not the time of day.

Question #11:
You notice that some of your queries aren't leveraging result caching, even though the same

data is being queried multiple times. Which two factors might be causing the cache not to be used?
A. The queries are using different session variables.
B. The queries are being executed with different query structures.
C. The data has been updated since the previous query.
D. The warehouse size has been changed since the last execution.
E. The session timeout value has been changed.

Question #12:
A business unit uses queries with date functions (CURRENT_DATE(), DATEADD()) and notices that result caching is not being utilized. Which two actions would most likely resolve this issue?
A. Replace date functions with a static date value or session variable.
B. Use a stable date value in the WHERE clause instead of the CURRENT_DATE() function.
C. Increase the warehouse size to improve performance.
D. Create a materialized view for queries with date functions.
E. Use CURRENT_TIMESTAMP() instead of CURRENT_DATE().

Question #13:
A report is running with the same data every day at the same time, but you notice that the queries do not leverage result caching. Which two reasons could explain this behavior?
A. The data has been modified since the last execution.
B. The query uses dynamic session variables such as USER() or CURRENT_TIMESTAMP().
C. The query is being executed by different users.
D. The report is run at different times of the day.
E. The warehouse size has been modified.

Question #14:
Your queries are running slower than expected, and you have verified that result caching should be used. Which two situations might prevent result caching from being applied?
A. The query includes dynamic session variables such as USER() or CURRENT_TIMESTAMP().
B. The query joins multiple tables in the SELECT statement.
C. The warehouse has a scaling policy configured.
D. The query includes complex functions like DATEADD().
E. The query has a different structure from the previously executed one.

Question #15:
A user queries the same table multiple times over a period of days, but the query does not benefit from result caching. Which two possible reasons could explain this behavior?
A. The query includes session-specific variables such as CURRENT_TIMESTAMP().
B. The table data has been updated since the last query.
C. The warehouse is in multi-cluster mode.
D. The warehouse size has been changed.
E. The query structure differs from the original query.

Answers and Explanations:

Question #11:
Correct Answers: A, B
Explanation:
A is correct. **Session-specific variables** (such as USER() or CURRENT_TIMESTAMP) invalidate result caching, as Snowflake treats each query with these variables as unique, even if the data hasn't changed.
B is correct. **Query structure differences** (e.g., adding or removing whitespace, changing column order) can prevent Snowflake from identifying queries as identical and therefore bypass result caching.
C is incorrect because result caching isn't impacted by data freshness unless data changes.
D is incorrect because scaling the warehouse does not impact whether result caching is used.
E is incorrect because result caching does not depend on the warehouse size.

Question #12:
Correct Answers: A, B
Explanation:
A is correct. **Replacing date functions** like CURRENT_DATE() with a static date or a session variable would ensure that the same query structure is used across executions, allowing result caching to be utilized.
B is correct. **Using a stable date in the WHERE clause** would prevent the query from changing each time the current date is evaluated, enabling result caching.
C is incorrect because changing warehouse size does not affect result caching.
D is incorrect because result caching can still be leveraged without specific optimizations for date functions.
E is incorrect because materialized views aren't necessary for result caching when the data is unchanged.

Question #13:
Correct Answers: A, B
Explanation:
A is correct. **Data modifications** invalidate result caching. If the data changes (even if it's the same table), the cache will be invalidated and the query will be recomputed.
B is correct. **Query-specific session variables**, such as USER() or CURRENT_TIMESTAMP, can prevent result caching, as Snowflake considers each execution a different query.
C is incorrect because the time of execution does not affect result caching as long as the query structure remains the same.
D is incorrect because result caching is valid if the query is identical across runs, irrespective of when the report is generated.
E is incorrect because result caching does not depend on the time of day.

Question #14:
Correct Answers: A, E

Explanation:
A is correct. **Dynamic session variables** (like CURRENT_TIMESTAMP or USER()) cause Snowflake to treat each query as a new query, preventing result caching.
E is correct. **Changes in query structure**, such as whitespace, function usage, or different ordering of columns, can prevent result caching because Snowflake detects the queries as distinct.
B is incorrect because result caching doesn't depend on query concurrency; it's based on query similarity.
C is incorrect because query performance is affected by compute resources but does not necessarily prevent result caching.
D is incorrect because caching is unrelated to session timeout settings; it's about the query structure.

Question #15:
Correct Answers: A, E
Explanation:
A is correct. **Session-specific variables** (e.g., USER() or CURRENT_TIMESTAMP) lead Snowflake to treat queries as different, preventing caching from being used even when the data is unchanged.
E is correct. **Changes in query structure**, such as whitespace, function usage, or different ordering of columns, can prevent result caching because Snowflake detects the queries as distinct.
B is incorrect because result caching can still be applied even across different days as long as the query and session context remain the same.
C is incorrect because result caching is not affected by how many times the query is run.
D is incorrect because Snowflake can still cache results for ad-hoc queries if they match the exact structure.

Question #16:
You are optimizing a Snowflake warehouse for performance and need to ensure that the warehouse maintains fast response times while still utilizing result caching. Which two actions should you take?
A. Use a larger warehouse to ensure sufficient compute resources.
B. Increase the **AUTO_SUSPEND** time to avoid repeated startup delays.
C. Set **RESULT_CACHE_MAX_SIZE** to a larger value.
D. Enable multi-cluster mode to handle larger concurrent workloads.
E. Use **QUERY_RESULT_CACHING** to control caching settings at the session level.

Question #17:
A query is running slower than expected, and result caching is not being used. Which two factors could be negatively impacting the warehouse's performance and prevent result caching from being applied?
A. The warehouse is in **multi-cluster mode** and has a **large scaling factor**.
B. The query involves **multiple joins** between large tables.
C. The query is executed by **multiple users** with different session variables.
D. The query is part of a **larger batch processing pipeline** with dynamic data.
E. The warehouse size is **too small** to handle the required workload.

Question #18:
You are tasked with optimizing query performance in Snowflake, and you want to make sure that result caching works effectively without scaling the warehouse too aggressively. Which two configurations would you change?
A. Enable **auto-suspend** to free up resources when queries are idle.
B. Use **smaller-sized warehouses** for frequent, lightweight queries.
C. Increase the warehouse **size** for all queries to guarantee faster execution.
D. Enable **multi-cluster** mode to automatically scale resources.
E. Use **materialized views** to optimize query performance for frequently used data.

Question #19:
You notice that result caching is not effective for queries involving **large datasets** and complex **aggregations**. Which two actions should you take to improve performance and utilize result caching?
A. **Optimize** the warehouse size to better handle large queries and aggregations.
B. **Break down** large queries into smaller ones to reduce the complexity of each execution.
C. Use **query pruning** techniques to limit the amount of data processed by the query.
D. **Increase** the RESULT_CACHE_MAX_SIZE to hold more query results in the cache.
E. Use **snowflake streams** to track changes in the dataset and optimize the cache.

Question #20:
A high-priority dashboard query runs every hour with a high level of concurrency. Result caching is enabled, but the query performance is not optimal. Which two actions should you take to improve the performance and caching efficiency?
A. Use **larger warehouses** to accommodate high concurrency without delays.
B. Enable **multi-cluster mode** to ensure that there are sufficient resources for concurrent execution.
C. Configure **QUERY_RESULT_CACHING** to set cache settings per query.
D. Modify the **AUTO_SUSPEND** time to a lower value to keep the warehouse running longer.
E. Use **materialized views** to precompute and cache frequent query results.

Answers and Explanations:

Question #16:
Correct Answers: A, D
Explanation:
A is correct. Using a **larger warehouse** ensures sufficient compute resources, improving query performance and enabling caching for larger, more complex queries.
D is correct. **Multi-cluster mode** can help with larger concurrent workloads, ensuring that result caching is used without causing delays due to lack of compute capacity.
B is incorrect because increasing **AUTO_SUSPEND** time would not directly improve caching or performance.
C is incorrect because **RESULT_CACHE_MAX_SIZE** is not a valid configuration parameter in Snowflake.

E is incorrect because **QUERY_RESULT_CACHING** is already enabled by default, and session-level adjustments are not needed to ensure result caching.

Question #17:
Correct Answers: B, C
Explanation:
B is correct. **Multiple joins** between large tables can slow down queries and prevent result caching from being effectively applied. To improve performance, you might consider optimizing the query or using materialized views.
C is correct. **Session variables** can change between users, preventing caching if the same query is executed by multiple users with different session settings.
A is incorrect because **multi-cluster mode** and **large scaling factors** are generally used to handle concurrent workloads and won't necessarily prevent result caching from being applied.
D is incorrect because **dynamic data** in a batch process doesn't impact result caching unless data changes, invalidating the cache.
E is incorrect because **warehouse size** only affects execution speed, but doesn't directly impact result caching.

Question #18:
Correct Answers: A, E
Explanation:
A is correct. **Auto-suspend** helps by freeing up resources when queries are idle, thus reducing the cost of running queries without affecting result caching.
E is correct. **Materialized views** can improve performance for frequently run queries by precomputing results and reducing the complexity of queries that are run repeatedly.
B is incorrect because using **smaller-sized warehouses** for frequent queries may not improve performance or caching efficiency; instead, it could degrade performance.
C is incorrect because **increasing warehouse size** may improve performance but does not directly affect the caching mechanism itself.
D is incorrect because **multi-cluster mode** is used for high concurrency, not for optimizing caching.

Question #19:
Correct Answers: A, C
Explanation:
A is correct. **Optimizing warehouse size** can help improve performance for queries involving large datasets, ensuring that result caching is used effectively.
C is correct. **Query pruning** reduces the amount of data processed, which can significantly speed up the query and make result caching more efficient by ensuring that only relevant data is processed.
B is incorrect because breaking down large queries may not necessarily improve caching performance. It might reduce the complexity but could introduce overhead.
D is incorrect because **RESULT_CACHE_MAX_SIZE** is not a configuration for controlling result caching at the warehouse level in Snowflake.
E is incorrect because **snowflake streams** track data changes but don't directly optimize result caching.

Question #20:
Correct Answers: A, B
Explanation:

A is correct. Using **larger warehouses** ensures that high concurrency workloads are executed more efficiently, improving the likelihood of result caching being used.
B is correct. **Multi-cluster mode** ensures that there are enough resources to handle concurrent queries without impacting performance or cache utilization.
C is incorrect because **QUERY_RESULT_CACHING** is not typically required to be configured for basic caching functionality as it's already enabled by default.
D is incorrect because **AUTO_SUSPEND** time is irrelevant to improving query performance or result caching in a high-concurrency environment.
E is incorrect because **materialized views** are useful for optimizing specific queries but are not the best solution for high-concurrency dashboard queries.

Question #21:
You have a reporting dashboard with frequently running queries and need to ensure that result caching is used effectively for the best performance. Which configuration will help achieve this?
A. Set **QUERY_RESULT_CACHING** to FALSE for the session.
B. Enable **auto-suspend** with a low value to keep the warehouse always running.
C. Increase the **warehouse size** to ensure faster execution times.
D. Use **materialized views** to precompute results for frequently accessed data.

Question #22:
A query is performing slower than expected, and you suspect that result caching is not being used due to data changes. What would be the best course of action to optimize the situation?
A. Enable **multi-cluster mode** for better scalability.
B. Use **result caching** explicitly in the query settings to optimize performance.
C. Use **materialized views** to optimize caching for large datasets.
D. Change the query structure to use **non-aggregated** data to improve caching efficiency.

Question #23:
You are configuring your Snowflake warehouse to maximize performance with result caching enabled. Which configuration change will help ensure that result caching is effectively utilized?
A. Set **QUERY_RESULT_CACHING** to TRUE at the warehouse level.
B. Set **RESULT_CACHE_MAX_SIZE** to a high value.
C. Increase the **AUTO_SUSPEND** time for the warehouse.
D. Disable **auto-suspend** to prevent the warehouse from idling and invalidating cache.

Question #24:
You want to optimize query performance for highly concurrent users without compromising result caching. What configuration will help you achieve this?
A. Increase **auto-suspend** time to ensure the warehouse is always running.
B. Enable **multi-cluster mode** and set the scaling policy to **Economy**.
C. Set **RESULT_CACHE_MAX_SIZE** to a low value.
D. Use **query profiling** to identify performance bottlenecks and adjust the warehouse size.

Question #25:
You are using Snowflake for large data processing and want to optimize performance while ensuring that result caching is used whenever possible. Which configuration will achieve this?
A. Use a **larger warehouse size** for better performance and faster query execution.

B. Disable **auto-suspend** to keep the warehouse running constantly.
C. Set **QUERY_RESULT_CACHING** to TRUE to force caching for all queries.
D. Enable **materialized views** for complex queries to ensure results are cached.

Answers and Explanations:

Question #21:
Correct Answer: D
Explanation:
D is correct. **Materialized views** precompute and store results for frequently accessed data, allowing result caching to be more effective for those queries.
A is incorrect because **QUERY_RESULT_CACHING** is enabled by default, and setting it to **FALSE** would prevent caching.
B is incorrect because **auto-suspend** should be used judiciously, not with a low value, to avoid unnecessary costs.
C is incorrect because increasing the warehouse size alone doesn't directly optimize caching.

Question #22:
Correct Answer: C
Explanation:
C is correct. **Materialized views** are the best way to optimize caching for frequently queried data, especially when the data structure involves complex joins or aggregations.
A is incorrect because enabling **multi-cluster mode** helps with concurrency but does not specifically improve result caching.
B is incorrect because **explicit result caching** settings are not typically needed for optimal performance when caching is already enabled.
D is incorrect because **non-aggregated data** may not be relevant for optimizing caching, as result caching works better with repeated queries over static datasets.

Question #23:
Correct Answer: A
Explanation:
A is correct. Setting **QUERY_RESULT_CACHING** to TRUE ensures that result caching is enabled at the warehouse level.
B is incorrect because **RESULT_CACHE_MAX_SIZE** is not a valid Snowflake configuration for controlling result caching.
C is incorrect because **AUTO_SUSPEND** impacts warehouse suspension behavior but does not directly affect result caching.
D is incorrect because disabling **auto-suspend** may prevent the warehouse from releasing resources when idle, but it doesn't guarantee better caching.

Question #24:
Correct Answer: B
Explanation:
B is correct. **Multi-cluster mode** with an **Economy** scaling policy ensures that the warehouse can handle higher concurrency without adding unnecessary cost, thus improving performance and caching efficiency.
A is incorrect because **auto-suspend** time doesn't directly help with caching or concurrency; it only controls idle behavior.

C is incorrect because **RESULT_CACHE_MAX_SIZE** should be configured based on usage needs, not set to low values.

D is incorrect because **query profiling** helps diagnose performance issues but doesn't directly optimize caching.

Question #25:
Correct Answer: A
Explanation:
A is correct. Using a **larger warehouse size** ensures that queries are processed quickly, and result caching can be more effective, especially for large datasets.

B is incorrect because **disabling auto-suspend** increases costs without improving caching or performance.

C is incorrect because **QUERY_RESULT_CACHING** is enabled by default, so explicitly setting it to TRUE does not have a significant impact.

D is incorrect because **materialized views** help with complex queries, but for larger datasets, increasing warehouse size is a more effective approach to optimize performance.

SECURED VIEWS

Question #01.
You are designing a secured view in Snowflake for sensitive financial data. Which configuration ensures that the view cannot be altered to expose underlying data?
Options:
A. Use the GRANT SELECT ON VIEW command for secure permissions.
B. Use the ALTER VIEW ... SECURE command to enforce immutability.
C. Use the ENABLE_SECURE_VIEW_POLICY parameter in the session.
D. Use a role hierarchy to restrict access to the underlying tables.

Question #02.
A team requests access to data via a secured view. How can you ensure that the view respects role-based access control while limiting direct access to the underlying tables?
Options:
A. Grant access to the secured view only to specific roles.
B. Enable Row Access Policies on the secured view.
C. Configure the secured view with DEFINER's rights.
D. Use a multi-cluster warehouse to restrict table access.

Question #03.
When creating a secured view, what happens if you attempt to include columns from a table that the current role lacks access to?
Options:
A. The secured view is created, but the restricted columns will show as NULL.
B. Snowflake raises an error indicating insufficient privileges.
C. The secured view creation succeeds, but the unauthorized columns are excluded.
D. Snowflake creates the view with warnings but includes all columns.

Question #04.
A secured view is being used in a business intelligence tool. Which Snowflake feature ensures that data remains encrypted during access?
Options:
A. Enabling encryption at rest for the tables used in the view.
B. Applying the TRANSPARENT_ENCRYPTION option on the secured view.

C. Using end-to-end encryption via the Snowflake driver and client.
D. Configuring secure materialized views for BI usage.

Question #05.
How does Snowflake enforce the security of a secured view when it is queried by a role without direct access to the underlying table?
Options:
A. By restricting access at the storage layer for unauthorized roles.
B. By ensuring the query executes under the privileges of the view's owner.
C. By checking permissions for every role accessing the secured view.
D. By dynamically rewriting queries to exclude unauthorized data.

Answers:

Question #01:
Correct Answer: B
Explanation:
B is correct. The ALTER VIEW ... SECURE command enforces immutability, ensuring the view cannot be modified to expose underlying data.
A is incorrect because GRANT SELECT does not enforce the view's secure property.
C is incorrect because ENABLE_SECURE_VIEW_POLICY is not a valid Snowflake parameter.
D is incorrect because role hierarchy only restricts access but does not secure the view itself.

Question #02:
Correct Answer: A
Explanation:
A is correct. Granting access to specific roles ensures that role-based access control is enforced while limiting table access through the view.
B is incorrect because Row Access Policies are not applied to views directly.
C is incorrect because DEFINER's rights do not align with Snowflake's access model.
D is incorrect because multi-cluster warehouses are unrelated to logical access control.

Question #03:
Correct Answer: B
Explanation:
B is correct. Snowflake raises an error if the current role lacks the necessary privileges for any columns included in a secured view.
A is incorrect because Snowflake does not substitute restricted columns with NULL values.
C is incorrect because unauthorized columns are not silently excluded.
D is incorrect because warnings are not issued; the operation fails outright.

Question #04:
Correct Answer: C
Explanation:
C is correct. Snowflake's driver and client use end-to-end encryption to ensure data security during access, complementing secured views.
A is incorrect because encryption at rest protects stored data, not accessed data.
B is incorrect because TRANSPARENT_ENCRYPTION is not a Snowflake feature.
D is incorrect because materialized views do not inherently add encryption for BI tools.

Question #05:
Correct Answer: B
Explanation:
B is correct. Queries against a secured view execute under the privileges of the view's owner, enforcing data security.
A is incorrect because storage layer restrictions do not handle logical access for secured views.
C is incorrect because permissions are not dynamically checked for every querying role.
D is incorrect because query rewriting is not how Snowflake secures views.

Question #06.
You need to create a secured view for a sensitive dataset to ensure that users with access to the view cannot modify the underlying data. What is the correct approach?
Options:
A. Set the secured view as READ_ONLY.
B. Use GRANT SELECT on the underlying table to restrict modifications.
C. Define the view using the CREATE SECURE VIEW command.
D. Apply a Row Access Policy directly to the secured view.

Question #07.
A secured view is required to display aggregated sales data while restricting individual transaction details. What is the best way to implement this?
Options:
A. Create a secured view with a SELECT statement containing aggregations.
B. Use masking policies on the underlying table columns.
C. Apply a Row Access Policy to limit the data included in the view.
D. Enable time travel to review aggregated historical data securely.

Question #08.
Your organization mandates that a secured view's SQL definition should remain hidden even from users with access to the view. How can you achieve this?
Options:
A. Use the CREATE SECURE VIEW command.
B. Mask the SQL definition by granting SELECT privileges only.
C. Disable the SHOW VIEW privilege for all roles.
D. Store the SQL definition in a separate, restricted schema.

Question #09.
An analyst queries a secured view but receives an error indicating a privilege issue on the underlying table. What could be the cause?
Options:
A. The analyst's role lacks SELECT privileges on the secured view.
B. The secured view does not inherit access permissions from its creator.
C. The analyst's role lacks usage privileges on the schema containing the view.
D. The secured view requires additional privileges to access the underlying table.

Question #10.
A secured view is shared with an external organization using a Snowflake data share. What ensures that the data remains secure during sharing?
Options:
A. Enable multi-factor authentication for shared users.
B. Use the CREATE SECURE VIEW command to enforce restrictions.

C. Encrypt the data in the shared database manually.
D. Apply masking policies to the data before creating the secured view.

Answers:

Question #06:
Correct Answer: C
Explanation:
C is correct. The CREATE SECURE VIEW command ensures that the view cannot be altered to modify the underlying data.
A is incorrect because there is no READ_ONLY property for views in Snowflake.
B is incorrect because GRANT SELECT restricts access but does not create a secured view.
D is incorrect because Row Access Policies apply to tables, not directly to views.

Question #07:
Correct Answer: A
Explanation:
A is correct. Creating a secured view with a SELECT statement that includes aggregations ensures that only aggregated data is exposed.
B is incorrect because masking policies protect individual column data but do not enforce aggregation.
C is incorrect because Row Access Policies are unnecessary when the view itself defines the aggregation.
D is incorrect because time travel does not relate to the creation of aggregated secured views.

Question #08:
Correct Answer: A
Explanation:
A is correct. The CREATE SECURE VIEW command hides the SQL definition of the view, even from users with access.
B is incorrect because granting SELECT privileges does not mask the SQL definition.
C is incorrect because disabling SHOW VIEW privilege is not a standard Snowflake feature.
D is incorrect because storing the SQL definition in a separate schema does not meet the requirement directly.

Question #09:
Correct Answer: D
Explanation:
D is correct. A secured view requires its creator or a privileged role to have access to the underlying table; otherwise, it cannot query the table's data.
A is incorrect because a lack of SELECT privilege on the view would not result in a privilege issue on the table.
B is incorrect because secured views do not automatically inherit creator permissions.
C is incorrect because usage privileges on the schema are separate from table access issues.

Question #10:
Correct Answer: B
Explanation:
B is correct. The CREATE SECURE VIEW command enforces restrictions, ensuring that only the

shared secured view's data is accessible.

A is incorrect because multi-factor authentication does not specifically protect data in a secured view.

C is incorrect because manual encryption is redundant when Snowflake automatically encrypts data.

D is incorrect because masking policies are not required if the secured view already limits data exposure

---

Question #11.
You need to ensure that specific sensitive columns in a table are not directly accessible via a secured view but can still be included in aggregate calculations. How should this be implemented?
Options:
A. Apply a masking policy to the sensitive columns.
B. Exclude the sensitive columns from the view definition entirely.
C. Use the CREATE SECURE VIEW command with column-level masking.
D. Include the sensitive columns only in aggregate expressions in the view.

Question #12.
A data-sharing agreement requires masking sensitive data dynamically based on the querying user's role. How can you implement this in Snowflake?
Options:
A. Create a Row Access Policy for the secured view.
B. Apply masking policies to the relevant columns in the underlying table.
C. Define conditional logic in the secured view to mask the data dynamically.
D. Use a combination of Row Access Policies and masking policie

Question #13.
You want to enforce column-level data privacy in a secured view that displays customer information. How can you achieve this?
Options:
A. Grant SELECT privileges on specific columns of the table.
B. Apply masking policies to the relevant columns in the secured view.
C. Use CREATE SECURE VIEW to define a view that excludes sensitive columns.
D. Use masking policies on the underlying table columns accessed by the view.

Question #14.
A business unit requires that a secured view displays data for users from different regions, but each user must only see data specific to their region. What approach ensures compliance with data privacy rules?
Options:
A. Define a Row Access Policy on the underlying table.
B. Use the CREATE SECURE VIEW command with conditional logic for regions.
C. Apply masking policies to sensitive data based on the region.
D. Use separate secured views for each region and share them accordingly.

Question #15.
A secured view is shared with a third-party organization. You want to ensure that sensitive data is masked dynamically based on the third party's specific access level. What solution should you implement?

Options:
A. Create the secured view with conditional masking logic based on the querying user's role.
B. Apply masking policies to the underlying table columns.
C. Enable column-level encryption in the secured view.
D. Use Row Access Policies and masking policies together.

Answers:

Question #11:
Correct Answer: A, D
Explanation:
A is correct. Masking policies applied to the sensitive columns allow secure aggregation without exposing raw data.
D is correct. Including sensitive columns only in aggregate expressions ensures they are not directly accessible.
B is incorrect because excluding the sensitive columns entirely limits the utility of the view.
C is incorrect because column-level masking is not a feature of the CREATE SECURE VIEW command.

Question #12:
Correct Answer: D
Explanation:
D is correct. Combining Row Access Policies for row-level filtering and masking policies for column-level protection provides dynamic, role-based masking.
A is incorrect because Row Access Policies do not mask sensitive column values.
B is incorrect because masking policies alone do not consider the user's role.
C is incorrect because conditional logic in the view is less flexible and harder to manage than policies.

Question #13:
Correct Answer: D
Explanation:
D is correct. Masking policies applied to the underlying table columns enforce consistent data privacy rules across all queries, including through secured views.
A is incorrect because Snowflake does not support granting SELECT privileges on specific table columns for views.
B is incorrect because masking policies cannot be directly applied to views.
C is incorrect because excluding sensitive columns does not allow for role-based data privacy.

Question #14:
Correct Answer: A
Explanation:
A is correct. Row Access Policies dynamically filter data based on the querying user's region, ensuring compliance with data privacy rules.
B is incorrect because conditional logic in the secured view is less robust and more difficult to

maintain than Row Access Policies.
C is incorrect because masking policies apply to sensitive data, not row-level restrictions.
D is incorrect because maintaining separate secured views for each region is not scalable.

Question #15:
Correct Answer: A, B
Explanation:
A is correct. Conditional masking logic in the secured view enables dynamic data masking based on the querying user's role.
B is correct. Masking policies applied to the underlying table enforce data privacy at the source level, ensuring consistent behavior across all accesses.
C is incorrect because Snowflake does not support column-level encryption in secured views.
D is incorrect because while combining Row Access Policies and masking policies is valid, it is unnecessary for this specific scenario.

Question #16.
A team of analysts requires access to a secured view that contains sensitive data, but their access should be revoked after a specific project deadline. How can you ensure restricted access?
Options:
A. Use the GRANT command with an expiration date.
B. Schedule a revocation of privileges using a task in Snowflake.
C. Apply a Row Access Policy to restrict data after the deadline.
D. Manually revoke their access when the deadline is reached.

Question #17.
A secured view is shared with an external partner, but they should only see a subset of data based on specific criteria. How can you implement this restriction?
Options:
A. Create a Row Access Policy for the secured view.
B. Use the GRANT command with filtering conditions.
C. Build the secured view with WHERE clauses limiting the data.
D. Apply masking policies to filter rows dynamically.

Question #18.
A user group needs temporary access to a secured view but should not have access to the underlying table. How do you enforce this restriction?
Options:
A. Grant SELECT on the secured view only.
B. Use a masking policy on the secured view to prevent access to raw data.
C. Apply Row Access Policies to the underlying table.
D. Use GRANT USAGE on the database containing the view.

Question #19.
A business requirement mandates that only managers can view salary details through a secured view. What is the most effective way to implement this?
Options:
A. Apply a masking policy to salary columns in the secured view.
B. Create a Row Access Policy on the underlying table that restricts salary data based on the

user's role.
C. Use the CREATE SECURE VIEW command with a WHERE clause to filter data for managers.
D. Grant SELECT privileges on the secured view only to manager roles.

Question #20.
You need to provide a contractor with access to a secured view for auditing purposes but prevent them from exporting data. What approach ensures this restriction?
Options:
A. Create a secured view with a limit on the number of rows displayed.
B. Use Snowflake's network policies to restrict access from non-approved devices.
C. Apply the GRANT SELECT privilege without the ability to copy or export data.
D. Use a masking policy to partially hide sensitive data while allowing access to the view.

Answers:

Question #16:
Correct Answer: B
Explanation:
B is correct. Scheduling a revocation of privileges using a Snowflake task ensures access is automatically removed after the deadline.
A is incorrect because Snowflake does not natively support an expiration date with the GRANT command.
C is incorrect because Row Access Policies restrict data visibility, not privilege duration.
D is incorrect because manual revocation increases the risk of human error or missed deadlines.

Question #17:
Correct Answer: C
Explanation:
C is correct. Using WHERE clauses in the secured view definition restricts the data visible to the external partner.
A is incorrect because Row Access Policies are applied to tables, not views.
B is incorrect because the GRANT command does not support filtering conditions.
D is incorrect because masking policies do not filter rows; they obfuscate column data.

Question #18:
Correct Answer: A
Explanation:
A is correct. Granting SELECT on the secured view only ensures users cannot access the underlying table directly.
B is incorrect because masking policies are applied to columns, not views.
C is incorrect because Row Access Policies affect table data, not access to views.
D is incorrect because GRANT USAGE does not provide data access; it only allows accessing the database or schema.

Question #19:
Correct Answer: B
Explanation:
B is correct. A Row Access Policy on the underlying table filters salary data for users based on

their role, enforcing role-based access control dynamically.
A is incorrect because masking policies cannot control row visibility.
C is incorrect because adding a WHERE clause in the secured view is less flexible and harder to maintain than Row Access Policies.
D is incorrect because granting SELECT privileges alone does not dynamically enforce role-based restrictions.

Question #20:
Correct Answer: B
Explanation:
B is correct. Snowflake's network policies can enforce IP whitelisting or other restrictions, preventing unauthorized data exports.
A is incorrect because row limits in a secured view do not prevent exporting available data.
C is incorrect because the GRANT command does not natively limit data copying or exporting.
D is incorrect because masking policies do not restrict exporting data; they obfuscate sensitive data.

Question #21.
A secured view is used to hide sensitive data. During query execution, how does Snowflake ensure enhanced security to prevent exposing underlying data?
Options:
A. By disallowing query rewriting and optimization for the secured view.
B. By applying masking policies automatically on all columns.
C. By encrypting query results at rest.
D. By requiring manual approval for secured view queries.

Question #22.
An analyst queries a secured view and notices a performance lag. What is the most likely reason for this lag?
Options:
A. The secured view prevents query caching for enhanced security.
B. The secured view uses additional storage for row-level security.
C. The secured view is not optimized by Snowflake's query engine.
D. The secured view applies dynamic masking policies at runtime.

Question #23.
A user needs access to aggregated sales data but must not have access to individual transaction details. How can this be achieved while maintaining enhanced security?
Options:
A. Create a secured view with aggregated data only.
B. Apply Row Access Policies to the transaction table.
C. Use dynamic masking policies to hide sensitive columns.
D. Grant SELECT on the table and instruct users to aggregate data manually.

Question #24.
You notice that a query involving a secured view is slower compared to a standard view. How should you address this performance concern without compromising security?
Options:
A. Replace the secured view with a standard view.

B. Pre-aggregate the data and use it to build the secured view.
C. Enable query optimization for secured views.
D. Reduce the dataset size by applying stricter masking policies.

Question #25.
A manager is concerned that a secured view might expose sensitive data through indirect access patterns. How does Snowflake mitigate this risk?
Options:
A. By disabling query optimizations that might expose data indirectly.
B. By forcing encryption for all queries involving secured views.
C. By rejecting queries that include potentially sensitive joins.
D. By monitoring and logging every query for compliance audits.

Answers:

Question #21:
Correct Answer: A
Explanation:
A is correct. Secured views disable internal optimizations like query rewriting to ensure no underlying data is exposed indirectly.
B is incorrect because masking policies are not automatically applied to secured views.
C is incorrect because encryption at rest is a separate feature and does not affect secured view processing.
D is incorrect because secured views do not require manual query approval.

Question #22:
Correct Answer: C
Explanation:
C is correct. Secured views are not optimized by Snowflake's query engine to maintain enhanced security, which may result in slower performance.
A is incorrect because secured views do not disable query caching outright; they only prevent certain optimizations.
B is incorrect because row-level security does not inherently increase storage.
D is incorrect because dynamic masking policies are unrelated to secured view performance.

Question #23:
Correct Answer: A
Explanation:
A is correct. Creating a secured view with aggregated data ensures that sensitive individual transaction details are hidden.
B is incorrect because Row Access Policies filter rows but do not aggregate data.
C is incorrect because masking policies obfuscate column values but do not summarize or aggregate data.
D is incorrect because granting direct access to the table would expose sensitive data, violating the requirement.

Question #24:
Correct Answer: B
Explanation:

B is correct. Pre-aggregating data ensures the secured view operates on a smaller dataset, reducing query time while maintaining security.
A is incorrect because replacing a secured view with a standard view would compromise security.
C is incorrect because query optimization is deliberately disabled for secured views to enhance security.
D is incorrect because masking policies do not improve query performance in this scenario.

Question #25:
Correct Answer: A
Explanation:
A is correct. Snowflake mitigates the risk of exposing sensitive data through indirect access patterns by disabling query optimizations that could reveal underlying data structures.
B is incorrect because encryption ensures data safety but does not address indirect exposure.
C is incorrect because Snowflake does not reject valid queries involving secured views.
D is incorrect because monitoring and logging do not actively prevent data exposure.

MATERIALIZED VIEWS

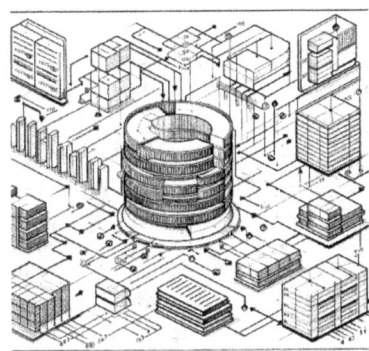

Question #01:
Your organization has a large dataset, and you've created a materialized view to optimize query performance. However, you notice that the materialized view is not being refreshed as expected. Which of the following could be the reason for this behavior?
A. The materialized view refreshes only when the base table data changes.
B. The materialized view is using a non-clustered warehouse, which doesn't support automatic refresh.
C. The materialized view is disabled due to insufficient storage resources.
D. The refresh interval is set too high, preventing automatic updates.

Question #02:
A Snowflake administrator is tasked with setting up a materialized view to optimize the performance of frequently run aggregate queries. The materialized view needs to be kept up-to-date with the base table in real-time. Which configuration would be most effective for this scenario?
A. Enable auto-refresh with a short interval and ensure the base table has clustering keys aligned with the materialized view.
B. Use a manual refresh schedule every 24 hours.
C. Create the materialized view without any clustering and rely on Snowflake's automatic refresh.
D. Create a stream on the base table and trigger the refresh of the materialized view using an external tool.

Question #03:
You have a materialized view in Snowflake that is regularly refreshed. However, you notice that after a certain update, the view shows outdated data. What could be the most likely cause of this issue?
A. The view is created with a filter condition that excludes updated rows.
B. The refresh on the materialized view was manually paused or failed during the last execution.

C. The underlying data is not partitioned correctly, preventing the view from being refreshed.
D. The materialized view is disabled due to query load constraints.

Question #04:
Your Snowflake environment is configured with a materialized view that is frequently queried for performance optimization. The materialized view is based on multiple tables, and you observe slow refresh times, impacting performance. Which approach would you take to optimize the refresh process for the materialized view?
A. Increase the size of the warehouse to speed up the refresh.
B. Introduce clustering keys on the base tables involved in the materialized view.
C. Manually refresh the materialized view during off-peak hours.
D. Disable automatic refresh to avoid unnecessary delays and refresh manually.

Question #05:
You are creating a materialized view for a reporting dashboard that aggregates large amounts of data daily. The dashboard needs to show up-to-date results while keeping query times fast. Which feature will most help in maintaining the performance of the materialized view over time?
A. Enable clustering keys on the base table columns used in the materialized view.
B. Increase the auto-suspend time for the warehouse used by the materialized view.
C. Use a manual refresh schedule with a time interval of 1 hour.
D. Use a dedicated virtual warehouse for materialized view queries.

Question #01:
Correct Answer: A
Explanation:
A is correct because materialized views in Snowflake only refresh when the underlying base table data changes, not on a set schedule unless explicitly triggered.
B is incorrect because Snowflake supports automatic refresh for materialized views regardless of warehouse clustering type.
C is incorrect because materialized views are not disabled due to storage resources; they may encounter refresh issues if there are resource constraints, but this isn't the primary cause.
D is incorrect because the refresh interval does not control automatic refresh behavior; it is set by Snowflake's refresh mechanism based on data changes.

Question #02:
Correct Answer: A
Explanation:
A is correct. Enabling auto-refresh with a short interval and ensuring the base table has clustering keys aligned with the materialized view will optimize both refresh efficiency and query performance.
B is incorrect because a manual refresh schedule does not provide real-time updates, which is critical for this scenario.
C is incorrect because clustering the materialized view alone is not sufficient to optimize refresh performance. The base tables also need to be well-structured.
D is incorrect because an external tool is not necessary; Snowflake provides native support for automatic refresh without external dependencies.

Question #03:
Correct Answer: B
Explanation:
B is correct. A manual pause or failure during the refresh process can cause outdated data to persist in the materialized view.
A is incorrect because filters are not the main cause of outdated data unless data in the base table doesn't meet the filter condition.
C is incorrect because materialized views in Snowflake can work with unpartitioned data, though clustering may improve performance.
D is incorrect because materialized views are not disabled due to query load constraints unless the system is overloaded.

Question #04:
Correct Answer: B
Explanation:
B is correct. Introducing clustering keys on the base tables will optimize data storage and query performance, reducing the time needed for the materialized view to refresh.
A is incorrect because increasing warehouse size impacts query performance but does not directly optimize refresh processes.
C is incorrect because manually refreshing during off-peak hours is not a long-term solution; clustering keys are a better way to optimize refresh times.
D is incorrect because automatic refreshes should be allowed to run when needed; manual refresh only adds overhead.

Question #05:
Correct Answer: A
Explanation:
A is correct. Enabling clustering keys on base table columns improves query performance and refresh efficiency by reducing the data scanned during aggregation.
B is incorrect because increasing the auto-suspend time does not improve performance or refresh speed.
C is incorrect because manual refresh intervals do not automatically address performance; clustering keys and auto-refresh are more effective.
D is incorrect because dedicating a warehouse for materialized views may improve query performance but does not solve the refresh issues.

Question #06:
You are building a dashboard that requires quick access to aggregated data from a large dataset. Instead of querying the base tables every time, you decide to use a materialized view to store pre-computed results. Which of the following best explains the benefit of using a materialized view in this scenario?
A. Materialized views allow for the aggregation of data on-the-fly, ensuring real-time data retrieval.
B. Materialized views store pre-computed data, significantly improving query performance by avoiding the need to scan large base tables.
C. Materialized views increase the storage cost of queries but provide more flexibility for ad-hoc reporting.
D. Materialized views perform better with non-aggregated, real-time data queries.

Question #07:

Your team frequently runs complex aggregation queries on a large sales table, but the queries take too long to execute. You decide to create a materialized view for performance optimization. After creating the materialized view, you notice that the queries are faster. Why does this happen?

A. The materialized view pre-computes the aggregate results, reducing the need to re-scan large datasets.
B. The materialized view directly reads from the base table, making the query faster.
C. Materialized views automatically index the underlying data for faster queries.
D. The materialized view reduces the number of queries that are needed to access data, speeding up report generation.

Question #08:

Your organization uses a materialized view for performance optimization in reporting. However, the data in the materialized view is not always up-to-date because it only refreshes periodically. Which of the following is a key benefit of materialized views in terms of query performance, despite this limitation?

A. Materialized views store pre-computed results, which means that queries can access data faster, even if they are not fully up-to-date.
B. Materialized views automatically refresh in real-time, ensuring that the data is always accurate.
C. Materialized views perform data cleansing operations during each refresh, ensuring consistent results.
D. Materialized views do not require manual intervention to update, ensuring that reports are always based on the latest data.

Question #09:

You are building a report that requires data to be aggregated from multiple tables. To speed up query performance, you decide to create a materialized view that pre-computes the aggregated data. However, you are concerned about the additional storage costs associated with storing pre-computed data. What is the best way to address these concerns?

A. Use a single large materialized view that aggregates all necessary data, minimizing the number of materialized views.
B. Monitor the refresh frequency of the materialized view to ensure that it is not consuming excessive storage resources.
C. Create smaller materialized views with the most important aggregates to optimize storage, while keeping other data in base tables.
D. Disable materialized views to avoid any extra storage costs, and query the base tables directly each time.

Question #10:

Your organization has implemented materialized views to pre-compute data for reporting purposes. However, you need to ensure that data freshness is balanced with performance optimization. Which of the following configurations would best maintain this balance?

A. Configure the materialized view to refresh every minute to ensure real-time accuracy.
B. Configure the materialized view to refresh periodically (e.g., once per day), while using the pre-computed data for fast query performance during reporting hours.
C. Manually refresh the materialized view before every report query to ensure the latest data.
D. Set up a multi-cluster warehouse to handle large report queries, bypassing the need for materialized views.

Question #06:
Correct Answer: B
Explanation:
B is correct. Materialized views store pre-computed data, which significantly speeds up query performance by avoiding the need to scan large base tables repeatedly.
A is incorrect because materialized views don't compute data on-the-fly; they store pre-computed results for faster access.
C is incorrect because materialized views are a performance optimization strategy, not a source of increased storage costs.
D is incorrect because materialized views are not optimized for non-aggregated queries; they are best for pre-aggregated data.

Question #07:
Correct Answer: A
Explanation:
A is correct because materialized views pre-compute aggregate results, reducing the need to re-scan large datasets for every query.
B is incorrect because while the materialized view may read from the base table, the key benefit is pre-computing results, not simply reading from the base table.
C is incorrect because materialized views do not automatically index the underlying data.
D is incorrect because materialized views optimize query performance by pre-computing results, not by reducing the number of queries needed.

Question #08:
Correct Answer: A
Explanation:
A is correct because materialized views store pre-computed results, making queries faster even if the data is not fully up-to-date.
B is incorrect because materialized views do not refresh in real-time; they refresh periodically.
C is incorrect because materialized views do not perform data cleansing.
D is incorrect because materialized views need to be refreshed periodically and are not automatically updated in real-time.

Question #09:
Correct Answer: C
Explanation:
C is correct. By creating smaller materialized views with the most critical aggregates, you can optimize storage usage while keeping query performance high.
A is incorrect because a large materialized view can lead to increased storage costs and may not be the most efficient use of resources.
B is incorrect because monitoring the refresh frequency is useful, but creating smaller materialized views is a more effective storage optimization strategy.
D is incorrect because querying base tables directly negates the benefits of materialized views.

Question #10:
Correct Answer: B
Explanation:
B is correct because refreshing the materialized view periodically (e.g., once per day) while

using pre-computed data for fast queries is the most efficient way to balance performance and data freshness.

A is incorrect because refreshing every minute would be expensive and unnecessary for most use cases.

C is incorrect because manually refreshing before each query would defeat the purpose of using a materialized view and add unnecessary overhead.

D is incorrect because a multi-cluster warehouse does not address the issue of pre-computed data, which is the core benefit of materialized views.

Question #11:
Your team has created a materialized view to optimize the performance of your reporting dashboard. You want to ensure that the materialized view always stays up-to-date without manual intervention. Which of the following benefits of Snowflake's automatic maintenance for materialized views apply in this case?
A. The materialized view will automatically refresh whenever a change occurs in the base table.
B. The materialized view will only refresh when queried, ensuring minimal resource usage.
C. Snowflake automatically detects changes to the base table and refreshes the materialized view in the background.
D. The materialized view refresh process is manually triggered via a scheduled job.
E. Snowflake automatically creates an index on the materialized view to enhance its performance.

Question #12:
You notice that your materialized view is not being updated when changes occur in the base table. Which of the following would best explain this issue?
A. The materialized view is disabled for automatic refresh due to a configuration setting.
B. Snowflake only refreshes materialized views after the base table has accumulated a significant amount of data.
C. The materialized view is not configured to automatically refresh upon changes to the base table.
D. Snowflake's automatic refresh functionality is only available during certain maintenance windows.
E. The materialized view only refreshes after the data in the base table exceeds a predefined size threshold.

Question #13:
Your team is working with large datasets, and you want to leverage the automatic maintenance feature of materialized views for real-time reporting. Which of the following is true regarding Snowflake's automatic maintenance of materialized views?
A. The materialized view refreshes automatically when there is a change in the base table, ensuring up-to-date results.
B. Automatic refresh is limited to when the base table undergoes major schema changes, not minor inserts or updates.
C. Materialized views refresh automatically in the background, which may result in slight delays in query results.
D. You must configure the materialized view to use a specific refresh interval to ensure it stays up-to-date.

E. Snowflake may suspend the automatic refresh of materialized views during periods of low query activity to conserve resources.

Question #14:
Your team uses materialized views for performance optimization, and you've noticed that the materialized view refresh process is causing occasional query delays. Which of the following could be contributing to this issue?
A. The materialized view is being refreshed too frequently, which may overload the system with unnecessary refresh operations.
B. The materialized view is not being refreshed automatically due to insufficient resources allocated to the compute warehouse.
C. The materialized view refresh is happening during heavy workloads, leading to resource contention.
D. Materialized views are not designed to refresh automatically, so manual refresh operations must be scheduled.
E. Snowflake only refreshes materialized views during maintenance windows, so the refresh might not be immediate.

Question #15:
You are managing a Snowflake data warehouse with materialized views. You want to ensure that the views stay up-to-date without putting undue pressure on system resources. Which of the following configurations will optimize the automatic maintenance of materialized views in Snowflake?
A. Use a larger warehouse size to ensure materialized views refresh more quickly.
B. Configure the materialized views to refresh only when necessary, rather than at fixed intervals.
C. Leverage the automatic background refresh feature of materialized views to ensure data is always up-to-date without manual intervention.
D. Avoid using materialized views with large datasets, as they can slow down refresh operations.
E. Set the refresh interval for materialized views to a short time window to ensure timely updates.

Question #11:
Correct Answer: A, C
Explanation:
A is correct because Snowflake automatically refreshes materialized views whenever changes are made to the base table.
C is correct because Snowflake detects changes to the base table and performs the refresh in the background without requiring manual intervention.
B is incorrect because the materialized view refreshes based on changes to the base table, not when queried.
D is incorrect because materialized views are automatically refreshed; they do not require scheduled jobs for updates.
E is incorrect because Snowflake does not automatically create indexes on materialized views; instead, it handles automatic maintenance, including refreshing the view.

Question #12:
Correct Answer: A, C

Explanation:
A is correct because the issue could be that the automatic refresh of the materialized view has been disabled through a configuration setting.
C is correct because the materialized view may not be configured for automatic refresh on changes to the base table.
B is incorrect because Snowflake refreshes materialized views upon any change to the base table, not just when a large volume of data is added.
D is incorrect because automatic refresh does not rely on maintenance windows.
E is incorrect because Snowflake refreshes materialized views automatically regardless of the data size in the base table.

Question #13:
Correct Answer: A, C
Explanation:
A is correct because Snowflake's automatic maintenance ensures that materialized views refresh when there are changes to the base table, making the data up-to-date.
C is correct because the automatic refresh occurs in the background, which may introduce minor delays in results but avoids manual intervention.
B is incorrect because materialized views refresh automatically with any change to the base table, regardless of the size or type of change.
D is incorrect because manual configuration of refresh intervals is not required for automatic refresh.
E is incorrect because Snowflake does not suspend automatic refresh during low query activity.

Question #14:
Correct Answer: A, C
Explanation:
A is correct because refreshing the materialized view too frequently can result in unnecessary system load and performance degradation.
C is correct because refresh operations may coincide with heavy workloads, which could cause resource contention, slowing down queries.
B is incorrect because the issue is likely related to refresh frequency or timing, not insufficient resources for compute warehouses.
D is incorrect because materialized views are designed to refresh automatically and do not require manual refresh operations.
E is incorrect because materialized views refresh automatically in the background as changes occur, not during maintenance windows.

Question #15:
Correct Answer: B, C
Explanation:
B is correct because configuring materialized views to refresh only when necessary helps optimize resource usage and reduces unnecessary refreshes.
C is correct because leveraging the automatic background refresh ensures the views are always up-to-date without requiring manual intervention or constant resource usage.
A is incorrect because increasing the warehouse size may not directly affect the automatic refresh process of materialized views.
D is incorrect because Snowflake can handle large datasets with materialized views and refresh them efficiently.

E is incorrect because setting a short refresh interval may increase system load unnecessarily and does not optimize automatic maintenance.

Question #16:
You are using materialized views to optimize the performance of reports in your organization. However, the base tables are frequently updated, and you need to ensure that the materialized view reflects the latest changes. Which of the following strategies would help maintain data freshness in your materialized views?
A. Set the materialized view to refresh automatically whenever the base table is updated.
B. Configure the materialized view to refresh periodically (e.g., once per hour) to ensure up-to-date data.
C. Use the AUTOMATIC_REFRESH setting to automatically refresh the materialized view whenever a query is executed.
D. Manually refresh the materialized view after every batch update to the base tables.
E. Set the materialized view to refresh based on a specific schedule to avoid refreshing it too often.

Question #17:
You need to ensure that a materialized view is always up-to-date with the latest data from the base tables, but you want to avoid unnecessary costs associated with too frequent refreshes. Which combination of actions should you take to strike a balance between data freshness and cost-efficiency?
A. Use a scheduled refresh interval that balances the need for up-to-date data with cost considerations.
B. Enable automatic refresh for all materialized views to ensure they always contain the latest data.
C. Manually refresh the materialized view only when critical changes occur to the base tables.
D. Set up a data monitoring system to track when the base tables change and trigger a refresh only when necessary.
E. Set the materialized view to refresh every minute for the most accurate data at all times.

Question #18:
Your team has implemented materialized views to enhance query performance. The materialized views should always return the most recent data even if the base tables change frequently. Which of the following options will ensure that the materialized views are always up-to-date?
A. Set the materialized view to refresh upon every query execution.
B. Schedule a refresh for the materialized view at a specific time of the day based on query usage.
C. Enable Snowflake's built-in auto-refresh feature, which automatically keeps materialized views in sync with changes to the base tables.
D. Manually refresh the materialized view after every significant update to the base tables.
E. Use incremental refreshes for the materialized view to minimize the performance overhead of full refreshes.

Question #19:
To ensure that your materialized view is always up-to-date and reflects recent changes in the base table, which actions should you take? (Choose all that apply.)
A. Enable automatic refresh to update the materialized view whenever changes occur in the

base table.
B. Set a high frequency refresh interval to refresh the materialized view every minute.
C. Use the refresh history feature to monitor when the materialized view was last refreshed.
D. Use the REFRESH command to manually update the materialized view after a significant update in the base table.
E. Schedule the materialized view to refresh only during off-peak hours when there is less load on the system.

Question #20:
You are working with materialized views that reflect data changes in real-time. However, your organization wants to reduce costs while maintaining accurate and fresh data. Which approach would be best to balance freshness and costs? (Choose all that apply.)
A. Set up a scheduled refresh interval that is based on the frequency of base table updates.
B. Enable automatic refresh on every query to guarantee the freshest data at all times.
C. Implement incremental refreshes to only update the changed portions of the materialized view.
D. Set the refresh interval to daily, depending on when your business processes require the most up-to-date data.
E. Use manual refresh triggers based on the specific needs of the business.

Question #16:
Correct Answer: B, E
Explanation:
B is correct because configuring the materialized view to refresh periodically (e.g., once per hour) ensures that the data remains current without incurring excessive refresh costs.
E is correct because scheduling a refresh helps balance the need for up-to-date data while preventing unnecessary refreshes.
A is incorrect because automatic refresh on every update may lead to higher costs and unnecessary refreshes.
C is incorrect because the AUTOMATIC_REFRESH setting does not exist in Snowflake, and such a feature is not available for materialized views.
D is incorrect because manual refreshing after each batch update can be error-prone and inefficient.

Question #17:
Correct Answer: A, D
Explanation:
A is correct because using a scheduled refresh interval allows you to keep the materialized view fresh without incurring excessive costs from frequent updates.
D is correct because setting up a data monitoring system and triggering refreshes only when necessary ensures that the materialized view stays up-to-date while minimizing the refresh frequency.
B is incorrect because enabling automatic refresh for all materialized views may incur high costs for frequent updates.
C is incorrect because manually refreshing materialized views on every change would be impractical and resource-intensive.
E is incorrect because refreshing every minute would unnecessarily increase costs without adding significant value.

Question #18:
Correct Answer: A, C
Explanation:
A is correct because setting the materialized view to refresh upon every query execution ensures it always reflects the latest data.
C is correct because Snowflake's built-in auto-refresh feature ensures that the materialized view stays in sync with changes to the base tables.
B is incorrect because scheduling a refresh may not guarantee the most up-to-date data.
D is incorrect because manually refreshing the materialized view on every significant update is inefficient and error-prone.
E is incorrect because incremental refreshes are not supported by materialized views in Snowflake.

Question #19:
Correct Answer: A, D
Explanation:
A is correct because enabling automatic refresh ensures that the materialized view is updated whenever there are changes in the base table.
D is correct because manually refreshing the materialized view when necessary is an effective way to keep data fresh without unnecessary costs.
B is incorrect because a high-frequency refresh interval may lead to unnecessary costs, especially if the data does not change that often.
C is incorrect because the refresh history feature is for tracking refresh times, not for updating the materialized view.
E is incorrect because refreshing only during off-peak hours does not ensure that the materialized view is always up-to-date.

Question #20:
Correct Answer: A, C, D
Explanation:
A is correct because setting a scheduled refresh interval based on the frequency of base table updates ensures that the materialized view stays fresh while keeping costs manageable.
C is correct because incremental refreshes are a good way to reduce the performance overhead of full refreshes while maintaining data freshness.
D is correct because scheduling daily refreshes can be an effective strategy if the business only requires up-to-date data on a daily basis.
B is incorrect because enabling automatic refresh on every query may lead to high costs for frequently updated tables.
E is incorrect because relying on manual triggers increases the risk of missing necessary refreshes and adds operational complexity.

Question #21:
Your team is experiencing performance issues with slow aggregation queries on a large dataset. After analyzing the query patterns, you decide to implement materialized views. What is the primary reason materialized views are useful for improving the performance of aggregation queries?
A. Materialized views store data in a compressed format, reducing the query time for aggregation.

B. Materialized views store pre-computed results for aggregation, avoiding the need to scan large datasets repeatedly.
C. Materialized views increase the concurrency of query execution, allowing more users to access data at the same time.
D. Materialized views automatically partition data to optimize queries involving large datasets.

Question #22:
You have a query that frequently selects data from multiple tables and aggregates it into a summary report. The query takes too long to execute due to the complexity of the joins and aggregations. How can materialized views help in this case?
A. By storing pre-aggregated results, materialized views can reduce the need to compute complex joins and aggregations on the fly.
B. Materialized views automatically rewrite the query to optimize the join operations, improving query performance.
C. Materialized views split the query into smaller queries, each of which executes faster.
D. Materialized views cache intermediate query results, improving the performance of complex queries.

Question #23:
You are working on a report that frequently aggregates large amounts of sales data. The aggregation process is slow because the data is spread across multiple tables. You decide to create a materialized view to speed up the process. What benefit does the materialized view provide?
A. It reduces storage costs by eliminating the need for multiple copies of the data.
B. It reduces query execution time by storing the pre-aggregated data, avoiding repeated computation of the same aggregation.
C. It ensures that the data is always up-to-date by automatically refreshing every time a query is run.
D. It optimizes the base table schema to make the aggregation process faster.

Question #24:
You have a query that selects a large volume of data with complex calculations on a regular basis. The query performance is poor, and you need to optimize it. How can using materialized views help you in this situation?
A. Materialized views will store pre-calculated results, allowing queries to return results more quickly by avoiding recalculation.
B. Materialized views reduce the storage requirements by compressing large datasets.
C. Materialized views optimize join operations on base tables, improving query performance.
D. Materialized views cache query results to improve overall performance without changing the query structure.

Question #25:
You are optimizing query performance for a reporting system that aggregates and filters data from large tables frequently. Which of the following best explains why materialized views are a suitable optimization for this scenario?
A. Materialized views store the pre-filtered and pre-aggregated results, allowing the reporting system to query the materialized view instead of the base tables.
B. Materialized views automatically update data in real-time, ensuring that the reporting system always accesses the most current information.
C. Materialized views distribute query load across multiple servers, enhancing scalability.

D. Materialized views perform better because they eliminate the need for filtering and aggregation altogether.

Answer Key:

Question #21:
Correct Answer: B
Explanation:
B is correct. Materialized views store pre-computed results for aggregation, which significantly reduces query time by avoiding the need to scan large datasets and recompute aggregates for each query.
A is incorrect because materialized views don't inherently store data in a compressed format. Compression would be an additional benefit but not the main reason for performance optimization.
C is incorrect because materialized views don't affect concurrency directly, though they can reduce the load on the database.
D is incorrect because materialized views do not automatically partition data, although partitioning strategies could help performance.

Question #22:
Correct Answer: A
Explanation:
A is correct. Materialized views store pre-aggregated results, reducing the need to recompute complex joins and aggregations, thus speeding up query performance.
B is incorrect because materialized views do not rewrite queries automatically; they simply store pre-computed results.
C is incorrect because materialized views do not split queries into smaller ones, but they optimize query execution by storing pre-computed results.
D is incorrect because materialized views do not cache intermediate results, they store final pre-computed data to optimize queries.

Question #23:
Correct Answer: B
Explanation:
B is correct because materialized views store pre-aggregated data, which allows you to skip repeated computations of the same aggregation, improving query performance.
A is incorrect because materialized views increase storage due to the pre-computed data being stored, but the benefit is in speed, not cost reduction.
C is incorrect because materialized views don't automatically refresh on every query run; they refresh periodically.
D is incorrect because materialized views don't optimize the base table schema; they only store pre-aggregated data.

Question #24:
Correct Answer: A
Explanation:
A is correct because materialized views store pre-calculated results of the query, meaning that subsequent queries can return results faster since they avoid recalculating complex calculations.

B is incorrect because while materialized views might have some compression, their main benefit is speed optimization, not storage reduction.

C is incorrect because materialized views do not optimize joins; they only optimize by storing pre-computed query results.

D is incorrect because materialized views do not cache query results; they store pre-computed results for faster query performance.

Question #25:
Correct Answer: A
Explanation:

A is correct because materialized views store pre-filtered and pre-aggregated results, meaning the reporting system can query the materialized view directly instead of the base tables, which reduces computation time.

B is incorrect because materialized views do not update in real-time but refresh periodically.

C is incorrect because materialized views do not distribute query load across servers, though they may reduce query load on the base tables.

D is incorrect because materialized views do not eliminate filtering and aggregation but optimize their performance by pre-calculating these operations.

ROLE BASED ACCESS CONTROL

Question #1:
An organization in the financial industry needs strong encryption, enhanced audit logging, and HIPAA compliance for handling sensitive data. Which Snowflake account type(s) would you recommend?

Options:
A. Enterprise
B. Business Critical
C. Virtual Private Snowflake
D. Standard

Question #2:
A global enterprise wants to ensure its Snowflake metadata services are completely isolated and does not share infrastructure with other Snowflake customers. Which account type should they use?

Options:
A. Standard
B. Business Critical
C. Virtual Private Snowflake
D. Enterprise

Question #3:
A healthcare organization needs to comply with HIPAA regulations but does not require a completely isolated infrastructure. Which Snowflake account type is the best fit?

Options:
A. Enterprise
B. Business Critical
C. Virtual Private Snowflake
D. Standard

Question #4:
A tech company is looking for an entry-level account with standard governance, data sharing, and scalability. They do not need advanced compliance features. Which account type should they choose?

Options:
A. Standard
B. Business Critical
C. Virtual Private Snowflake
D. Premium

Question #5:
Which of the following account types support customer-managed encryption keys through Tri-Secret Secure?

Options:
A. Enterprise
B. Business Critical
C. Virtual Private Snowflake
D. Standard

Answers and Explanations

Question #1:
Correct Answer: B, C
Explanation:
A is incorrect because the Enterprise (or Standard) account does not include the enhanced security features required for stringent compliance like HIPAA.
B is correct because Business Critical accounts provide enhanced security, end-to-end encryption, and compliance options like HIPAA.
C is correct because Virtual Private Snowflake provides the highest level of security and isolation, which may be suitable for extremely sensitive environments.
D is incorrect because "Standard" is synonymous with Enterprise and lacks the required features.

Question #2:
Correct Answer: C
Explanation:

A is incorrect because the Standard account does not provide dedicated infrastructure or isolated metadata services.
B is incorrect because Business Critical enhances security but does not offer complete infrastructure isolation.
C is correct because Virtual Private Snowflake offers a fully isolated environment, including metadata services, ideal for organizations requiring extreme data separation.
D is incorrect because Enterprise (Standard) accounts do not provide isolation features.

Question #3:
Correct Answer: B
Explanation:

A is incorrect because Enterprise accounts do not include HIPAA compliance features.
B is correct because Business Critical accounts are designed for industries with regulatory compliance requirements like HIPAA.
C is incorrect because Virtual Private Snowflake offers more security than necessary for this scenario, leading to potential over-investment.
D is incorrect because Standard (Enterprise) accounts lack compliance-specific features.

Question #4:
Correct Answer: A
Explanation:

A is correct because the Standard (Enterprise) account provides scalability and data sharing for general business use.
B is incorrect because Business Critical accounts include additional security features not required in this scenario.
C is incorrect because Virtual Private Snowflake is an over-engineered solution for this use case.
D is incorrect because "Premium" is not an account type in Snowflake.

Question #5:
Correct Answer: B, C
Explanation:

A is incorrect because Enterprise accounts do not include Tri-Secret Secure functionality.
B is correct because Business Critical accounts support Tri-Secret Secure, enabling customer-managed encryption keys.
C is correct because Virtual Private Snowflake also supports Tri-Secret Secure as part of its advanced security features.
D is incorrect because Standard is another name for Enterprise, which does not offer this feature.

Question #6:
A user needs to manage the creation of roles and grant privileges to other roles in Snowflake. Which role should be assigned to this user?

Options:
A. ACCOUNTADMIN
B. SYSADMIN
C. SECURITYADMIN
D. PUBLIC

Question #7:
A database developer needs to create and manage tables and schemas in a specific database but should not have access to account-wide configurations. Which role is most appropriate for this user?

Options:
A. ACCOUNTADMIN
B. SYSADMIN

C. SECURITYADMIN
D. PUBLIC

Question #8:
Which of the following roles has the highest level of administrative privileges in Snowflake, allowing access to all objects and configurations within the account?

Options:
A. SYSADMIN
B. ACCOUNTADMIN
C. SECURITYADMIN
D. PUBLIC

Question #9:
You want to grant a role the ability to monitor user activities and query execution statistics but not modify any data or configuration. Which role should you assign?

Options:
A. SECURITYADMIN
B. SYSADMIN
C. MONITORING_ROLE
D. PUBLIC

Question #10:
A user with the SYSADMIN role attempts to create a new user in Snowflake. However, they encounter an error stating they lack the necessary privileges. What additional role or privilege is required to perform this action?

Options:
A. ACCOUNTADMIN
B. SECURITYADMIN
C. ROLEADMIN
D. PUBLIC

Answers and Explanations

Question #6:
Correct Answer: C
Explanation:

A is incorrect because ACCOUNTADMIN has broader privileges than required, including account-wide management, which is unnecessary in this scenario.
B is incorrect because SYSADMIN focuses on managing objects like tables and warehouses, not roles.
C is correct because SECURITYADMIN is responsible for managing roles and granting privileges to roles.
D is incorrect because PUBLIC is a default role with minimal privileges, unsuitable for role management.

Question #7:
Correct Answer: B
Explanation:

A is incorrect because ACCOUNTADMIN has excessive privileges for this scenario.
B is correct because SYSADMIN is designed for managing database objects like tables, schemas, and warehouses.
C is incorrect because SECURITYADMIN is focused on role and privilege management, not database object management.
D is incorrect because PUBLIC has minimal privileges and cannot manage database objects.

Question #8:
Correct Answer: B
Explanation:

A is incorrect because SYSADMIN, while powerful, does not have account-wide administrative privileges.
B is correct because ACCOUNTADMIN has the highest level of administrative control, including all objects and configurations in the account.
C is incorrect because SECURITYADMIN focuses on roles and privileges, not overall account management.
D is incorrect because PUBLIC has minimal privileges and no administrative capabilities.

Question #9:
Correct Answer: C
Explanation:

A is incorrect because SECURITYADMIN is focused on managing roles and privileges, not monitoring activities.
B is incorrect because SYSADMIN is focused on database and warehouse management.
C is correct because a custom MONITORING_ROLE can be created to grant monitoring-related privileges like viewing query execution statistics and session information.
D is incorrect because PUBLIC has minimal privileges and cannot monitor activities.

Question #10:
Correct Answer: B
Explanation:

A is incorrect because ACCOUNTADMIN has broader privileges than required for creating users.
B is correct because SECURITYADMIN is responsible for managing user accounts and roles, which includes creating new users.
C is incorrect because ROLEADMIN focuses on managing role hierarchies, not user accounts.
D is incorrect because PUBLIC has no privileges related to user creation.

Question #11:
A user is assigned a role that grants access to a schema but cannot access a specific table within that schema. What should be done to resolve this issue?

Options:
A. Grant the table privileges directly to the user.
B. Grant the table privileges to the user's role.
C. Assign the ACCOUNTADMIN role to the user.
D. Grant schema privileges to the user's role.

Question #12:
A security administrator needs to grant the SELECT privilege on a table to a specific role but does not want to manage user access directly. Which statement correctly describes this approach?

Options:
A. Privileges must always be granted to users directly.
B. Privileges should be granted to roles, which are then assigned to users.
C. Users should be granted direct access to the table and bypass roles.
D. Privileges cannot be granted to roles in Snowflake.

Question #13:
Which of the following actions requires the USAGE privilege on a database or schema in Snowflake?

Options:
A. Querying tables within a schema.
B. Creating a new table in a schema.
C. Viewing the list of tables in a schema.
D. Dropping a schema.

Question #14:
A developer wants to access multiple tables across schemas without being granted individual permissions for each table. What is the best approach?

Options:
A. Grant SELECT on each table to the developer's role.
B. Grant SELECT at the schema level to the developer's role.
C. Assign the ACCOUNTADMIN role to the developer.
D. Grant the PUBLIC role to the developer.

Question #15:
A user reports that they cannot query a table despite having the required SELECT privilege through a role. What could be the reason?

Options:
A. The SELECT privilege was granted to the PUBLIC role.
B. The user is not set as the owner of the table.
C. The role with the SELECT privilege is not set as the user's active role.
D. The user does not have the USAGE privilege on the schema.

Answers and Explanations

Question #11:
Correct Answer: B
Explanation:

A is incorrect because privileges should be granted to roles, not directly to users, to maintain RBAC principles.
B is correct because privileges are best granted to roles, which are then assigned to users, ensuring scalable access control.
C is incorrect because assigning ACCOUNTADMIN is excessive and violates the principle of least privilege.
D is incorrect because the schema-level privileges might already exist, but specific table-level access is required.

Question #12:
Correct Answer: B
Explanation:

A is incorrect because privileges should not be granted to users directly; RBAC encourages privilege management through roles.
B is correct because Snowflake's RBAC model relies on granting privileges to roles, which can then be assigned to users.
C is incorrect because directly granting privileges to users bypasses the role-based structure and reduces scalability.
D is incorrect because privileges can be granted to roles in Snowflake.

Question #13:
Correct Answer: C
Explanation:

A is incorrect because querying tables requires the SELECT privilege, not just USAGE.
B is incorrect because creating a new table requires the CREATE TABLE privilege.
C is correct because the USAGE privilege is required to view schema objects like the list of tables.
D is incorrect because dropping a schema requires ownership or a specific DROP privilege.

Question #14:
Correct Answer: B
Explanation:

A is incorrect because granting privileges on each table individually is inefficient.
B is correct because granting SELECT at the schema level simplifies access control for all tables within the schema.
C is incorrect because assigning ACCOUNTADMIN is excessive and against the principle of least privilege.
D is incorrect because the PUBLIC role has minimal privileges and cannot provide broad access.

Question #15:
Correct Answer: C, D
Explanation:

A is incorrect because granting privileges to the PUBLIC role would not necessarily ensure access if other conditions are unmet.
B is incorrect because ownership is not required to query a table; privileges are sufficient.
C is correct because roles need to be set as active to access their associated privileges.
D is correct because the USAGE privilege on the schema is necessary to access objects within it.

Question #16:
A user has been assigned the ANALYST role, which inherits privileges from the REPORTING_ROLE. The REPORTING_ROLE has SELECT privileges on a specific schema. Can the user with the ANALYST role query tables in that schema?

Options:
A. Yes, because ANALYST inherits all privileges from REPORTING_ROLE.
B. No, because privileges do not propagate through inheritance.
C. Yes, but only if ANALYST is explicitly granted USAGE on the schema.
D. No, because the user needs direct SELECT privileges.

Question #17:
A security administrator grants the DATA_SCIENCE_ROLE to the DATA_ENGINEERING_ROLE. Which of the following is true about privilege inheritance?

Options:
A. DATA_ENGINEERING_ROLE inherits all privileges of DATA_SCIENCE_ROLE.
B. DATA_SCIENCE_ROLE inherits all privileges of DATA_ENGINEERING_ROLE.
C. Users with the DATA_ENGINEERING_ROLE must still be granted privileges individually.
D. Privileges cannot be inherited between roles.

Question #18:
The FINANCE_ROLE has been granted the HR_ROLE, which has INSERT privileges on an employee table. What is required for a user with FINANCE_ROLE to insert data into the employee table?

Options:
A. The user must set HR_ROLE as their active role.
B. The user must set FINANCE_ROLE as their active role.
C. The user must be explicitly granted INSERT privileges.
D. The user must have ACCOUNTADMIN privileges.

Question #19:
A role hierarchy is established where PROJECT_MANAGER_ROLE is granted TEAM_LEAD_ROLE, which in turn is granted DEVELOPER_ROLE. Which of the following is true?

Options:
A. A user with PROJECT_MANAGER_ROLE can access all privileges of DEVELOPER_ROLE.
B. Privileges propagate only one level, so PROJECT_MANAGER_ROLE cannot inherit

from DEVELOPER_ROLE.
C. Each user must directly inherit the DEVELOPER_ROLE for access.
D. Users with TEAM_LEAD_ROLE do not inherit privileges from DEVELOPER_ROLE.

Question #20:
A data administrator creates a new role, SUPERVISOR_ROLE, and grants it to EMPLOYEE_ROLE. What happens if the administrator grants additional privileges to SUPERVISOR_ROLE later?

Options:
A. Users with EMPLOYEE_ROLE automatically gain those privileges.
B. Users with EMPLOYEE_ROLE must be reassigned the role to inherit the privileges.
C. Privileges granted to SUPERVISOR_ROLE do not affect EMPLOYEE_ROLE.
D. Users with EMPLOYEE_ROLE need explicit grants to gain new privileges.

Answers and Explanations

Question #16:
Correct Answer: A
Explanation:

A is correct because privileges granted to REPORTING_ROLE propagate to ANALYST through inheritance.
B is incorrect because privilege inheritance is a core feature of Snowflake RBAC.
C is incorrect because schema USAGE privileges are inherited by ANALYST from REPORTING_ROLE.
D is incorrect because users do not require direct privileges when roles inherit them.

Question #17:
Correct Answer: A
Explanation:

A is correct because DATA_ENGINEERING_ROLE inherits all privileges from DATA_SCIENCE_ROLE.
B is incorrect because inheritance flows only from the granted role (DATA_SCIENCE_ROLE) to the grantee role (DATA_ENGINEERING_ROLE).
C is incorrect because privileges are managed through roles, not users, in RBAC.
D is incorrect because Snowflake supports privilege inheritance between roles.

Question #18:
Correct Answer: B
Explanation:

A is incorrect because HR_ROLE does not need to be set as active; the privileges propagate to FINANCE_ROLE.
B is correct because the active role (FINANCE_ROLE) includes all inherited privileges, allowing the user to insert data.
C is incorrect because explicit grants are unnecessary when roles inherit privileges.
D is incorrect because ACCOUNTADMIN is not required for this operation.

Question #19:
Correct Answer: A
Explanation:

A is correct because inheritance allows privileges to propagate through multiple levels, from DEVELOPER_ROLE to PROJECT_MANAGER_ROLE.
B is incorrect because privileges propagate across all levels of the hierarchy.
C is incorrect because inheritance eliminates the need for direct assignment of DEVELOPER_ROLE to each user.
D is incorrect because TEAM_LEAD_ROLE does inherit privileges from DEVELOPER_ROLE.

Question #20:
Correct Answer: A
Explanation:

A is correct because any additional privileges granted to SUPERVISOR_ROLE automatically propagate to EMPLOYEE_ROLE through inheritance.
B is incorrect because reassignment is not needed; inheritance works dynamically.
C is incorrect because privilege inheritance ensures that changes to SUPERVISOR_ROLE impact EMPLOYEE_ROLE.
D is incorrect because explicit grants are not required when roles are linked through inheritance.

Question #21:
A user with the DB_OWNER role has OWNERSHIP on a database. They want to transfer ownership of the database to another role, NEW_OWNER. What command should they use?

Options:
A. GRANT OWNERSHIP ON DATABASE my_db TO ROLE NEW_OWNER;
B. ALTER DATABASE my_db TRANSFER TO ROLE NEW_OWNER;
C. ALTER DATABASE my_db SET OWNER = NEW_OWNER;
D. ALTER DATABASE my_db CHANGE OWNER TO NEW_OWNER;

Question #22:
If a role owns a table, which of the following is true about that role's privileges on the table?

Options:
A. The role can only grant SELECT and INSERT privileges to other roles.
B. The role can grant all available privileges on the table to other roles.
C. The role cannot revoke privileges it has granted to other roles.
D. The role cannot drop the table without additional privileges.

Question #23:
What happens if a role with OWNERSHIP of a table grants OWNERSHIP to another role?

Options:
A. The original owner role retains all privileges on the table.
B. The original owner role loses all privileges on the table.
C. Both roles share ownership of the table.
D. The original owner role automatically gets the ALL PRIVILEGES grant on the table.

Question #24:
A role DATA_ADMIN owns a schema and grants USAGE and CREATE privileges on it to another role, DEVELOPER. Which of the following actions can DEVELOPER perform?

Options:
A. Create new tables in the schema.
B. Grant CREATE privilege on the schema to another role.
C. Drop the schema.
D. Transfer ownership of the schema to another role.

Question #25:
Which of the following is true about ownership in Snowflake?

Options:
A. Ownership cannot be transferred once assigned.
B. A role with OWNERSHIP on an object can revoke privileges granted by other roles.
C. Only the ACCOUNTADMIN role can transfer ownership of objects.
D. Ownership provides privileges beyond what can be explicitly granted

---

Answers and Explanations

Question #21:
Correct Answer: A
Explanation:

A is correct because GRANT OWNERSHIP is the proper syntax for transferring ownership of an object in Snowflake.
B is incorrect as they do not match the correct syntax for ownership transfer in Snowflake.
C is incorrect as they do not match the correct syntax for ownership transfer in Snowflake.
D is incorrect as they do not match the correct syntax for ownership transfer in Snowflake.

Question #22:
Correct Answer: B
Explanation:

B is correct because ownership grants the ability to manage all privileges on the object, including granting and revoking them.
A is incorrect because OWNERSHIP is not limited to specific privileges like SELECT or INSERT.
C is incorrect because owners can revoke privileges they have granted.
D is incorrect because owners inherently have the ability to drop the object they own.

Question #23:
Correct Answer: B
Explanation:

B is correct because granting OWNERSHIP to another role removes all privileges of the original owner, as only one role can own an object at a time.
A is incorrect because ownership transfer eliminates the original owner's privileges.
C is incorrect because ownership cannot be shared between roles.
D is incorrect because privileges are not retained automatically when ownership is transferred.

Question #24:
Correct Answer: A
Explanation:

A is correct because the CREATE privilege allows DEVELOPER to create new objects within the schema.
B is incorrect because DEVELOPER cannot grant privileges they do not own.
C is incorrect because only the owner can drop the schema.
D is incorrect because only the owner can transfer ownership.

Question #25:
Correct Answer: B
Explanation:

B is correct because ownership allows the role to manage privileges, including revoking grants made by other roles.
A is incorrect because ownership can be transferred using the GRANT OWNERSHIP command.
C is incorrect because any role with appropriate privileges can transfer ownership.
D is incorrect because ownership does not provide undefined or implicit privileges; it enables full management of the object.

SNOWFLAKE SCHEMA

Question #1:
You want to create a zero-copy clone of a large table for a data migration process. What key considerations must you account for to ensure the cloning process does not impact the performance of the original table?
Choose two:
A) Cloning uses significant compute resources, so you should provision additional warehouses.
B) The clone operation only involves metadata, so it will not impact performance.
C) Any updates to the original table will reflect on the clone unless explicitly blocked.
D) The size of the dataset determines the duration of the clone operation.
E) Cloning large datasets requires suspending operations on the original table during the process.

Question #2:
A team needs to run multiple experiments on the same dataset without modifying the original data. They decide to use cloning for this purpose. Which statements about cloning in Snowflake are accurate?
Choose two:
A) Cloning allows instant creation of a duplicate with no additional storage cost initially.
B) Clones automatically inherit privileges from the original object.
C) Clones and the original share the same underlying storage until data is modified.
D) Any modifications made to the clone propagate back to the original.
E) Cloning impacts the performance of the original data during the operation.

Question #3:
After creating a clone of a database, the team notices unexpected behavior in their cloned objects. What could explain this behavior?
Choose two:
A) Views in the cloned database retain references to the original database.
B) The clone inherits user-defined stages from the original database.
C) Row-level security policies in the original database are copied to the clone.
D) The cloned database contains snapshots of the data at the time of cloning.
E) Changes made to the clone are instantly synchronized with the original.

Question #4:

You've cloned a table to test updates, and now you want to track the changes. Which Snowflake feature can you use to monitor modifications in the clone?
Choose two:
A) Time Travel to compare the original and clone over time.
B) Access History to track user activities on the clone.
C) Table Metadata to log all changes made to the clone.
D) Streams to capture DML operations on the cloned table.
E) Clone Synchronization Logs to identify data divergence.

Question #5:
A zero-copy clone of a Snowflake table is created to test new transformations. Which of the following operations will directly impact storage costs?
Choose two:
A) Deleting rows in the original table after cloning.
B) Modifying rows in the cloned table.
C) Running SELECT queries on both the original and cloned tables.
D) Altering the schema of the cloned table.
E) Inserting rows into the original table post-cloning.

Answers and Explanations

Question #1:
Correct Answers: B, C
Explanation:
B is correct because cloning is a metadata operation that does not require significant compute resources, ensuring no performance impact on the original object.
C is correct because changes made to the original will not affect the clone unless explicitly configured.
A is incorrect because cloning does not require additional warehouses or compute resources.
D is incorrect because the cloning operation's duration is not determined by dataset size.
E is incorrect because the original table remains fully operational during the cloning process.

Question #2:
Correct Answers: A, C
Explanation:
A is correct because clones are created instantly and use no additional storage initially.
C is correct because clones share underlying storage with the original until changes are made.
B is incorrect because privileges are not automatically inherited; they need to be granted separately.
D is incorrect because modifications to the clone do not affect the original.
E is incorrect because cloning does not impact the performance of the original object.

Question #3:
Correct Answers: A, D
Explanation:
A is correct because views in a clone still reference objects in the original database unless explicitly redirected.

D is correct because cloning creates a snapshot of the data as it existed at the time of the operation.
B is incorrect because user-defined stages are not automatically cloned.
C is incorrect because row-level security policies are not copied by default.
E is incorrect because changes in the clone do not propagate back to the original.

Question #4:
Correct Answers: A, D
Explanation:
A is correct because Time Travel allows you to compare versions of the original and cloned tables.
D is correct because Streams can track DML operations on cloned tables.
B is incorrect because Access History does not track specific changes to the data itself.
C is incorrect because Table Metadata does not log detailed data changes.
E is incorrect because there is no feature called "Clone Synchronization Logs."

Question #5:
Correct Answers: B, E
Explanation:
B is correct because modifying rows in the clone incurs additional storage costs due to the creation of new data blocks.
E is correct because inserting rows into the original table post-cloning increases storage costs as the data is not shared with the clone.
A is incorrect because deleting rows in the original table does not affect shared storage immediately.
C is incorrect because SELECT queries do not impact storage costs.
D is incorrect because schema changes do not directly affect storage usage.

Question #6:
You have revoked the READ role from a user. However, the user can still query data within a specific schema. What could be the reason?
A) The user still has another role with necessary privileges.
B) The user has direct permissions on the schema.
C) Snowflake does not support revoking schema-level privileges.
D) Revoking a role does not affect permissions immediately.

Question #7:
To completely remove the ability of a role to grant privileges on a specific object to other roles, which command should be used?
A) REVOKE OWNERSHIP ON <object> FROM ROLE <role_name>;
B) REVOKE GRANT OPTION FOR SELECT ON <object> FROM ROLE <role_name>;
C) REVOKE ALL PRIVILEGES ON <object> FROM ROLE <role_name>;
D) REMOVE GRANT OPTION FOR ALL PRIVILEGES FROM ROLE <role_name> ON <object>;

Question #8:
You want to limit access to a specific sensitive column in a table. Which privilege should you grant to allow a role to access only that column, while restricting access to other columns in the same table?
A) GRANT SELECT ON TABLE <table_name> TO ROLE <role_name>;

B) GRANT SELECT ON COLUMN <column_name> IN TABLE <table_name> TO ROLE <role_name>;
C) GRANT USAGE ON COLUMN <column_name> IN TABLE <table_name> TO ROLE <role_name>;
D) GRANT READ ON COLUMN <column_name> IN TABLE <table_name> TO ROLE <role_name>;

Question #9:
If you need to revoke access to a sensitive column that was previously granted to a role, which command should you use?
A) REVOKE ALL PRIVILEGES ON COLUMN <column_name> FROM ROLE <role_name>;
B) REVOKE SELECT ON COLUMN <column_name> IN TABLE <table_name> FROM ROLE <role_name>;
C) REVOKE USAGE ON COLUMN <column_name> IN TABLE <table_name> FROM ROLE <role_name>;
D) REVOKE READ ON COLUMN <column_name> IN TABLE <table_name> FROM ROLE <role_name>;

Question #10:
To comply with data privacy regulations, you need to apply masking policies on certain columns to ensure sensitive data is only visible to authorized roles. Which feature in Snowflake supports this requirement?
A) Column-level Access Control
B) Dynamic Data Masking
C) Virtual Private Database (VPD)
D) Row-level Security

Answers and Explanations

Question #6:
Correct Answers: A, B
Explanation:
A is correct because the user may still have another role that provides the necessary privileges to query the schema.
B is correct because direct permissions granted to the user on the schema will remain effective even after the role is revoked.
C is incorrect because Snowflake does support revoking schema-level privileges.
D is incorrect because permissions in Snowflake are updated immediately upon revocation.

Question #7:
Correct Answer: B
Explanation:
B is correct because the REVOKE GRANT OPTION command removes the ability of a role to delegate privileges to other roles.
A is incorrect because revoking ownership does not specifically target the GRANT OPTION.
C is incorrect because revoking all privileges does not address the grant delegation.
D is incorrect because it uses an invalid syntax for Snowflake.

Question #8:
Correct Answer: B
Explanation:
B is correct because GRANT SELECT ON COLUMN is the appropriate privilege to restrict access to a specific column in a table.
A is incorrect because it grants SELECT on the entire table.
C is incorrect because USAGE is not valid at the column level.
D is incorrect because READ is not a valid privilege in Snowflake.

Question #9:
Correct Answer: B
Explanation:
B is correct because the REVOKE SELECT ON COLUMN command is the proper syntax to remove access to a specific column.
A is incorrect because revoking "ALL PRIVILEGES" at the column level is not valid syntax.
C is incorrect because USAGE is not a valid privilege at the column level.
D is incorrect because READ is not a valid privilege in Snowflake.

Question #10:
Correct Answer: B
Explanation:
B is correct because Dynamic Data Masking in Snowflake allows sensitive data to be masked for unauthorized roles, ensuring compliance with data privacy regulations.
A is incorrect because Column-level Access Control is not a specific Snowflake feature for masking data.
C is incorrect because Virtual Private Database (VPD) is not a Snowflake feature.
D is incorrect because Row-level Security applies to rows, not individual columns.

Question #11:
Which command would allow you to grant a role conditional access to a masked column, only revealing unmasked data to specific roles?
A) GRANT USAGE ON MASKING POLICY <policy_name> TO ROLE <role_name>;
B) APPLY MASKING POLICY <policy_name> ON COLUMN <column_name> TO ROLE <role_name>;
C) CREATE MASKING POLICY <policy_name> AS (val string) -> CASE WHEN current_role() = '<role_name>' THEN val ELSE 'MASKED' END;
D) GRANT SELECT ON MASKING POLICY <policy_name> TO ROLE <role_name>;

Question #12:
Which privilege must a role have in order to alter or apply a masking policy on a column in a Snowflake table?
A) USAGE on the schema and SELECT on the column
B) OWNERSHIP on the table
C) APPLY MASKING POLICY on the column
D) ALL PRIVILEGES on the database

Question #13:
You need to restrict access to certain rows in a table based on the role of the user querying

the data. Which feature in Snowflake is specifically designed to manage this type of access control?
A) Row-Level Security
B) Column-Level Security
C) Row Access Policy
D) Dynamic Data Masking

Question #14:
If you want to create a masking policy that masks data by replacing sensitive information with the string "MASKED" unless accessed by an authorized role, which of the following would be a valid policy definition?
A) CREATE MASKING POLICY my_policy AS (val string) -> CASE WHEN current_role() IN ('authorized_role') THEN val ELSE 'MASKED' END;
B) CREATE MASKING POLICY my_policy AS (val string) -> IF role() = 'authorized_role' THEN val ELSE 'MASKED';
C) CREATE MASKING POLICY my_policy FOR (val string) RETURN CASE WHEN role() = 'authorized_role' THEN val ELSE 'MASKED';
D) CREATE MASKING POLICY my_policy FOR COLUMN (val string) RETURN CASE WHEN current_role() IS 'authorized_role' THEN val ELSE 'MASKED' END;

Question #15:
What privilege does a role need to apply a masking policy to a column within a table?
A) OWNERSHIP on the column
B) APPLY MASKING POLICY on the table
C) MODIFY on the table
D) OWNERSHIP on the table

Answers and Explanations

Question #11:
Which command would allow you to grant a role conditional access to a masked column, only revealing unmasked data to specific roles?
Correct Answer: A) GRANT USAGE ON MASKING POLICY <policy_name> TO ROLE <role_name>;
Explanation:
A is correct because granting **USAGE ON MASKING POLICY** to a role allows that role to use a masking policy on the designated column, ensuring the column's data is only unmasked when specific conditions (such as role checks) are met.
B is incorrect because **APPLY MASKING POLICY** is not a valid command in Snowflake.
C is incorrect because **CREATE MASKING POLICY** is used for creating a masking policy, not for granting access to it.
D is incorrect because **GRANT SELECT ON MASKING POLICY** does not apply to masking policies in Snowflake.

Question #12:
Which privilege must a role have in order to alter or apply a masking policy on a column in a Snowflake table?

Correct Answer: B) OWNERSHIP on the table
Explanation:
B is correct because the role must have **OWNERSHIP** privileges on the table to alter or apply masking policies on columns within that table. Without **OWNERSHIP**, a role cannot manage masking policies.
A is incorrect because **USAGE on the schema** and **SELECT on the column** are insufficient for managing masking policies.
C is incorrect because **APPLY MASKING POLICY** is not a valid privilege in Snowflake.
D is incorrect because **ALL PRIVILEGES on the database** do not grant the ability to modify or apply masking policies on a specific table.

Question #13:
You need to restrict access to certain rows in a table based on the role of the user querying the data. Which feature in Snowflake is specifically designed to manage this type of access control?
Correct Answer: C) Row Access Policy
Explanation:
C is correct because **Row Access Policy** allows you to restrict access to specific rows based on conditions, such as the role of the user querying the data.
A is incorrect because **Row-Level Security** is a general term and not a specific Snowflake feature.
B is incorrect because **Column-Level Security** controls access to specific columns, not rows.
D is incorrect because **Dynamic Data Masking** pertains to column-level data masking, not row-level access control.

Question #14:
If you want to create a masking policy that masks data by replacing sensitive information with the string "MASKED" unless accessed by an authorized role, which of the following would be a valid policy definition?
Correct Answer: A) CREATE MASKING POLICY my_policy AS (val string) -> CASE WHEN current_role() IN ('authorized_role') THEN val ELSE 'MASKED' END;
Explanation:
A is correct because it follows the correct syntax for creating a masking policy with conditional logic, revealing unmasked data only to the specified roles (current_role() IN ('authorized_role')).
B is incorrect because **IF role()** is not a valid function in Snowflake's policy syntax.
C is incorrect because **RETURN CASE** is not valid syntax in Snowflake for creating a masking policy.
D is incorrect because **current_role() IS 'authorized_role'** is an incorrect way to check for a role in Snowflake masking policy definitions.

Question #15:
What privilege does a role need to apply a masking policy to a column within a table?
Correct Answer: D) OWNERSHIP on the table
Explanation:
D is correct because **OWNERSHIP** is the only privilege that allows a role to apply or modify a masking policy on a table column.
A is incorrect because **OWNERSHIP on the column** is not required to apply a masking policy—ownership of the table is required instead.

B is incorrect because **APPLY MASKING POLICY** is not a valid privilege in Snowflake.
C is incorrect because **MODIFY on the table** is insufficient for applying masking policies; the role must have **OWNERSHIP** of the table.

Question #16:
A user needs to create a clone of a schema in Snowflake to perform testing without affecting the original data. They are concerned about storage costs. What is the key advantage of Snowflake's zero-copy cloning for this scenario?
Options:
A. The schema clone requires a full copy of the data to be created, resulting in additional storage costs.
B. The schema clone is instantaneous and does not require duplicating the underlying data, resulting in minimal storage impact.
C. The cloned schema is a physical copy of the original schema, consuming the same storage as the original schema.
D. The schema clone allows for a logical copy of the data, reducing the storage usage but maintaining the integrity of the original schema.

Question #17:
You have cloned a schema in Snowflake for development purposes. What happens when you update a table in the original schema after cloning it?
Options:
A. The cloned schema is immediately updated to reflect changes made to the original schema.
B. The changes to the original schema do not affect the cloned schema unless explicitly synchronized.
C. The cloned schema will automatically update every 24 hours to reflect changes from the original schema.
D. The cloned schema will remain static as of the time of cloning and will not reflect any changes made to the original schema.

Question #18:
A team cloned a schema for testing purposes in Snowflake and later deleted the original schema. What happens to the cloned schema?
Options:
A. The cloned schema is deleted automatically when the original schema is deleted.
B. The cloned schema remains intact and independent of the original schema.
C. The cloned schema will stop functioning if the original schema is deleted.
D. The cloned schema will lose its data if the original schema is deleted.

Question #19:
You need to create a clone of a schema that includes tables, views, and stages in Snowflake. What is a key benefit of using Snowflake's zero-copy cloning for this purpose?
Options:
A. The clone will include the data, but with separate storage for each cloned object.
B. The clone will include all objects (tables, views, stages) from the original schema without duplicating the data, resulting in efficient storage use.
C. The clone will create a physical copy of each object, consuming more storage than the original schema.

D. Only tables and views are cloned; stages and file formats are not included in the clone.

Question #20:
You have cloned a schema in Snowflake, and now you want to test changes to a table. What is true about the relationship between the cloned schema and the original schema?
Options:
A. Changes made to the original schema, including tables and views, will automatically be reflected in the cloned schema.
B. Changes made to the original schema after the clone are not reflected in the cloned schema unless the clone is refreshed.
C. The cloned schema is a read-only snapshot, and changes cannot be made to the clone.
D. The cloned schema is an independent copy and can be modified without affecting the original schema.

Answers and Explanations

Question #16:
Correct Answer: B, D
Explanation:
B is correct because Snowflake's zero-copy cloning is instantaneous and does not require duplicating the underlying data. This results in minimal storage impact.
D is correct because cloning in Snowflake creates a logical copy without duplicating the original data, minimizing storage costs while preserving the integrity of the schema.
A is incorrect because Snowflake does not require copying the underlying data when cloning a schema.
C is incorrect because the cloned schema does not involve a physical copy of the data.

Question #17:
Correct Answer: B, D
Explanation:
B is correct because any changes made to the original schema after the clone will not automatically affect the cloned schema unless explicitly refreshed.
D is correct because the cloned schema remains static at the time of cloning and does not reflect any changes unless re-cloned.
A is incorrect because Snowflake cloning creates an independent copy; changes in the original schema do not propagate automatically to the clone.
C is incorrect because there is no automatic synchronization between the original and cloned schema on a scheduled basis.

Question #18:
Correct Answer: B
Explanation:
B is correct because the cloned schema is independent of the original schema, meaning it remains intact even after the original schema is deleted.
A is incorrect because deleting the original schema does not affect the cloned schema.
C is incorrect because the cloned schema continues to function after the original schema is deleted.

D is incorrect because the deletion of the original schema does not impact the data in the cloned schema.

Question #19:
Correct Answer: B
Explanation:
B is correct because Snowflake's zero-copy cloning creates an efficient copy of all objects (tables, views, stages) from the original schema without duplicating the underlying data, saving on storage.
A is incorrect because the clone does not create separate storage for each object; it operates with logical references to the original data.
C is incorrect because the cloned schema does not create physical copies of the objects.
D is incorrect because stages and file formats are also cloned along with tables and views

Question #20:
Correct Answer: B, D
Explanation:
B is correct because changes made to the original schema do not affect the cloned schema unless it is explicitly refreshed or re-cloned.
D is correct because the cloned schema is an independent copy and can be modified without affecting the original schema.
A is incorrect because changes made to the original schema do not automatically propagate to the cloned schema.
C is incorrect because the cloned schema is not read-only; it can be modified independently of the original schema.

Question #21:
You are working on a Snowflake project where you have created a schema to organize your data. You are now setting up access controls for different roles in Snowflake. Which of the following statements accurately describes Snowflake's approach to data and metadata management in schemas?
Options:
A. Snowflake stores both data and metadata in the same physical location for faster access and management.
B. Snowflake allows for the separation of data storage and metadata management, ensuring flexibility and scalability.
C. The schema in Snowflake automatically includes both data and metadata, which must be managed together.
D. Metadata is stored outside of Snowflake, and the schema only manages data storage.
E. Snowflake schemas manage metadata separately from the data, enabling independent transformations and access controls.

Question #22:
You are tasked with designing a schema in Snowflake that will scale efficiently for large amounts of structured and semi-structured data. Which of the following characteristics of Snowflake schemas are most relevant to ensuring performance and scalability?

Options:
A. Data and metadata are tightly coupled in a Snowflake schema, leading to better query performance.
B. Metadata is decoupled from data storage, allowing for more efficient data transformations and access management.
C. Snowflake allows you to store data in one schema while managing metadata separately, enhancing performance.
D. The schema can automatically partition data to improve scalability, independent of metadata storage.
E. Snowflake supports a single, global metadata storage location for all schemas to optimize performance.

Question #23:
You are managing a Snowflake schema for a project involving sensitive data. Which of the following options best describes how Snowflake's separation of data and metadata can benefit compliance and security?
Options:
A. By separating data storage from metadata, Snowflake allows for granular control over access to sensitive data and metadata.
B. Storing data and metadata together simplifies compliance, as all permissions and security measures are managed in a single location.
C. Metadata is not stored within Snowflake, ensuring that security measures are applied only to the data.
D. Snowflake allows metadata to be encrypted separately from data, providing enhanced security and compliance flexibility.
E. Snowflake's separation of data and metadata makes it easier to audit and control access, helping to meet regulatory requirements like GDPR.

Question #24:
You are working on a Snowflake schema that needs to integrate data from multiple sources. Which of the following features of Snowflake schemas best support this integration?
Options:
A. Data and metadata are tightly coupled in Snowflake, making integration more efficient.
B. The ability to store metadata separately from the data allows for easy integration of external datasets and systems.
C. Snowflake's separation of metadata and data simplifies data transformations and allows easier integration of new data sources.
D. Metadata in Snowflake must be pre-defined, preventing the integration of new data from dynamic or changing sources.
E. Snowflake schemas provide built-in tools for combining both structured and unstructured data in a single schema without metadata constraints.

Question #25:
You are designing a schema for an analytics solution in Snowflake. How does Snowflake's separation of data and metadata contribute to the flexibility and performance of your data architecture?
Options:
A. Storing data and metadata together ensures that queries are executed in the shortest time possible.

B. The separation of data storage and metadata allows for greater flexibility in managing large-scale datasets and optimizing query performance.
C. Since metadata is stored externally, Snowflake can perform queries much faster than traditional databases.
D. By managing metadata separately, Snowflake can scale more efficiently as data volumes grow, without impacting query performance.
E. Snowflake's architecture automatically optimizes metadata storage to improve data query speeds.

Answers and Explanations

Question #21:
Correct Answer: B, E
Explanation:
- **B** is correct because Snowflake's architecture allows for the separation of data storage and metadata management, enhancing scalability, flexibility, and performance.
- **E** is correct because Snowflake's design ensures that metadata is managed independently from data, which aids in applying separate access controls and transformations.
- **A** is incorrect because Snowflake separates data and metadata storage, not keeping them in the same physical location.
- **C** is incorrect because while Snowflake uses schemas for organizing data, data and metadata are managed independently.
- **D** is incorrect because metadata is stored within Snowflake and not externally.

Question #22:
Correct Answer: B, C
Explanation:
- **B** is correct because Snowflake separates metadata from data storage, which allows for better efficiency in transformations and access management, crucial for scalability.
- **C** is correct because Snowflake allows independent storage and management of data and metadata, improving performance and scalability.
- **A** is incorrect because data and metadata are not tightly coupled in Snowflake, as this would reduce flexibility and scalability.
- **D** is incorrect because the automatic partitioning of data is separate from metadata management.
- **E** is incorrect because Snowflake doesn't store metadata globally but manages it separately for each schema.

Question #23:
Correct Answer: A, E
Explanation:
- **A** is correct because separating data from metadata allows Snowflake to control access at a granular level, improving security and compliance.

220

- **E is correct** because the independent management of data and metadata simplifies auditing and access control, making it easier to comply with regulations such as GDPR.
- **B is incorrect** because storing data and metadata together would not provide the flexibility required for granular access control.
- **C is incorrect** because metadata is stored within Snowflake, ensuring that security is applied to both data and metadata.
- **D is incorrect** because Snowflake does not store metadata separately; instead, it applies different management rules to metadata.

Question #24:
Correct Answer: B, C
Explanation:
- **B is correct** because separating metadata from data allows Snowflake to integrate data from external sources more easily, without requiring changes to the metadata structure.
- **C is correct** because this separation simplifies data transformations and enables seamless integration of external datasets.
- **A is incorrect** because tightly coupling data and metadata would hinder integration by limiting flexibility.
- **D is incorrect** because metadata in Snowflake is dynamic and can be modified to accommodate new data sources.
- **E is incorrect** because metadata management in Snowflake is critical for organizing and accessing structured and unstructured data.

Question #25:
Correct Answer: B, D
Explanation:
- **B is correct** because the separation of data storage and metadata allows Snowflake to scale efficiently without impacting query performance.
- **D is correct** because managing metadata separately from the data helps Snowflake scale without affecting performance, especially as data volumes grow.
- **A is incorrect** because separating data and metadata actually provides flexibility and scalability, rather than ensuring the shortest query times.
- **C is incorrect** because Snowflake stores both data and metadata internally, not externally.
- **E is incorrect** because metadata optimization in Snowflake helps manage the architecture but does not directly improve query speed by itself.

EXTERNAL TABLES

Question #1:
You are tasked with creating an external table in Snowflake that points to a set of data files stored in an S3 bucket. The data is stored in CSV format. After creating the external table, you notice that the query performance is suboptimal when accessing the data. Which of the following could improve the query performance?
A. Convert the CSV files into Parquet format and recreate the external table.
B. Use a larger virtual warehouse to run the queries more efficiently.
C. Configure the external table with a cluster key to optimize query performance.
D. Convert the CSV files into JSON format and recreate the external table.

Question #2:
You have an external table in Snowflake that is based on data stored in Google Cloud Storage. The table is accessed regularly for reporting purposes. Which of the following actions can help reduce the cost of querying this external table?
A. Enable auto-scaling on the virtual warehouse used for querying the external table.
B. Partition the external table by columns that are frequently queried.
C. Use an internal stage for storing temporary data before querying.
D. Convert the external table to an internal table to optimize cost.

Question #3:
Your Snowflake external table references a set of files in an S3 bucket. The files have been updated frequently, and you are observing that the external table does not reflect the latest changes. What could be the most likely reason for this issue?
A. Snowflake caches the data in the external table, so new files need to be manually refreshed.
B. The external table needs to be recreated after each file update to reflect the latest data.
C. External tables automatically detect and update changes in the files as long as the file format remains the same.
D. The external table is not configured with proper permissions to read the updated files.

Question #4:
You are tasked with creating an external table on data stored in an S3 bucket. The data is partitioned by year and month. Which configuration would you use to optimize query performance on this external table?
A. Set the **FILE_FORMAT** property to **CSV** and set a partition key for the year and month.

B. Enable **Automatic Clustering** on the external table.
C. Use the **EXTERNAL_STAGE** object to specify partitioning based on year and month.
D. Use **partition pruning** by creating partitioned views on the external table.

Question #5:
Your organization is working with large datasets stored in a remote cloud storage location. You want to create an external table in Snowflake that provides access to these datasets without physically copying the data into Snowflake storage. Which of the following is a key benefit of using an external table in this scenario?
A. External tables can be queried directly, allowing for on-the-fly transformation of data without requiring data movement.
B. External tables support automatic query optimization, improving performance without any additional configuration.
C. External tables always guarantee lower query costs compared to internal tables.
D. External tables can only be queried in the raw format without any transformations or schema changes.

Answers and Explanations

Question #1:
Correct Answer: A
Explanation:
A is correct. Converting the data to **Parquet** format can significantly improve query performance due to its columnar storage, which is optimized for read-heavy workloads in Snowflake.
B is incorrect because while using a larger virtual warehouse may help, it does not address the underlying inefficiency of the data format.
C is incorrect because external tables cannot be clustered in the same way as internal tables; they are designed to reference data directly in external storage.
D is incorrect because **JSON** format is not as efficient as **Parquet** for querying large datasets.

Question #2:
Correct Answer: B
Explanation:
B is correct. **Partitioning** the external table by columns such as date or region can optimize query performance and reduce costs by limiting the amount of data scanned during queries.
A is incorrect because auto-scaling may not significantly reduce costs unless the data is distributed effectively across queries.
C is incorrect because using an internal stage to store temporary data may introduce additional costs and doesn't necessarily reduce query costs on external tables.
D is incorrect because converting the external table to an internal table may increase costs, as it requires the data to be loaded into Snowflake storage, which is not the goal.

Question #3:
Correct Answer: A
Explanation:

A is correct. **Snowflake caches** the external table data, and it does not automatically refresh to reflect changes in the underlying files. Manual refreshes or reloading the table may be needed to pick up the latest data.
B is incorrect because recreating the external table every time new files are added is not necessary; manual refresh can be done.
C is incorrect because while external tables can detect new files, they do not automatically refresh or update to reflect data changes.
D is incorrect because permissions are typically not the issue unless specifically restricted by access policies.

Question #4:
Correct Answer: C
Explanation:
C is correct. Specifying **partitioning** in the **EXTERNAL_STAGE** object can optimize performance, particularly when working with partitioned data stored in cloud storage.
A is incorrect because specifying partition keys in the **FILE_FORMAT** property is not a valid configuration option.
B is incorrect because **Automatic Clustering** is not available for external tables in Snowflake.
D is incorrect because **partition pruning** is done through querying partitioned data directly; however, partitioning needs to be configured correctly within the **EXTERNAL_STAGE** object.

Question #5:
Correct Answer: A
Explanation:
A is correct. The primary advantage of external tables is that you can **query** the data directly from external storage without copying it into Snowflake, providing on-the-fly access without requiring data movement.
B is incorrect because external tables require explicit configurations for query optimization and do not automatically optimize queries.
C is incorrect because querying external tables may incur higher costs due to the need to scan data in external storage.
D is incorrect because external tables can support transformations, schema modifications, and various file formats, making them flexible for analytics.

Question #6:
You have created an external table in Snowflake that references large data files stored in AWS S3. You are running SQL queries on this table and notice that the query performance is slower than expected. Which of the following actions would **most likely** improve query performance when accessing the external table data?
A. Use **Clustering Keys** on the external table to optimize query performance.
B. Use **Materialized Views** to pre-compute and store the results of frequently accessed queries.
C. Use **Automatic Query Caching** to improve the speed of repetitive queries.
D. Convert the data format from **CSV** to **Parquet** and recreate the external table.

Question #7:

You are working with a large dataset stored in Google Cloud Storage and want to create an external table in Snowflake. Your company frequently queries this external data and wants to optimize both performance and cost. Which of the following is **most beneficial** when working with external tables in Snowflake to achieve both performance and cost efficiency?
A. Store the data as **JSON** format to allow flexible querying.
B. Use **partitioning** on the external table to reduce the volume of data scanned during queries.
C. Use an internal stage to load the data into Snowflake before querying.
D. Use **manual scaling** of the virtual warehouse to speed up queries.

Question #8:
Your team is querying an external table in Snowflake that references data stored in AWS S3. The queries are working well, but you notice that they are sometimes slow when the underlying data files are large. What is **one potential strategy** to improve the query performance when querying large external tables?
A. **Change the virtual warehouse size** to a larger one for more compute resources.
B. **Repartition the data** into smaller files and adjust the external table configuration.
C. **Create an internal table** to copy the data into Snowflake and then query it for better performance.
D. **Use result caching** for the external table queries to speed up performance.

Question #9:
You are analyzing sales data stored in an external table in Snowflake. The data is stored as Parquet files in AWS S3 and is partitioned by year and month. You run a query that only filters the data by the year but are noticing that the query performance is suboptimal.
Which **optimization** could help improve the performance for this type of query?
A. **Increase the size of the virtual warehouse** used for querying the external table.
B. **Use partition pruning** by specifying the partitioned columns (year, month) in the query.
C. **Convert the external table to an internal table** for improved query performance.
D. **Reorganize the S3 bucket** to store the data in a non-partitioned structure.

Question #10:
You are working with an external table in Snowflake that references large CSV files stored in AWS S3. The data is queried frequently, but you notice that the queries take longer as the dataset grows. Which of the following actions **most likely** explains why the query performance is degrading as the dataset increases?
A. External tables automatically scale with the size of the data, so there is no performance degradation.
B. CSV files in S3 are row-based, and as the dataset grows, the query engine has to scan more rows, which can slow down performance.
C. External tables in Snowflake do not support compression, which leads to performance issues with large datasets.
D. Snowflake's query engine can cache the data from external tables automatically, eliminating performance degradation.

Answers and Explanations

Question #6:
Correct Answer: D
Explanation:
D is correct. Converting the data from **CSV** to **Parquet** significantly improves performance when querying external tables because **Parquet** is a columnar storage format, which is more efficient for querying large datasets.
A is incorrect because **Clustering Keys** are not supported on external tables.
B is incorrect because **Materialized Views** cannot be created on external tables.
C is incorrect because **Automatic Query Caching** is more effective for internal tables and data stored in Snowflake's managed storage.

Question #7:
Correct Answer: B
Explanation:
B is correct. **Partitioning** the data in the external table (especially by frequently queried columns) helps Snowflake efficiently prune partitions during query execution, reducing the amount of data scanned.
A is incorrect because **JSON** format is less efficient for querying large datasets compared to **Parquet** or **ORC**.
C is incorrect because copying the data into an internal stage or table would incur additional costs and reduce the benefits of using external tables.
D is incorrect because scaling the virtual warehouse doesn't optimize the underlying data structure or reduce data scanning.

Question #8:
Correct Answer: B
Explanation:
B is correct. **Repartitioning** the external table data into smaller files (e.g., splitting large files into smaller, manageable parts) and adjusting the external table configuration for optimal performance can significantly improve query execution time.
A is incorrect because simply changing the warehouse size might not address the core issue, which is related to data structure optimization.
C is incorrect because **internal tables** require loading data into Snowflake, which negates the benefits of external tables.
D is incorrect because **result caching** is not applicable to external tables; results of external table queries aren't cached.

Question #9:
Correct Answer: B
Explanation:
B is correct. **Partition pruning** ensures that only the relevant partitions are scanned when querying an external table. In this case, querying by **year** would benefit from partition pruning, making the query more efficient.
A is incorrect because **increasing the warehouse size** will not improve query performance unless the data is partitioned correctly.

C is incorrect because converting the external table to an **internal table** would not improve performance and would result in additional costs.
D is incorrect because **partitioned data** is typically more efficient to query, and reorganizing the S3 bucket to remove partitions is counterproductive.

Question #10:
Correct Answer: B
Explanation:
B is correct. **CSV files** are **row-based**, meaning the query engine must scan all rows, leading to slower performance as the dataset grows. Columnar formats like **Parquet** are better for performance because they allow for more efficient data reading and querying.
A is incorrect because external tables do not automatically scale to handle large datasets without optimizations like partitioning.
C is incorrect because **compression** is supported in external tables, but CSV files are still less efficient than columnar formats for large datasets.
D is incorrect because Snowflake does not automatically cache external table data, which is why query performance can degrade with large datasets.

Question #11:
You are working with an external table in Snowflake that references data stored in AWS S3. The data format is **CSV**, and you have created a schema for the table. However, you later realize that you need to change the column data type for a field in the schema. Which of the following actions do you need to take?
A. Reload the external data into Snowflake after modifying the schema.
B. Modify the external table schema directly without needing to reload the data.
C. Drop and recreate the external table with the new schema, and reload the data.
D. Change the S3 data to match the new schema and then query it again.

Question #12:
Your team is using Snowflake external tables for querying data stored in AWS S3. The external table schema was initially set to reference a VARCHAR field, but you now need to change the field type to STRING. Since Snowflake uses a schema-on-read approach, which of the following statements is true regarding this change?
A. You must reload the external data into Snowflake after changing the field type.
B. You can modify the table schema in Snowflake without reloading the data.
C. You must drop the external table and recreate it with the new schema, then reload the data.
D. You cannot change the field type for an external table after it has been defined.

Question #13:
You are working with an external table in Snowflake that references Parquet files stored in Azure Blob Storage. The data format is columnar, and you need to modify the schema. Since Snowflake uses a schema-on-read approach, which of the following
scenarios **requires** reloading the data?
A. Modifying the schema to add a new column.
B. Changing the data type of an existing column.
C. Modifying the column order in the schema.

227

D. All of the above.

Question #14:
You are querying an external table in Snowflake that is connected to data stored in AWS S3 in **Parquet** format. The data is not changing, but you need to add a new column to the external table schema. Which of the following is the best course of action, given the schema-on-read feature of Snowflake external tables?
A. Reload the data into Snowflake and update the schema.
B. Modify the external table schema to add the new column without reloading the data.
C. Drop the external table and reload all the data with the new schema.
D. The new column must be added in the Parquet files themselves before modifying the schema.

Question #15:
You have an external table in Snowflake that is reading data stored in AWS S3 as Parquet files. The schema has been applied to the data, but your team now needs to query a subset of the data with a slightly different structure (additional columns and changes). Which of the following is true about this scenario, given the schema-on-read approach?
A. You need to reload the data with the new schema structure.
B. You can modify the query to ignore the new columns in the external table without reloading the data.
C. You must drop the external table and recreate it with the new schema and reload the data.
D. The new schema must be applied to the Parquet files directly before it can be read in Snowflake.

Answers and Explanations

Question #11:
Correct Answer: B
Explanation:
B is correct. With Snowflake's **schema-on-read** approach, you can modify the schema directly within Snowflake without needing to reload the data. The schema is applied when the data is queried, so the underlying data in S3 doesn't need to be reloaded.
A is incorrect because you don't need to reload the data to modify the schema in Snowflake.
C is incorrect because the schema can be adjusted without needing to drop and recreate the table.
D is incorrect because the schema change only applies to how Snowflake reads the data, not to how it is stored in S3.

Question #12:
Correct Answer: B
Explanation:
B is correct. Since Snowflake uses a **schema-on-read** approach, you can modify the schema (such as changing the data type from VARCHAR to STRING) directly in Snowflake without having to reload the external data.
A is incorrect because reloading the data is not required for schema changes.
C is incorrect because you don't need to drop the external table to modify the schema.
D is incorrect because Snowflake allows schema changes on external tables without needing to reload data.

Question #13:
Correct Answer: B
Explanation:
B is correct. In Snowflake, you don't need to reload the external data when adding a new column to the external table schema. However, **changing the data type of an existing column** or modifying the column order may require reloading the data to reflect these changes.
A is incorrect because adding a new column does not require reloading the data.
C is incorrect because column order changes do not require reloading.
D is incorrect because Snowflake's schema-on-read capability allows schema changes without reloading the data, except in cases of more complex structural changes like data type modifications.

Question #14:
Correct Answer: B
Explanation:
B is correct. In Snowflake, when you add a new column to the external table schema, you can modify the schema directly in Snowflake without needing to reload the data. The schema is applied when you query the data.
A is incorrect because reloading the data is not necessary when you just modify the schema to add new columns.
C is incorrect because dropping the external table and reloading the data is unnecessary for adding a new column to the schema.
D is incorrect because Snowflake does not require changes to the Parquet files themselves when modifying the schema to add a column.

Question #15:
Correct Answer: B
Explanation:
B is correct. Since Snowflake uses a **schema-on-read** approach, you can modify your query to ignore the new columns in the external table, and you do not need to reload the data with the new schema.
A is incorrect because reloading the data is not needed for querying with a modified schema.
C is incorrect because there is no need to drop and recreate the table or reload the data.
D is incorrect because changes to the schema don't require modifying the source Parquet files themselves.

Question #16:
You have an external table in Snowflake that reads data stored in AWS S3 as **CSV** files. The data is in a format that is slightly different from your target schema. Given that Snowflake supports multiple file formats, which of the following file formats would **NOT** require any significant transformations in Snowflake if you wanted to switch the external table from CSV to **Parquet**?
A. CSV to Parquet is a straightforward transformation in Snowflake.

B. You will need to transform the data to match Parquet's columnar format before reading it in Snowflake.
C. Parquet files are already optimized for Snowflake queries, so no transformation is needed.
D. You must convert the Parquet files back to CSV before using them.

Question #17:
You are tasked with creating an external table in Snowflake to query data from a **JSON** file stored in AWS S3. The JSON structure contains nested data that you need to query. Which of the following statements is true about querying nested JSON data in Snowflake?
A. Snowflake automatically flattens the nested JSON data for querying.
B. You need to manually flatten the nested JSON data before querying.
C. Snowflake cannot query nested JSON data; it requires transformation into a flat structure.
D. You must use a special schema for JSON data before querying.

Question #18:
You are integrating external data into Snowflake stored in **Avro** format in AWS S3. The data includes multiple records with the same schema but may contain different field names. What should you expect when querying the Avro data in Snowflake?
A. Snowflake will automatically map and reconcile different field names between records.
B. You must manually reconcile the field names before querying the Avro data.
C. Snowflake will reject the data if the field names differ between records.
D. You need to reload the data to standardize the field names across records before querying.

Question #19:
You need to create an external table in Snowflake that reads data from an **ORC** file stored in AWS S3. Which of the following is an advantage of using **ORC** format over **CSV** for external tables in Snowflake?
A. ORC is a columnar storage format, which optimizes query performance and reduces storage costs compared to CSV.
B. CSV is optimized for large-scale querying and offers better performance than ORC.
C. ORC files cannot be used in Snowflake external tables.
D. CSV files require fewer resources to query compared to ORC files in Snowflake.

Question #20:
You are integrating multiple external data sources into Snowflake using different file formats (CSV, Parquet, Avro). Snowflake allows you to work with these file formats with minimal transformation. Which of the following is the most important consideration when working with these diverse formats in Snowflake external tables?
A. Ensuring that all file formats are converted into a uniform format before loading into Snowflake.
B. Ensuring that all the data formats have the same compression settings for optimal performance.
C. Ensuring the external table is configured with the correct **FILE_FORMAT** for each data source.
D. Ensuring the file formats are manually flattened before querying.

Answers and Explanations

Question #16:
Correct Answer: C
Explanation:
C is correct. **Parquet** is a columnar format, and Snowflake can query it natively without any significant transformation needed. This is one of the benefits of using Parquet, as it is highly optimized for analytical queries.
A is incorrect because the transition from CSV to Parquet does not involve straightforward transformations in Snowflake.
B is incorrect because Snowflake supports Parquet natively without the need for transformations before querying.
D is incorrect because **CSV** files do not need to be converted to **Parquet** before use in Snowflake.

Question #17:
Correct Answer: A
Explanation:
A is correct. Snowflake can automatically flatten nested **JSON** data when querying, using its **variant** data type and **flatten** function, allowing you to work with complex JSON structures seamlessly.
B is incorrect because Snowflake automatically flattens nested JSON, so you don't need to manually flatten it before querying.
C is incorrect because Snowflake supports querying nested JSON data without requiring transformation.
D is incorrect because Snowflake does not require a special schema for JSON data beyond defining the appropriate **FILE_FORMAT**.

Question #18:
Correct Answer: A
Explanation:
A is correct. Snowflake can automatically map and reconcile fields across different records in **Avro** files, allowing for flexible handling of different field names.
B is incorrect because Snowflake handles differing field names in Avro files automatically.
C is incorrect because Snowflake will not reject the data based on differing field names between records; it handles it internally.
D is incorrect because Snowflake can handle varying field names without needing to reload or standardize the data.

Question #19:
Correct Answer: A
Explanation:
A is correct. **ORC** is a columnar format that is optimized for analytical queries, providing faster query performance and reducing storage costs compared to row-based formats like CSV.
B is incorrect because **CSV** is a row-based format and does not offer the same level of optimization as **ORC** for querying.
C is incorrect because **ORC** files can be used in Snowflake external tables.
D is incorrect because **ORC** provides better performance than **CSV** in Snowflake due to its columnar structure.

Question #20:
Correct Answer: C
Explanation:
C is correct. The most important consideration when working with multiple file formats is ensuring that the **FILE_FORMAT** is correctly configured for each data source. Snowflake needs to know the format (e.g., CSV, Parquet, Avro, etc.) to properly read and interpret the data.
A is incorrect because Snowflake allows you to use multiple formats without requiring conversion to a uniform format.
B is incorrect because Snowflake handles compression settings automatically for different file formats.
D is incorrect because Snowflake handles nested data structures in formats like **JSON** and **Avro** without requiring them to be flattened before querying.

Question #21:
You are working with Snowflake external tables that are reading data from files stored in Amazon S3. The data is stored in JSON format and includes nested structures. Which of the following statements about querying this data in Snowflake is true? (Select two)
Options:
A. Snowflake automatically flattens nested JSON data for querying.
B. You need to transform the JSON data into a flat structure before querying.
C. Snowflake can query JSON data directly from Amazon S3 without loading it into Snowflake storage.
D. You must manually map the fields in the JSON structure before querying.
E. Querying JSON data in external tables is slower than querying internal Snowflake tables.

Question #22:
You have configured an external table in Snowflake to query Parquet data stored in Google Cloud Storage. Which of the following benefits does using Parquet format with external tables provide in Snowflake? (Select two)
Options:
A. Parquet is a columnar storage format, so it improves query performance by only reading relevant columns.
B. Parquet files are stored in Snowflake's internal storage for faster querying.
C. Parquet files allow Snowflake to scan data directly from Google Cloud Storage without the need for loading into Snowflake storage.
D. Parquet is slower for query performance in Snowflake than row-based formats like CSV.
E. Parquet is a row-based format and is ideal for large-scale analytical queries in Snowflake.

Question #23:
Your organization is using Snowflake external tables to read CSV files stored in Microsoft Azure Blob Storage. The data is large and frequently updated. Which of the following statements about using CSV files with external tables is correct? (Select two)
Options:
A. Snowflake can query CSV files directly from Microsoft Azure Blob Storage without loading them into Snowflake storage.
B. External tables with CSV files require all data to be loaded into Snowflake before querying.

C. Using CSV files in external tables can save Snowflake storage costs because data is not stored in internal Snowflake storage.
D. Querying CSV files from external tables is faster than querying Parquet files.
E. CSV files in external tables may require manual data transformation for performance optimization due to their row-based nature.

Question #24:
You are setting up external tables in Snowflake to query data stored in Amazon S3 in both Parquet and ORC formats. Which of the following benefits are associated with using ORC and Parquet formats for external tables? (Select two)
Options:
A. Both ORC and Parquet are columnar storage formats, optimizing Snowflake's query performance.
B. ORC and Parquet require Snowflake to load the data into internal storage before querying.
C. Both formats support efficient compression and faster queries by only reading relevant columns.
D. ORC and Parquet provide slower query performance than row-based formats like CSV for large datasets.
E. Using ORC and Parquet formats in external tables helps reduce the need for data transformation.

Question #25:
You have external tables set up in Snowflake that read JSON and CSV data from Microsoft Azure Blob Storage. Which of the following are advantages of using external tables with JSON and CSV file formats in Snowflake? (Select two)
Options:
A. External tables with CSV and JSON allow Snowflake to query data without needing to load it into Snowflake's internal storage.
B. Snowflake external tables automatically transform CSV and JSON data into a structured format when querying.
C. CSV files in external tables provide better performance than JSON files for querying in Snowflake.
D. JSON files are optimized for analytical queries, whereas CSV files are better suited for operational workloads.
E. Using external tables for CSV and JSON data allows you to scale without incurring additional storage costs in Snowflake.

Answers with Explanations

Question #21:
Correct Answers: C, E
Explanation:
C is correct because Snowflake external tables can directly query data from Amazon S3 without loading it into Snowflake's storage, as they use pointers to the data.
E is correct because external tables typically perform slower than internal tables due to the additional network and storage access overhead.
A is incorrect because Snowflake does not automatically flatten JSON data; users must use functions like FLATTEN for this purpose.
B is incorrect because no prior transformation is required; Snowflake can query the nested structure directly.

D is incorrect because field mapping is unnecessary when querying JSON data directly.

Question #22:
Correct Answers: A, C
Explanation:
A is correct because Parquet's columnar format enables Snowflake to scan only relevant columns, improving query performance.
C is correct because Parquet files can be queried directly from Google Cloud Storage without loading them into Snowflake.
B is incorrect because external tables do not load data into Snowflake's internal storage.
D is incorrect because Parquet is optimized for query performance, unlike row-based formats.
E is incorrect because Parquet is a columnar format, not a row-based format.

Question #23:
Correct Answers: A, C
Explanation:
A is correct because Snowflake external tables can directly query CSV files from Azure Blob Storage without importing them into Snowflake storage.
C is correct because external tables reduce storage costs since the data remains outside Snowflake's internal storage.
B is incorrect because external tables do not require data to be loaded into Snowflake for querying.
D is incorrect because Parquet, a columnar format, generally outperforms CSV in terms of query speed.
E is correct because CSV, as a row-based format, may require additional optimization for better query performance.

Question #24:
Correct Answers: A, C
Explanation:
A is correct because both ORC and Parquet are columnar formats that optimize Snowflake's query performance.
C is correct because both formats support efficient compression and selective column reads, enhancing query efficiency.
B is incorrect because Snowflake does not load data from ORC/Parquet formats into internal storage for querying.
D is incorrect because columnar formats like ORC/Parquet generally provide faster performance than row-based formats.
E is incorrect because Snowflake does not rely on these formats to reduce data transformation needs.

Question #25:
Correct Answers: A, E
Explanation:
A is correct because Snowflake external tables can query JSON and CSV data directly from external storage without loading into Snowflake's internal storage.
E is correct because external tables help scale without additional storage costs since the data resides in external storage.

234

B is incorrect because Snowflake does not automatically transform data into a structured format; the user must define the structure.
C is incorrect because CSV files typically perform slower than JSON files for querying in analytical workloads.
D is incorrect because Snowflake does not differentiate operational vs. analytical workloads by format type.

DATA MARKETPLACE

Question #1:
You are exploring Snowflake Data Marketplace to access a dataset from a healthcare provider. The data is stored in a Parquet format and will be accessed through an external table. Which of the following is a key benefit of using Snowflake Data Marketplace for this healthcare dataset?
A. You need to manually format the data before using it.
B. You can seamlessly access the data from multiple external providers without worrying about infrastructure setup.
C. You can only access the data within the Snowflake ecosystem and not use it for external analytics tools.
D. You have to store the data internally in Snowflake to access it for queries.

Question #2:
You are working with a marketing dataset from a provider in the Snowflake Data Marketplace that is in CSV format. You want to query the data using external tables. What is a major advantage of using external tables with this data?
A. The data is stored and processed directly in the Snowflake environment, increasing performance.
B. You can query the data directly without loading it into Snowflake storage, reducing storage costs.
C. The external data can only be used for one-time analytics and cannot be updated.
D. The data can only be accessed from the Snowflake Data Marketplace and not externally.

Question #3:
You are exploring a finance dataset from Snowflake Data Marketplace and wish to integrate it with your Snowflake account for analysis. Which feature does Snowflake offer to enable this integration for efficient querying?
A. You must download the data and upload it to your local storage before querying.
B. You can create an external table to query the data directly from the marketplace, avoiding data duplication.
C. The data can only be used once and cannot be reused in multiple queries.
D. Snowflake automatically loads the data into your internal storage before any queries are performed.

Question #4:
You are working with a healthcare dataset in the Snowflake Data Marketplace that is available in JSON format. The dataset is large, and you want to perform advanced analytics using

Snowflake's capabilities. Which of the following features of Snowflake's integration with external tables will help with this?

A. Snowflake will convert JSON data into a relational format automatically, making it ready for analysis.
B. The JSON data will be automatically optimized for fast querying when it is queried through external tables.
C. You can query the data directly from the marketplace without storing it in Snowflake, but you may need to flatten the JSON structure manually.
D. You must store the JSON data in Snowflake's internal storage for optimization before querying.

Question #5:
You are setting up an analytics project that requires access to data from multiple providers in the Snowflake Data Marketplace, including finance, healthcare, and marketing datasets. What is a major advantage of using external tables with data from different providers in the marketplace?

A. The data is automatically standardized across all datasets from different providers, making it easy to analyze.
B. You can combine and query data from multiple external sources in a single query without needing to replicate the data in Snowflake's internal storage.
C. You can only query one external dataset at a time from Snowflake Data Marketplace.
D. External tables only support structured data formats like CSV and Parquet, making integration with non-structured data difficult.

Answers and Explanations

Question #1:
Correct Answer: B
Explanation:
B: Correct. Snowflake Data Marketplace provides seamless access to data from various external providers, meaning users do not need to worry about infrastructure setup. The marketplace streamlines the process of finding, sharing, and accessing diverse datasets.
A: Incorrect. Snowflake Data Marketplace allows you to access data in the format provided (e.g., Parquet) without requiring manual formatting.
C: Incorrect. You can access the data both within Snowflake and integrate it with external analytics tools, offering flexibility.
D: Incorrect. The data can be accessed via external tables without needing to store it internally, reducing storage costs.

Question #2:
Correct Answer: B
Explanation:
B: Correct. Using external tables allows Snowflake to query external data directly without loading it into internal storage, which reduces storage costs.
A: Incorrect. The data remains external and is not processed directly in the Snowflake environment unless explicitly loaded.
C: Incorrect. External data can be updated and queried multiple times as long as it is accessible from the Snowflake Data Marketplace.

D: Incorrect. Data accessed from Snowflake Data Marketplace can be queried within Snowflake and can also be integrated with external systems.

Question #3:
Correct Answer: B
Explanation:
B: Correct. External tables allow Snowflake to access and query external data directly without duplicating it in Snowflake's internal storage.
A: Incorrect. Snowflake allows querying data directly from the marketplace using external tables without needing to download or upload the data manually.
C: Incorrect. The data is accessible as long as it remains in the marketplace, and it can be reused in multiple queries without restriction.
D: Incorrect. Data in Snowflake Data Marketplace can be queried via external tables, and it is not automatically loaded into internal storage unless explicitly done by the user.

Question #4:
Correct Answer: C
Explanation:
C: Correct. You can query JSON data directly from the marketplace using external tables, but you might need to flatten the JSON structure manually for easier analysis.
A: Incorrect. Snowflake does not automatically convert JSON into a relational format, but it does provide the ability to flatten JSON data using the FLATTEN() function if needed.
B: Incorrect. While Snowflake can query JSON data directly, it does not automatically optimize the data for querying.
D: Incorrect. Data in Snowflake Data Marketplace can be queried via external tables without needing to store it internally in Snowflake.

Question #5:
Correct Answer: B
Explanation:
B: Correct. You can query data from multiple providers in the marketplace using external tables without needing to replicate the data into Snowflake's internal storage, which allows efficient data integration.
A: Incorrect. While Snowflake can work with various data formats, the data may not be automatically standardized. You may need to perform transformations to align the datasets for analysis.
C: Incorrect. Snowflake allows querying multiple external datasets simultaneously in a single query if they are referenced through external tables.
D: Incorrect. External tables in Snowflake support various structured and semi-structured data formats, including CSV, Parquet, JSON, ORC, and Avro.

Question #6:
You are working on a project where you need to query data from Snowflake Data Marketplace. The data is in JSON format, and you want to access it directly in Snowflake without storing it internally. Which of the following best describes the benefit of Snowflake's native integration with external data?
A. Snowflake requires you to load the JSON data into internal storage before querying it.

B. You can query the external JSON data directly without the need to load it into internal storage, reducing duplication and management overhead.
C. External data must be processed by an external ETL tool before it can be used in Snowflake.
D. You can only query JSON data by converting it into a structured format first.

Question #7:
You are working on a healthcare analytics project and want to access external data for analysis from the Snowflake Data Marketplace. How does Snowflake's native integration benefit your workflow?
A. By requiring external data to be copied into Snowflake's internal storage before it can be queried.
B. By allowing you to access the external data directly via external tables, streamlining data workflows and eliminating data silos.
C. By forcing you to set up an external ETL pipeline to manage the data.
D. By limiting the types of external data that can be queried.

Question #8:
You are integrating data from multiple external providers in the Snowflake Data Marketplace for your organization. Which of the following advantages does Snowflake's native integration provide for querying external tables?
A. You can query the external data directly from within Snowflake, combining data from multiple sources without needing to move the data into Snowflake's internal storage.
B. You need to manually load the external data into Snowflake storage before querying.
C. External data must be processed by a third-party tool before it can be accessed in Snowflake.
D. You can only query data from one external provider at a time.

Question #9:
You are working on a business intelligence project where you need to analyze marketing data from the Snowflake Data Marketplace. How does Snowflake's native integration with external tables help streamline this project?
A. By requiring all data to be loaded into Snowflake's internal storage before it can be queried.
B. By enabling you to query and analyze the data directly from external storage, reducing the need for replication and duplication.
C. By requiring an external data warehouse to process the data before importing it into Snowflake.
D. By restricting the ability to query external data unless it's converted into a different format.

Question #10:
You are working on an analytics pipeline that uses external data from Snowflake Data Marketplace. How does Snowflake's native integration improve your data management and workflow?
A. It eliminates the need to replicate the external data into Snowflake's internal storage, reducing redundancy and management overhead.
B. It requires that all external data be replicated into Snowflake's internal storage before any processing can occur.
C. External data cannot be queried directly and must be pre-processed externally.
D. Snowflake restricts access to external data, only allowing users to view it without querying.

Answers and Explanations

Question #6:
Correct Answer: B
Explanation:
A: Incorrect. Snowflake allows querying external data directly without needing to load it into internal storage.
B: Correct. Snowflake's native integration allows you to query the external JSON data directly, avoiding the need to duplicate or load it into internal storage.
C: Incorrect. External data can be accessed directly via external tables without the need for external ETL processing.
D: Incorrect. Snowflake can query JSON data directly, so there's no need to convert it into a structured format first.

Question #7:
Correct Answer: B
Explanation:
A: Incorrect. With Snowflake's native integration, external data can be queried directly without needing to be loaded into internal storage.
B: Correct. Snowflake's native integration allows external data to be queried directly via external tables, reducing the need for data movement and simplifying workflows.
C: Incorrect. External data can be queried directly from Snowflake, so there is no need for an external ETL pipeline.
D: Incorrect. Snowflake supports querying various types of external data, including JSON, CSV, Parquet, etc.

Question #8:
Correct Answer: A
Explanation:
A: Correct. Snowflake's native integration allows you to query data from multiple external providers directly, without needing to move the data into Snowflake's internal storage.
B: Incorrect. Data in external tables can be queried directly, without the need for manual loading into internal storage.
C: Incorrect. Snowflake enables direct querying of external data without needing a third-party tool for processing.
D: Incorrect. Snowflake allows querying data from multiple external providers simultaneously.

Question #9:
Correct Answer: B
Explanation:
A: Incorrect. Snowflake allows querying external data directly via external tables, eliminating the need for it to be loaded into internal storage.
B: Correct. Snowflake's native integration enables you to query external data directly, streamlining analysis and reducing the need for data replication.
C: Incorrect. Data can be queried directly within Snowflake without needing a separate data warehouse for processing.

D: Incorrect. Snowflake supports querying external data without requiring conversion into another format.

Question #10:
Correct Answer: A
Explanation:
A: Correct. Snowflake's native integration allows querying external data directly, avoiding unnecessary replication and reducing data management overhead.
B: Incorrect. Snowflake enables querying external data directly, without the need to replicate it into internal storage.
C: Incorrect. Snowflake supports direct querying of external data, eliminating the need for external preprocessing.
D: Incorrect. Snowflake enables querying and processing of external data, not just viewing

---

Question #11:
You have a project that requires access to healthcare data provided through the Snowflake Data Marketplace. What is the key advantage of secure data sharing when accessing this data?
A. It ensures that data is copied into your Snowflake environment, allowing for better processing and security.
B. It allows you to access the data in real-time without needing to replicate or move it into your system, maintaining privacy and compliance.
C. It forces you to manually validate the data every time you access it.
D. It requires your organization to transfer the data to a third-party storage provider for access.

Question #12:
Your organization needs to collaborate with an external partner to analyze financial data via the Snowflake Data Marketplace. How does secure data sharing simplify this collaboration?
A. The external partner has to replicate the data into their own Snowflake environment before they can use it.
B. Both organizations can access and query the shared data directly in real-time without duplicating or storing it.
C. Data access is restricted to specific geographic regions, limiting sharing across borders.
D. Only the data provider can modify the shared data; consumers can only view it without querying.

Question #13:
Your team needs to analyze marketing data from a third-party provider via the Snowflake Data Marketplace. What is the primary benefit of secure data sharing in this scenario?
A. It allows your team to load the data into a third-party storage location, making it easier to analyze.
B. It ensures the marketing data can be accessed in real-time without the need for replication, reducing storage costs and maintaining data privacy.
C. It automatically loads all shared data into your Snowflake environment every time a change occurs.
D. It forces you to manually download and process the data before querying it.

Question #14:
In your healthcare organization, you need to access patient data shared by a provider via the Snowflake Data Marketplace. Which of the following is a key feature of secure data sharing that helps maintain data privacy and compliance with regulations like HIPAA?

A. The data is always duplicated into your internal storage, where it can be processed according to your security policies.

B. The data is shared with you directly, and you can access it in real-time while ensuring it remains under the provider's control.

C. The data provider has to manually approve every query that your organization makes to access the data.

D. Your organization is allowed to modify the shared data to suit your needs.

Question #15:
You are part of a legal team that needs to access legal document data shared by a partner through the Snowflake Data Marketplace. Which of the following is true about Snowflake's secure data sharing?

A. The legal data is copied into your internal Snowflake storage every time a new document is added.

B. You can access the data directly in real-time from the partner's Snowflake environment without replicating it, ensuring data privacy.

C. You need to transfer the data to an external system before querying it.

D. You cannot access the data if your organization's geographic region does not match the partner's region.

Answers and Explanations

Question #11:
Correct Answer: B.
Explanation:
A: Incorrect. Snowflake's secure data sharing eliminates the need to copy data into your system, allowing direct access without replication.
B: Correct. Snowflake's secure data sharing ensures real-time access to data without duplication, helping to maintain privacy and compliance, such as with healthcare regulations.
C: Incorrect. There is no manual validation required when accessing shared data within Snowflake's ecosystem.
D: Incorrect. Snowflake's secure data sharing works directly between Snowflake environments without needing third-party storage providers.

Question #12:
Correct Answer: B.
Explanation:
A: Incorrect. Snowflake's secure data sharing eliminates the need for replication; both parties can access the data without duplicating it.
B: Correct. Secure data sharing allows direct real-time access to shared data from multiple organizations, promoting efficient collaboration without data duplication.

C: Incorrect. Snowflake does not limit data access based on geographic regions but on permissions and roles.
D: Incorrect. Secure data sharing enables both data providers and consumers to query the data, not just view it.

Question #13:
Correct Answer: B.
Explanation:
A: Incorrect. Snowflake's secure data sharing allows you to query shared data directly in your Snowflake environment without needing to load it into third-party storage.
B: Correct. Secure data sharing allows real-time access to shared marketing data without replication, reducing storage costs and maintaining privacy.
C: Incorrect. Snowflake does not require automatic loading; instead, you can query the data directly.
D: Incorrect. There is no manual download process required when using Snowflake's secure data sharing.

Question #14:
Correct Answer: B.
Explanation:
A: Incorrect. Snowflake's secure data sharing avoids data duplication, allowing you to access it directly without needing to replicate it internally.
B: Correct. Secure data sharing ensures that the data remains under the provider's control, and your organization can query it in real-time without duplication, which helps maintain privacy and compliance.
C: Incorrect. There is no manual approval required for every query; permissions are granted to allow access to data.
D: Incorrect. Secure data sharing does not allow you to modify the shared data; it only enables querying.

Question #15:
Correct Answer: B.
Explanation:
A: Incorrect. Snowflake's secure data sharing allows you to access shared data directly without copying it to your internal storage.
B: Correct. Secure data sharing allows you to access the shared data in real-time without duplication, ensuring privacy and maintaining data security.
C: Incorrect. There is no need to transfer the data to an external system before querying it; direct access within Snowflake is possible.
D: Incorrect. Snowflake does not restrict access based on geographic regions but on permissions and access controls.

Answers and Explanations

Question #16:
Your organization is using the **Snowflake Data Marketplace** to access data in both structured (tables) and semi-structured (JSON) formats for analysis. Which of the following is an advantage of this integration?

A. It allows seamless querying of both structured and semi-structured data within a single SQL query.
B. It requires separate storage for structured and semi-structured data, increasing complexity.
C. Semi-structured data cannot be analyzed within Snowflake and needs to be pre-processed externally.
D. Snowflake cannot integrate structured and semi-structured data within the same data pipeline.

Question #17:
Your team is analyzing financial data from a provider on the **Snowflake Data Marketplace**. The data consists of structured (tables) and semi-structured (Parquet) formats. How does **Snowflake's marketplace** simplify analysis for both types of data?
A. You must transform all data into a standard structured format before analyzing it.
B. Snowflake supports both formats natively, allowing you to query and analyze them together with no transformation.
C. Snowflake requires separate processing pipelines for structured and semi-structured data.
D. The marketplace only supports structured data, so semi-structured data needs to be loaded separately.

Question #18:
You have a project that requires analyzing a dataset consisting of structured and semi-structured data, available through the **Snowflake Data Marketplace**. What is the main advantage of Snowflake's approach to handling these two data types?
A. Snowflake requires you to process both structured and semi-structured data in separate storage locations, complicating data workflows.
B. Snowflake supports native querying of both data types within the same environment, simplifying analysis without complex transformations.
C. Semi-structured data must be converted into structured data before it can be queried in Snowflake.
D. Snowflake only supports structured data natively; semi-structured data must be analyzed externally.

Question #19:
A Snowflake customer is accessing external data from the **Snowflake Data Marketplace** that includes both structured (tables) and semi-structured (JSON, Parquet) data. What feature of Snowflake enables seamless integration and analysis of both data types?
A. The ability to load structured and semi-structured data into separate databases within Snowflake.
B. Snowflake automatically converts semi-structured data into structured data before it can be queried.
C. Snowflake's native support for both structured and semi-structured data within the same data warehouse.
D. Semi-structured data must be pre-processed into a compatible format before it can be loaded into Snowflake.

Question #20:

You want to use **Snowflake Data Marketplace** to analyze a large dataset that includes both structured data (tables) and semi-structured data (JSON). How does **Snowflake** enable the consumption of both types of data?

A. Both structured and semi-structured data must be pre-processed externally before analysis in Snowflake.
B. Snowflake requires separate warehouses for structured and semi-structured data analysis.
C. Snowflake provides native capabilities to query and analyze both structured and semi-structured data without needing complex transformations.
D. Semi-structured data cannot be analyzed using Snowflake's query engine.

Answers and Explanations

Question #16:
Correct Answer: A
Explanation:
A is correct because Snowflake allows seamless querying of both structured and semi-structured data within a single query, simplifying the analysis process.
B is incorrect because Snowflake does not require separate storage for structured and semi-structured data.
C is incorrect because Snowflake allows querying of semi-structured data directly without requiring external pre-processing.
D is incorrect because Snowflake fully supports both structured and semi-structured data, allowing integration in the same data pipeline.

Question #17:
Correct Answer: B
Explanation:
B is correct because Snowflake supports both structured and semi-structured data natively, enabling you to query and analyze them together without any transformation.
A is incorrect because Snowflake does not require transformation before querying semi-structured data.
C is incorrect because Snowflake can handle both types of data in the same pipeline.
D is incorrect because Snowflake supports both structured and semi-structured data in its marketplace without the need for separate loading.

Question #18:
Correct Answer: B
Explanation:
B is correct because Snowflake provides native support for both structured and semi-structured data, making analysis simple and efficient without the need for transformation.
A is incorrect because Snowflake allows analysis of both types of data within the same environment, reducing complexity.
C is incorrect because Snowflake does not require semi-structured data to be converted into structured data for querying.

D is incorrect because Snowflake does support both data types natively.

Question #19:
Correct Answer: C
Explanation:
C is correct because Snowflake supports native integration of both structured and semi-structured data within the same data warehouse, simplifying workflows.
A is incorrect because Snowflake does not require separate databases for structured and semi-structured data.
B is incorrect because Snowflake does not automatically convert semi-structured data into structured data; it can be queried directly in its native format.
D is incorrect because Snowflake supports querying semi-structured data using its native query engine.

Question #20:
Correct Answer: C
Explanation:
C is correct because Snowflake allows you to query and analyze both structured and semi-structured data natively, without complex transformations or external processing.
A is incorrect because Snowflake does not require external pre-processing before analysis.
B is incorrect because there is no need for separate warehouses for analyzing structured and semi-structured data in Snowflake.
D is incorrect because Snowflake fully supports the analysis of semi-structured data using its query engine.

Question #21:
A data analyst is exploring the **Snowflake Data Marketplace** for datasets to enhance their analysis. They need access to high-quality healthcare data for their business intelligence project. What is the most suitable option available in the marketplace?
A. Commercial datasets that offer specialized, high-quality data with a price tag.
B. Free datasets that are publicly available but may not provide the specialized data needed.
C. All datasets are free of charge, regardless of their quality or source.
D. The marketplace only offers free datasets for healthcare data.

Question #22:
You are working on a project that requires accessing both commercial and free datasets from the **Snowflake Data Marketplace**. What is the main advantage of having access to both types of datasets?
A. It eliminates the need for data transformation, as commercial datasets are ready to use.
B. The marketplace enables you to access valuable commercial datasets while controlling costs by using free datasets for certain analyses.
C. Free datasets are only available for a limited time, making commercial datasets the preferred choice.

D. All commercial datasets are automatically included for free once you subscribe to the marketplace.

Question #23:
A business analyst is analyzing data from the **Snowflake Data Marketplace** for a marketing campaign. They are using both commercial and free datasets in their analysis. Which of the following best explains why a mix of these datasets is beneficial?
A. Commercial datasets offer a higher quality of data, while free datasets can help offset costs by providing complementary data for exploratory analysis.
B. Commercial datasets are less reliable, so free datasets are used to ensure the accuracy of analysis.
C. Free datasets cannot be integrated with commercial datasets, limiting their use in the same analysis.
D. Only free datasets are compatible with Snowflake's query engine, making them preferable for all use cases.

Question #24:
A company is looking to use the **Snowflake Data Marketplace** to access financial datasets for a detailed analysis of global market trends. They are considering both commercial and free datasets. What would be a potential consideration when deciding between the two?
A. Free datasets generally contain outdated or incomplete information, whereas commercial datasets provide up-to-date and accurate market data.
B. Free datasets are automatically more accurate than commercial datasets because they are publicly available.
C. Commercial datasets are always free of charge, and free datasets may incur costs depending on usage.
D. Commercial datasets only provide raw data, whereas free datasets come with pre-processed insights.

Question #25:
Your organization is considering using the **Snowflake Data Marketplace** to enhance customer insights through access to commercial and free datasets. What is a key advantage of using both types of datasets?
A. Commercial datasets are much slower to query, while free datasets offer faster performance.
B. Using free datasets alongside commercial datasets helps control costs while still providing valuable data for comprehensive analysis.
C. Free datasets are only available for small-scale projects, making them unsuitable for large data analysis needs.
D. Commercial datasets are stored externally and cannot be queried within Snowflake, while free datasets are fully integrated with Snowflake's query engine.

Answers and Explanations

Question #21:
Correct Answer: A
Explanation:
A is correct because commercial datasets are typically high-quality, specialized datasets with a price tag, which is what the analyst needs for the business intelligence project.
B is incorrect because free datasets may not provide the specialized, high-quality data required for the analysis.
C is incorrect because not all datasets are free; commercial datasets are available for a price.
D is incorrect because there are both free and commercial datasets available in the marketplace.

Question #22:
Correct Answer: B
Explanation:
B is correct because having access to both commercial and free datasets allows businesses to optimize their costs while still gaining access to valuable data.
A is incorrect because commercial datasets may not always be "ready to use" without some data transformation, depending on the use case.
C is incorrect because free datasets are available indefinitely and do not have a limited time frame.
D is incorrect because not all commercial datasets are free when subscribing to the marketplace.

Question #23:
Correct Answer: A
Explanation:
A is correct because a mix of commercial and free datasets allows businesses to obtain high-quality data from commercial sources while utilizing free datasets for exploratory or complementary analysis, helping manage costs.
B is incorrect because commercial datasets are typically reliable and are intended to provide high-quality data for specific industries or needs.
C is incorrect because commercial and free datasets can be integrated together in Snowflake.
D is incorrect because both commercial and free datasets are compatible with Snowflake's query engine.

Question #24:
Correct Answer: A
Explanation:
A is correct because free datasets may lack the freshness and specificity of commercial datasets, making commercial data more appropriate for up-to-date, accurate market trend analysis.
B is incorrect because free datasets are not automatically more accurate than commercial datasets; commercial datasets are often more curated and up-to-date.
C is incorrect because commercial datasets are not free of charge; they are typically paid for, while free datasets are available at no cost.
D is incorrect because both commercial and free datasets can be processed and queried in Snowflake without restrictions on the type of data.

Question #25:

Correct Answer: B
Explanation:
B is correct because using a combination of free and commercial datasets allows businesses to optimize costs while still accessing a broad range of valuable data for deeper insights.
A is incorrect because performance is not generally affected by whether the dataset is commercial or free; both are accessible within Snowflake's query engine.
C is incorrect because free datasets are not limited to small-scale projects and can be used for large analyses.
D is incorrect because both commercial and free datasets can be queried within Snowflake without any compatibility issues

CRUD TRANSACTIONS

Question #01:
A data pipeline in Snowflake is implemented using a task that processes new data from a table. The task is set up with a schedule but does not seem to execute. What could be the reason for this behavior?
Options:
A. The task has been created without specifying a SQL statement to execute.
B. The task requires a parent task to be completed before it can execute.
C. The task is not enabled.
D. The warehouse associated with the task is suspended.
E. The task's schedule conflicts with other active tasks.

Question #02:
You are using Snowflake's MERGE statement to update data in a target table based on a source table. After executing the statement, you notice that the target table was not updated as expected. Which of the following could be the cause?
Options:
A. The MERGE statement was executed without a valid WHEN MATCHED or WHEN NOT MATCHED clause.
B. The source and target tables are not partitioned by the same columns, leading to mismatched data.
C. The MERGE statement requires explicit COMMIT to apply changes.
D. The target table has a stale flag that was not properly cleared.
E. The MERGE statement can only perform updates and cannot insert new rows.

Question #03:
A Snowflake table is using **micro-partitioning** and **versioning** for data storage. If a user performs an update on the data, what happens to the old data?
Options:
A. The old data is immediately overwritten in the storage layer.
B. The old data is moved to a separate storage location and is no longer accessible.
C. The old data is marked as stale and remains accessible through Time Travel.
D. The old data is removed and cannot be recovered.
E. The old data is archived and requires a special request for access.

Question #04:

250

A Snowflake administrator needs to implement a **stale flagging** mechanism for identifying obsolete records in a table. Which of the following would be an effective way to manage this flagging in a data pipeline?

Options:

A. Use **zero-copy cloning** to create a new version of the table without stale data.
B. Set up a scheduled task that periodically updates the records' status with a "stale" flag based on a timestamp.
C. Use the **MERGE** statement to flag records as stale by comparing against an external source.
D. Implement a stored procedure that uses **Micro-partition pruning** to filter stale records automatically.
E. Create a view that excludes stale records and rely on users to query only the view.

Question #05:

A Snowflake database is using **transactional consistency** to support OLTP workloads. When working with transactional tables, which of the following concepts will help ensure that concurrent queries do not read inconsistent data during updates?

Options:

A. Use **ACID** properties to guarantee consistency during reads and writes.
B. Use **Merge** operations to lock tables during read and write processes.
C. Use **optimistic concurrency control (OCC)** to manage concurrent access to data.
D. Use **Time Travel** and **cloning** to create consistent snapshots of the data.
E. Use **Materialized Views** to improve the consistency of read data during ongoing transactions.

Answers and Explanations

Question #01:
Correct Answer: C, D
Explanation:
C is correct because tasks in Snowflake do not execute unless they are explicitly enabled.
D is correct because if the associated warehouse is suspended, the task cannot execute as it requires compute resources.
A is incorrect because a task cannot be created without a SQL statement; it would fail at creation.
B is incorrect because not all tasks require a parent task; this depends on how the task chain is configured.

Question #02:
Correct Answer: A, D
Explanation:
A is correct because the MERGE statement requires a WHEN MATCHED or WHEN NOT MATCHED clause to specify the action to be taken on matched or unmatched records.
D is correct because if a **stale flag** is not cleared during the update, the data might not be considered for the operation, leading to unexpected behavior.
B is incorrect because partitioning does not directly affect MERGE operations unless the tables are very large and optimization strategies are required.
C is incorrect because Snowflake automatically commits MERGE statements; no

explicit COMMIT is needed.
E is incorrect because the MERGE statement can perform inserts, updates, and deletes, depending on the clauses.

Question #03:
Correct Answer: C
Explanation:
C is correct because Snowflake uses **Time Travel** to maintain old data versions, and updates to data do not overwrite but create new versions. The old data remains accessible through Time Travel for a specified period.
A is incorrect because Snowflake does not overwrite data; it creates new versions in the underlying storage.
B is incorrect because old data is not moved but retained in the same storage location.
D is incorrect because the old data is not removed unless the **Time Travel** retention period has expired.
E is incorrect because data is not archived or hidden unless it's purged after the **Time Travel** period ends.

Question #04:
Correct Answer: B, C
Explanation:
B is correct because setting up a scheduled task to update records with a "stale" flag based on a timestamp is an effective way to manage stale data.
C is correct because the **MERGE** statement can be used to compare data against an external source and flag records as stale when a mismatch is detected.
A is incorrect because **zero-copy cloning** creates a new version of a table but does not address flagging stale records.
D is incorrect because **micro-partition pruning** helps optimize query performance but does not directly flag stale records.
E is incorrect because relying on a view to exclude stale records may cause performance overhead and lack clarity on stale data status.

Question #05:
Correct Answer: A, D
Explanation:
A is correct because Snowflake guarantees transactional consistency using **ACID** properties, ensuring data consistency during concurrent reads and writes.
D is correct because using **Time Travel** and **cloning** ensures consistent snapshots of the data, which is essential in maintaining consistency for OLTP workloads during updates.
B is incorrect because **Merge** operations do not lock tables by default; they rely on atomic operations.
C is incorrect because **optimistic concurrency control (OCC)** is not a concept used by Snowflake.
E is incorrect because **Materialized Views** are used to cache query results but do not guarantee consistency during transactions.

Question #6:
You are tasked with integrating Snowflake with Amazon S3 to store large datasets, and you have enabled S3 versioning. How will enabling versioning on the S3 bucket impact Snowflake's ability to access and manage data?
Options:
A. Enabling S3 versioning allows Snowflake to access only the latest version of the object in the bucket.
B. Snowflake will be able to access historical versions of objects stored in the S3 bucket without requiring additional configuration.
C. S3 versioning ensures that Snowflake can only load the most recent version of the file, preventing data duplication.
D. Versioned objects in S3 are handled like immutable data for Snowflake, ensuring that no changes are made to them once loaded.
E. With S3 versioning enabled, Snowflake will treat each version of the file as a unique object, potentially leading to multiple copies of the same data.

Question #7:
You have a large dataset stored in S3 with versioning enabled. You've noticed that some of your Snowflake queries are returning outdated data. What could be the reason?
Options:
A. Snowflake does not support querying older versions of objects in an S3 bucket, even if versioning is enabled.
B. Snowflake is pulling the most recent version of the data, but the metadata associated with older versions is cached.
C. Snowflake queries by default always return the most recent version of the object unless explicitly configured to pull a previous version.
D. If S3 versioning is enabled, Snowflake will automatically pull the first available version, not necessarily the latest one.
E. Versioned files in S3 are not reflected in Snowflake until explicitly synced, leading to delays in returning updated data.

Question #8:
You are configuring external tables in Snowflake to read data stored in an S3 bucket with versioning enabled. What do you need to consider when accessing the data?
Options:
A. Snowflake automatically queries the most recent version of the files in the S3 bucket when accessing external tables.
B. The external table configuration must specify a specific S3 version if you need to query data from older versions of the object.
C. Snowflake can only query the latest version of the S3 object, and older versions will be ignored.
D. If data needs to be queried from a specific version, you must manually manage S3 version IDs in the external table definition.
E. The external table in Snowflake does not support S3 versioning; it will always point to the latest available file in the S3 bucket.

Question #9:

You are setting up a data pipeline in Snowflake that uses S3 as an external stage with versioning enabled. You've noticed that occasionally outdated data is being processed in your pipeline. What could be a potential cause?

Options:

A. S3 versioning causes Snowflake to always load the latest file, which might not be the correct version of the dataset.

B. Snowflake uses a versioned stage to always query the most recent data, but it could be fetching outdated metadata.

C. The data pipeline may be set up to pull specific file versions, but versioning on S3 causes inconsistencies.

D. Outdated data can occur if Snowflake is not configured to use version IDs when pulling data from versioned S3 objects.

E. The data pipeline may be pulling from the wrong schema in Snowflake, not necessarily related to S3 versioning.

Question #10:

You have a scenario where your Snowflake data warehouse is set to automatically process data from versioned files in an S3 bucket. Which of the following configurations would allow Snowflake to work effectively with S3 versioning?

Options:

A. Snowflake must be configured to query specific file versions explicitly when external tables are defined.

B. You must configure Snowflake to automatically use the latest version of the file, without needing manual intervention.

C. The external stage in Snowflake should use the VERSION_ID to identify which file version to query when accessing data.

D. Snowflake will automatically manage versioning and ensure that only the latest data is loaded, even without any additional configurations.

E. You need to specify the versioning configuration in the S3 stage to ensure that Snowflake fetches data from the appropriate version.

Answers and Explanations

Question #6:
Correct Answer: B, E
Explanation:
B is correct because with S3 versioning enabled, Snowflake can access older versions of files stored in S3, and there are no additional configurations required for this access.
E is correct because enabling S3 versioning means Snowflake will treat different versions of the file as separate objects, potentially leading to multiple copies.
A is incorrect because Snowflake can access any version of the object, not just the latest.
C is incorrect because Snowflake can access previous versions of a file if configured to do so.
D is incorrect because versioned objects are not immutable by default in Snowflake and can be queried like any other data object.

Question #7:
Correct Answer: C, B

Explanation:
C is correct because by default, Snowflake queries the most recent version of the object stored in the S3 bucket.
B is correct because it is possible that older versions are being cached or metadata has not been refreshed, leading to outdated results.
A is incorrect because Snowflake can query older versions of files when versioning is enabled.
D is incorrect because Snowflake does not automatically pull older versions unless explicitly configured to do so.
E is incorrect because S3 versioning updates reflect in Snowflake once properly synced.

Question #8:
Correct Answer: A, D
Explanation:
A is correct because Snowflake automatically pulls the most recent version of the file from S3 when versioning is enabled.
D is correct because if a specific version of data is required, the version ID must be included in the external table configuration.
B is incorrect because Snowflake does not require explicit version IDs unless targeting a specific version.
C is incorrect because Snowflake does not ignore older versions; it simply queries the latest version by default.
E is incorrect because external tables in Snowflake can access versioned files in S3.

Question #9:
Correct Answer: D, B
Explanation:
D is correct because Snowflake needs the version ID to query data from specific versions, especially if versioning causes inconsistencies in the data pipeline.
B is correct because metadata could cause outdated data if not refreshed, but Snowflake may still pull data from an earlier version due to the versioning configuration.
A is incorrect because Snowflake can query specific versions when required, and does not always pull the latest file.
C is incorrect because the issue is more related to how Snowflake is querying data from versioned files, not just the stage configuration.
E is incorrect because the data pipeline configuration could be pulling from the wrong schema, but this is not related to S3 versioning.

Question #10:
Correct Answer: A, C
Explanation:
A is correct because Snowflake can query specific versions of files in S3 when external tables are defined with explicit version IDs.
C is correct because the VERSION_ID parameter allows Snowflake to target specific versions of files in versioned S3 buckets.
B is incorrect because Snowflake does not automatically manage versioning unless explicitly configured.
D is incorrect because Snowflake requires explicit configuration to manage versioned data from S3.

E is incorrect because specifying versioning in the S3 stage is not the main factor in enabling Snowflake to query specific versions; the configuration involves using version IDs.

Question #11:
A Snowflake table is designed with **micro-partitioning**. After performing a DELETE operation, you notice that the space usage of the table does not decrease significantly. What could be the reason for this behavior?

Options:

A. Snowflake automatically reclaims the space used by deleted rows in micro-partitions immediately.
B. The data is not immediately purged from the micro-partitions due to Snowflake's automatic optimization processes.
C. The deleted data is retained in the micro-partitions for **Time Travel** purposes and will be removed after the retention period.
D. The table is not using **automatic clustering**, which is required to compact deleted data.

Question #12:
You are performing frequent **INSERT** operations on a Snowflake table with micro-partitioning. You notice that query performance has degraded over time. What could be a potential cause of this issue?

Options:

A. Snowflake uses **automatic clustering** to optimize performance, so no additional steps are needed.
B. Data in the table has been inserted in a way that creates a large number of small micro-partitions, which causes poor performance.
C. The **Time Travel** feature is using too much space due to frequent changes in the table.
D. The **micro-partition pruning** process is too slow due to a lack of partitioning by relevant columns.

Question #13:
In Snowflake, after performing multiple updates and deletes on a table using **micro-partitioning**, what happens to the previous versions of the data?

Options:

A. The data is immediately deleted and does not exist in any form after the update.
B. The data is retained for **Time Travel** purposes and can be accessed until the retention period expires.
C. The previous versions of data are automatically moved to a separate table.
D. The previous versions are overwritten, leaving no way to access the older data.

Question #14:
You are working with a Snowflake table that uses **micro-partitioning** for managing large volumes of data. Which of the following best practices will help optimize performance when performing frequent **CRUD** operations?

Options:
A. Increase the size of the micro-partitions manually to reduce the number of partitions Snowflake manages.
B. Perform regular **CLUSTER BY** operations to optimize the way Snowflake organizes micro-partitions.
C. Avoid using **Time Travel** to reduce storage and improve performance.
D. Insert new rows in bulk rather than in small increments to ensure efficient partitioning.

Question #15:
When performing a MERGE operation in Snowflake with **micro-partitioning**, what impact does the partitioning strategy have on the performance of the operation?

Options:
A. Partitioning has no effect on MERGE performance in Snowflake as it always processes data sequentially.
B. The MERGE operation is faster when the source and target tables are partitioned by the same columns, improving **micro-partition pruning**.
C. Using multiple partitioning columns in the MERGE operation can result in slower performance due to an increase in partition scans.
D. The MERGE operation automatically optimizes the partitioning strategy during execution, eliminating the need for manual intervention.

Answers and Explanations

Question #11:
Correct Answer: B, C
Explanation:
B is correct because Snowflake automatically handles micro-partition optimization, and space is not immediately reclaimed after a DELETE operation.
C is correct because deleted rows are retained for **Time Travel** purposes until the retention period expires, which can delay space reclamation.
A is incorrect because the reclamation is not immediate.
D is incorrect because **automatic clustering** is not required for the reclaiming of deleted data.

Question #12:
Correct Answer: B, D
Explanation:
B is correct because frequent inserts of small amounts of data can result in many small micro-partitions, which causes performance degradation.
D is correct because **micro-partition pruning** works best when data is partitioned by relevant columns, improving query performance by filtering out unnecessary partitions.
A is incorrect because **automatic clustering** does not guarantee performance improvement; it's helpful but not a catch-all.
C is incorrect because **Time Travel** does not directly affect performance during queries; it only impacts storage.

Question #13:
Correct Answer: B

Explanation:
B is correct because Snowflake retains the previous versions of data for **Time Travel** purposes, allowing access to past data until the retention period expires.
A is incorrect because deleted data is not immediately purged.
C is incorrect because data versions are not moved to separate tables; they are retained within the same table.
D is incorrect because older versions are not overwritten but retained for Time Travel purposes.

Question #14:
Correct Answer: B, D
Explanation:
B is correct because **CLUSTER BY** operations help organize data into more efficient micro-partitions, which improves query performance during CRUD operations.
D is correct because bulk inserts allow Snowflake to better optimize micro-partition creation, as opposed to many small inserts that can result in inefficient partitioning.
A is incorrect because manually increasing the size of micro-partitions is not a recommended practice; Snowflake manages this automatically.
C is incorrect because **Time Travel** should be used only when necessary, but it does not negatively impact performance unless retention periods are unnecessarily long.

Question #15:
Correct Answer: B
Explanation:
B is correct because **partitioning by the same columns** in both source and target tables improves **micro-partition pruning**, which optimizes the MERGE operation by reducing unnecessary scans of partitions.
A is incorrect because partitioning does impact performance by reducing unnecessary data scans.
C is incorrect because using multiple partitioning columns can still be effective if chosen carefully, and Snowflake optimizes this.
D is incorrect because Snowflake does not automatically change partitioning strategies during execution; optimization requires manual intervention.

Question #16:
You are tasked with performing a MERGE operation in Snowflake to update data in a target table based on matching records from a source table. The target table has a primary key constraint, and the source table contains records with duplicate keys. What will be the result of executing the MERGE statement?
Options:
A. The MERGE will fail because the source table contains duplicate keys.
B. The MERGE will automatically handle the duplicates in the source table by updating all matching records in the target table.
C. The MERGE will update only the first matching record from the source table for each key.
D. Snowflake will allow the MERGE to complete successfully but will update only the first row it encounters for each key in the source table.

258

E. The MERGE will update all records in the target table that match a key in the source table, even if there are duplicate keys.

Question #17:
You are running a MERGE operation in Snowflake to update records in a target table from a source table. The MERGE statement includes a WHEN MATCHED clause that updates the target table. However, after executing the MERGE, you notice that some rows were not updated as expected. What could be the reason for this?
Options:
A. The MERGE only updates rows where the source and target tables have an exact match on all columns.
B. The condition specified in the ON clause of the MERGE statement may not be correctly identifying matching rows.
C. The MERGE will only update the first match and ignore subsequent rows with the same key.
D. The MERGE operation does not support updating data from multiple source tables.
E. The target table must have an index on the column used in the ON clause for the MERGE to work correctly.

Question #18:
You are performing a MERGE operation in Snowflake to insert new records into a target table when no matching records are found in the target. However, you notice that some records are not being inserted. What could be the cause of this issue?
Options:
A. The MERGE statement does not support the INSERT operation, so no new records can be added to the target table.
B. The WHEN NOT MATCHED clause may not be correctly configured to handle the insert operation.
C. The MERGE statement requires the target table to have a primary key constraint to insert new records.
D. If the source table contains duplicate records, they will not be inserted into the target table.
E. The MERGE operation only inserts records when the source and target tables have matching column data types.

Question #19:
You are executing a MERGE operation in Snowflake to synchronize data between two tables. The MERGE statement is designed to update records in the target table and insert new records from the source table. What is the behavior when there is no match between the source and target tables for a particular row?
Options:
A. Snowflake will ignore the row and no action will be taken.
B. Snowflake will insert the unmatched row into the target table.
C. Snowflake will update the unmatched row in the target table with NULL values.
D. Snowflake will log the unmatched row but not perform any updates or inserts.
E. Snowflake will return an error if no matching row is found in the target table.

Question #20:

You are performing a MERGE operation in Snowflake, and you want to ensure that the operation updates records only when the values in the source table are different from the values in the target table. Which of the following approaches will help achieve this?

Options:

A. Add a WHERE clause inside the WHEN MATCHED section to filter for rows where the source and target values are different.

B. Snowflake automatically compares the values in the source and target tables and only updates records if the values differ.

C. Use a CASE statement inside the WHEN MATCHED clause to compare the source and target values and only update when necessary.

D. You cannot perform such an operation in Snowflake; MERGE will update records regardless of the data difference.

E. The MERGE operation requires the source and target tables to have identical column names and data types to work correctly.

Answers and Explanations

Question #16:
Correct Answer: A, D
Explanation:

A is correct because Snowflake will fail the MERGE operation if the source table contains duplicate keys, as this would create ambiguity in determining the correct row to update in the target table.

D is correct because if the source table contains duplicate keys, Snowflake will update only the first matching row for each key.

B is incorrect because Snowflake does not automatically handle duplicate keys in the source table; it requires unique keys to perform the MERGE operation correctly.

C is incorrect because Snowflake doesn't automatically update only the first matching record, even if duplicates exist.

E is incorrect because Snowflake will not update multiple target rows unless each source row corresponds to a unique target row.

Question #17:
Correct Answer: B, A
Explanation:

B is correct because the condition specified in the ON clause of the MERGE statement might not correctly identify matching rows, leading to some rows not being updated.

A is correct because if there is no exact match on all specified columns in the ON clause, the MERGE will not perform the update as expected.

C is incorrect because the MERGE operation will update all matching rows, not just the first one.

D is incorrect because Snowflake does support updating data from a single source table in a MERGE operation.

E is incorrect because Snowflake does not require an index on the columns used in the ON clause for the MERGE to work.

Question #18:
Correct Answer: B, D
Explanation:
B is correct because if the WHEN NOT MATCHED clause is not configured properly, the records from the source table will not be inserted into the target table.
D is correct because Snowflake will not insert records if the source table contains duplicate records with the same key, which would cause ambiguity in the insertion process.
A is incorrect because the MERGE statement does support the INSERT operation when no matching records are found.
C is incorrect because a primary key constraint on the target table is not required for the MERGE operation to insert new records.
E is incorrect because Snowflake does not require identical column data types between source and target tables to insert data during the MERGE.

Question #19:
Correct Answer: B, A
Explanation:
B is correct because when there is no match between the source and target tables, Snowflake will insert the unmatched row into the target table if the WHEN NOT MATCHED clause specifies an insert action.
A is correct because if no match is found and the WHEN NOT MATCHED clause does not specify an insert, Snowflake will simply ignore the unmatched row and not perform any action.
C is incorrect because Snowflake will not update unmatched rows with NULL values; it will insert them if the MERGE specifies an insert action.
D is incorrect because Snowflake does not log unmatched rows without taking action; it will insert or ignore the row as per the configuration.
E is incorrect because Snowflake does not return an error when there is no match; it will simply not perform any update or insert unless specified.

Question #20:
Correct Answer: A, C
Explanation:
A is correct because adding a WHERE clause inside the WHEN MATCHED section to filter for rows where the source and target values differ will ensure that only the records with different values are updated.
C is correct because using a CASE statement inside the WHEN MATCHED clause will allow Snowflake to compare the source and target values and update only when there is a difference.
B is incorrect because Snowflake does not automatically check for data differences before updating; it will update any matching row by default.
D is incorrect because you can perform operations that only update records when values differ in Snowflake, using either WHERE or CASE statements.
E is incorrect because Snowflake does not require identical column names and data types to perform a MERGE operation, although matching column names and data types help facilitate the process.

Question #21:

You are working with Snowflake and need to create a temporary table that is only available for the duration of the session. Which type of table should you use, and what is the main feature of this table type?

Options:

A. Use a **Temporary Table**; it is available only within the session and is dropped automatically when the session ends.

B. Use a **Transient Table**; it persists only during the session but can be accessed across multiple sessions.

C. Use a **Permanent Table**; it is available to all sessions and can be shared with other users.

D. Use a **Global Temporary Table**; it is available to all users but gets deleted when the session ends.

E. Use a **Session Table**; it is session-specific but requires manual cleanup.

Question #22:

You have created a temporary table in Snowflake and loaded data into it. However, when trying to access the table in a different session, you find that it no longer exists. What could be the reason?

Options:

A. Temporary tables in Snowflake are session-specific and are automatically dropped when the session ends.

B. Temporary tables are shared across all sessions and users until explicitly dropped.

C. Snowflake caches temporary tables in the background, and you need to refresh the cache to access them.

D. Temporary tables are automatically cloned when a session ends to persist across sessions.

E. Temporary tables require an explicit command to persist across multiple sessions.

Question #23:

You are configuring a pipeline that utilizes temporary tables in Snowflake. After several queries, you notice that the temporary table does not exist anymore. How can you ensure the table persists for the full session duration?

Options:

A. Temporary tables in Snowflake automatically persist throughout the entire session as long as the session remains active.

B. To ensure persistence, you must specify the **TRANSIENT** option when creating the temporary table.

C. Temporary tables can be recreated each time the session is restarted; however, there is no way to make them persist beyond the session.

D. Set the TIMEOUT parameter on the temporary table to prevent it from being dropped.

E. Temporary tables are dropped immediately after their first use; you need to recreate them each time.

Question #24:

You are implementing a scenario where temporary tables need to store intermediate results for a multi-step process in a data pipeline. The results need to be cleared after each session. Which type of table is the best choice for this situation?

Options:

A. **Temporary Table**, because it is session-specific and will automatically be dropped after the session ends.
B. **Permanent Table**, because it allows you to store data persistently across sessions.
C. **Global Temporary Table**, because it is available to all users and is dropped after the session ends.
D. **Transient Table**, because it allows for temporary storage but can persist beyond the session if needed.
E. **Stage Table**, because it stores data temporarily but allows for long-term querying.

Question #25:
You want to create a table in Snowflake that is only available to the current session, and the table should be dropped automatically at the end of the session. What is the correct SQL statement to achieve this?
Options:
A. CREATE TEMPORARY TABLE <table_name> (columns) AS SELECT * FROM <source>;
B. CREATE TRANSIENT TABLE <table_name> (columns) AS SELECT * FROM <source>;
C. CREATE GLOBAL TEMPORARY TABLE <table_name> (columns) AS SELECT * FROM <source>;
D. CREATE TABLE <table_name> (columns) WITH SESSION LIFETIME;
E. CREATE SESSION TABLE <table_name> (columns) AS SELECT * FROM <source>;

Answers and Explanations

Question #21:
Correct Answer: A
Explanation:
A is correct because a Temporary Table is session-specific and is dropped automatically when the session ends, making it the best choice for temporary storage during a session.
B is incorrect because a Transient Table persists beyond the session and is used for persistent storage across sessions.
C is incorrect because a Permanent Table is not session-specific and is used for storing data permanently.
D is incorrect because Global Temporary Tables are available across sessions for all users, and they are dropped when the session ends.
E is incorrect because Snowflake does not have a Session Table type.

Question #22:
Correct Answer: A
Explanation:
A is correct because Temporary Tables are session-specific and are automatically dropped when the session ends.
B is incorrect because temporary tables are not shared across sessions and users, they are session-bound.
C is incorrect because Snowflake does not require cache refreshing to access temporary tables within the same session.
D is incorrect because temporary tables are not automatically cloned; they are session-dependent and dropped after the session ends.

E is incorrect because temporary tables do not persist across sessions unless explicitly created in each session.

Question #23:
Correct Answer: A
Explanation:
A is correct because Temporary Tables in Snowflake automatically persist throughout the entire session until the session ends.
B is incorrect because specifying the TRANSIENT option does not apply to temporary tables. The TRANSIENT option is used for tables that persist beyond the session.
C is incorrect because temporary tables are not automatically recreated in new sessions. They exist only during the session they were created in.
D is incorrect because TIMEOUT parameters do not control the persistence of temporary tables.
E is incorrect because temporary tables do not require recreation after their first use unless the session ends.

Question #24:
Correct Answer: A
Explanation:
A is correct because Temporary Tables are perfect for storing session-specific intermediate results. They are automatically dropped at the end of the session.
B is incorrect because Permanent Tables are not session-bound and will persist across sessions, which is unnecessary for this scenario.
C is incorrect because Global Temporary Tables are accessible across all users and sessions, which is not needed in this case.
D is incorrect because Transient Tables can persist beyond the session, which is not the intended use case here.
E is incorrect because Stage Tables are used to load external data and are not meant for intermediate session-based storage.

Question #25:
Correct Answer: A
Explanation:
A is correct because the CREATE TEMPORARY TABLE statement is the correct SQL syntax for creating a temporary table in Snowflake, and it will be dropped automatically at the end of the session.
B is incorrect because the CREATE TRANSIENT TABLE statement is used for creating persistent tables that are not automatically dropped after the session ends.
C is incorrect because the CREATE GLOBAL TEMPORARY TABLE statement is used for creating tables that persist across sessions and users, not for session-specific temporary tables.
D is incorrect because the WITH SESSION LIFETIME clause is not a valid syntax in Snowflake for table creation.
E is incorrect because there is no SESSION TABLE in Snowflake; the correct syntax is TEMPORARY TABLE.

TIME TRAVEL

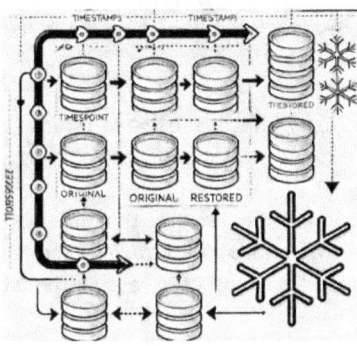

Question #01:
Your organization needs to access and analyze historical sales data that has been updated over time in Snowflake. How can Time Travel help in this scenario?
Options:
A. It allows you to query data as it existed at a specific point in time, even if it has been updated or deleted.
B. It enables you to restore deleted tables but only for a maximum of 7 days.
C. It requires the database administrator to manually create snapshots of the data to query the historical versions.
D. It allows querying historical data by specifying a timestamp or offset within the Time Travel retention period.
E. It ensures deleted data is completely removed and cannot be queried again.

Question #02:
A table in Snowflake is accidentally updated, and the team wants to recover its state as it was two days ago. Which of the following approaches can be used?
Options:
A. Use the SELECT * query with a specific timestamp using Time Travel to access the table's previous state.
B. Use the UNDO UPDATE command to reverse the update operation directly.
C. Use a cloning operation with the AT clause to create a new table from the historical state.
D. Restore the table using the RESTORE command to a specific point in time.
E. Query the Recycle Bin to locate the updated data and reverse the change.

Question #03:
You need to audit data changes in a critical table and ensure that any accidental updates or deletions can be investigated. How does Time Travel address this need?
Options:
A. It allows you to access historical data by querying previous versions of the table within the retention period.
B. It creates a backup of the table at regular intervals to maintain historical data versions.
C. It enables automatic notifications when data in the table is modified or deleted.
D. It requires integration with third-party backup solutions for maintaining historical data.
E. It stores historical data indefinitely, even beyond the Time Travel retention period.

Question #04:

Your team mistakenly dropped a table that was crucial for generating a report. However, the table was dropped only 12 hours ago. What is the best way to recover it using Snowflake Time Travel?

Options:
A. Query the data using Time Travel without the need for restoration.
B. Use the RESTORE command to recover the dropped table within the Time Travel retention period.
C. Use the CREATE TABLE AS command to recreate the table from scratch using its schema.
D. Request assistance from Snowflake Support to recover the table.
E. Clone the database from an earlier snapshot to recover the table.

Question #05:

A team is tasked with analyzing historical trends in a table where the data is frequently updated. They want to create a report showing how the data looked exactly 3 days ago. Which approach should they use?

Options:
A. Use a query with a specific timestamp and the AT clause to fetch the historical data.
B. Clone the table using the CLONE command with the BEFORE clause to capture its state from 3 days ago.
C. Query the table with the TIME MACHINE feature provided by Snowflake's Time Travel.
D. Use a stored procedure to iterate over changes in the data to recreate its historical state.
E. Restore the entire database to its state from 3 days ago using the RESTORE command.

Answers and Explanations

Question #01:
Correct Answer: A, D
Explanation:
A is correct because Snowflake's Time Travel allows querying historical data exactly as it existed at a specific point in time.
D is correct because you can use a timestamp or offset within the retention period to query historical data.
B is incorrect because the Time Travel retention period can be configured to exceed 7 days depending on the account settings.
C is incorrect because Time Travel operates without requiring manual snapshots.
E is incorrect because deleted data can be queried within the Time Travel retention period.

Question #02:
Correct Answer: A, C, D
Explanation:
A is correct because Time Travel allows querying data at a specific timestamp using SQL queries.
C is correct because cloning with the AT clause creates a new table from a historical state.
D is correct because the RESTORE command can revert a table to its historical state.
B is incorrect because Snowflake does not support an UNDO UPDATE command.
E is incorrect because the Recycle Bin only applies to dropped objects, not updated data.

Question #03:
Correct Answer: A
Explanation:
A is correct because Time Travel allows querying previous table versions to audit and investigate data changes.
B is incorrect because Time Travel does not create periodic backups; it retains data changes within the retention period.
C is incorrect because Time Travel does not send automatic notifications about changes.
D is incorrect because no third-party backup solutions are required for Time Travel.
E is incorrect because Time Travel only retains historical data for the configured retention period.

Question #04:
Correct Answer: B
Explanation:
B is correct because the RESTORE command can recover dropped tables within the Time Travel retention period.
A is incorrect because querying using Time Travel does not restore dropped tables; it only allows access to historical data.
C is incorrect because recreating the table would not recover its data.
D is incorrect because Snowflake Support is not required for recovering data within the Time Travel retention period.
E is incorrect because cloning requires an existing object to create a clone.

Question #05:
Correct Answer: A, B
Explanation:
A is correct because querying with a timestamp using the AT clause fetches historical data from 3 days ago.
B is correct because cloning with the BEFORE clause creates a copy of the table as it existed 3 days ago.
C is incorrect because there is no feature named TIME MACHINE in Snowflake; Time Travel provides this functionality.
D is incorrect because a stored procedure is unnecessary; Time Travel simplifies the process.
E is incorrect because restoring the entire database is not needed for analyzing a single table.

Question #06:
Your organization accidentally dropped a table containing customer records. They want to restore it to its state before deletion. What should they do?
Options:
A. Use the RESTORE command if the table is within the Time Travel retention period.
B. Query the INFORMATION_SCHEMA.DROPPED_TABLES view to directly recover the table.
C. Use the UNDROP command to restore the table.
D. Manually re-create the table using historical query results from the HISTORY function.
E. Submit a support ticket to Snowflake to restore the table.

Question #07:
An entire schema containing important reporting tables was dropped accidentally. The team needs to recover the schema without losing any data. Which steps should they take?
Options:
A. Use the UNDROP SCHEMA command if it is within the Time Travel retention period.
B. Use the RESTORE SCHEMA command after creating a replacement schema.
C. Query the HISTORY function to manually retrieve the dropped schema's metadata and data.
D. Use the CLONE command on an active backup schema.
E. Use the DROP SCHEMA command followed by RESTORE SCHEMA to reinitialize the schema.

Question #08:
A developer ran a DROP DATABASE command on a production database by mistake. How can the team recover the database quickly?
Options:
A. Execute the RESTORE DATABASE command immediately to recover the database.
B. Use the UNDROP DATABASE command to recover it if it falls within the retention period.
C. Clone the dropped database from a historical backup.
D. Query the HISTORY function and manually rebuild the database.
E. Use a previously exported data backup from external storage.

Question #09:
A user dropped a table and its data outside of the Time Travel retention period. How can they recover this table?
Options:
A. Use UNDROP to recover the table regardless of the Time Travel retention period.
B. Query the HISTORY function for past data and recreate the table manually.
C. Clone a backup of the table if a clone was created before the drop.
D. Use the RESTORE command to bring the table back to its previous state.
E. Recovery is not possible once the Time Travel retention period has expired.

Question #10:
Your organization accidentally dropped a database containing multiple schemas and tables. The team wants to recover the database to its last known state. What steps should they follow?
Options:
A. Use UNDROP DATABASE if the retention period allows.
B. Use RESTORE DATABASE to recover the deleted database.
C. Clone the entire database from the last snapshot before deletion.
D. Submit a support ticket to Snowflake for database restoration.
E. Manually rebuild the database using historical data queries.

Answers and Explanations
Question #06:
Correct Answer: A, C
Explanation:
A is correct because the RESTORE command can recover a table within the Time Travel retention period.
C is correct because the UNDROP command can recover a dropped table if within the

retention window.
B is incorrect because INFORMATION_SCHEMA.DROPPED_TABLES only provides metadata, not recovery functionality.
D is incorrect because manually re-creating the table is unnecessary if Time Travel is available.
E is incorrect because Snowflake's Time Travel allows self-service recovery without involving support.

Question #07:
Correct Answer: A, B
Explanation:
A is correct because UNDROP SCHEMA can restore the schema if within the retention period.
B is correct because RESTORE SCHEMA works for schemas if a replacement schema is created first.
C is incorrect because HISTORY does not restore schemas, only tracks query execution.
D is incorrect because CLONE does not apply to dropped schemas directly.
E is incorrect because DROP SCHEMA followed by RESTORE is not a valid recovery sequence.

Question #08:
Correct Answer: B, E
Explanation:
B is correct because UNDROP DATABASE restores the database if within the retention period.
E is correct as external backups are a last-resort recovery method outside of Snowflake's retention window.
A is incorrect because RESTORE DATABASE does not work directly for databases; UNDROP is needed.
C is incorrect because cloning requires a pre-existing database or backup.
D is incorrect as manually recreating a database is time-intensive and avoidable with Time Travel.

Question #09:
Correct Answer: C, E
Explanation:
C is correct because cloning a pre-existing backup is a viable recovery option.
E is correct because recovery is not possible once the retention window is exceeded without backups.
A is incorrect because UNDROP only works within the Time Travel retention period.
B is incorrect as HISTORY only provides query audit data, not data restoration.
D is incorrect because RESTORE also depends on the Time Travel retention window.

Question #10:
Correct Answer: A, C
Explanation:
A is correct because UNDROP DATABASE restores the database if within the retention period.
C is correct as cloning from a pre-existing snapshot is a valid way to recover the database.
B is incorrect because RESTORE DATABASE is not a valid Snowflake command.
D is incorrect because Snowflake's native tools negate the need for external support tickets for undropping objects.
E is incorrect because rebuilding the database manually is unnecessary with available recovery options.

Question #11:
A team accidentally deleted a critical table in Snowflake. They want to restore it using Time Travel to the state it was in before the deletion. What is the correct SQL command to achieve this?
Options:
A. CREATE OR REPLACE TABLE table_name AS SELECT * FROM table_name BEFORE (STATEMENT => 'query_id');
B. RESTORE TABLE table_name TO (BEFORE STATEMENT => 'query_id');
C. SELECT * FROM table_name AS OF TIME '2024-12-01 12:00:00';
D. CREATE TABLE table_name AS (SELECT * FROM table_name VERSION => 'previous');
E. UNDROP TABLE table_name;

Question #12:
An analyst needs to retrieve data from a table as it existed at a specific point in time, using a query timestamp. Which SQL syntax is appropriate?
Options:
A. SELECT * FROM table_name AT (TIME => '2024-11-30 10:00:00');
B. SELECT * FROM table_name AS OF TIMESTAMP '2024-11-30 10:00:00';
C. SELECT * FROM table_name BEFORE '2024-11-30 10:00:00';
D. SELECT * FROM table_name VERSION => '2024-11-30T10:00:00';
E. SELECT * FROM table_name WITH (TIMEPOINT '2024-11-30T10:00:00');

Question #13:
A developer wants to compare the current state of a table with its state before a specific query was executed. How can this be achieved?
Options:
A. SELECT * FROM table_name VERSION AS OF STATEMENT 'query_id';
B. SELECT * FROM table_name BEFORE (STATEMENT => 'query_id');
C. SELECT * FROM table_name AS OF QUERY_ID 'query_id';
D. SELECT * FROM table_name USING QUERY_ID 'query_id';
E. SELECT * FROM table_name WHERE query_id = 'query_id';

Question #14:
A Snowflake database was accidentally dropped, but it was restored using Time Travel. What SQL syntax should be used to restore a specific table from the recovered database to its state at a prior timestamp?
Options:
A. CREATE TABLE table_name_restored AS SELECT * FROM table_name AS OF '2024-12-01 08:00:00';
B. RESTORE TABLE table_name TO TIME '2024-12-01 08:00:00';
C. SELECT * FROM table_name BEFORE TIMESTAMP '2024-12-01 08:00:00';
D. CREATE TABLE table_name_restored AT TIME '2024-12-01 08:00:00';
E. CREATE OR REPLACE TABLE table_name_restored FROM TIME '2024-12-01 08:00:00';

Question #15:

A critical table in Snowflake was accidentally dropped and subsequently undropped using the UNDROP command. The team now wants to verify the table's data integrity by comparing its current state with the state from one day prior. What SQL syntax should they use?

Options:

A. SELECT * FROM table_name MINUS SELECT * FROM table_name AS OF '2024-11-30 12:00:00';
B. COMPARE table_name TO '2024-11-30 12:00:00';
C. SELECT * FROM table_name VERSION BEFORE TIMESTAMP '2024-11-30 12:00:00';
D. SELECT * FROM table_name EXCEPT (AS OF '2024-11-30 12:00:00');
E. SELECT * FROM table_name AS OF '2024-11-30 12:00:00';

Answers and Explanations

Question #11:
Correct Answer: B, E
Explanation:
B is correct because the RESTORE command is used with the BEFORE STATEMENT clause to restore a table to its state before a specific query execution.
E is correct because the UNDROP command can be used to recover a dropped table.
A is incorrect because CREATE OR REPLACE TABLE is not a valid command for restoring tables.
C is incorrect because AS OF TIME is used for querying, not restoring.
D is incorrect because the syntax VERSION => 'previous' does not exist in Snowflake.

Question #12:
Correct Answer: B
Explanation:
B is correct because AS OF TIMESTAMP retrieves the table state as it existed at a specific point in time.
A is incorrect because the AT (TIME =>) syntax is invalid in Snowflake.
C is incorrect because BEFORE is not a valid clause for querying historical data.
D is incorrect because VERSION is not a recognized keyword for time travel in Snowflake.
E is incorrect because WITH (TIMEPOINT) syntax does not exist.

Question #13:
Correct Answer: B
Explanation:
B is correct because BEFORE (STATEMENT => 'query_id') allows the table state to be queried as it existed before a specific query was executed.
A is incorrect because VERSION AS OF STATEMENT is not valid in Snowflake.
C is incorrect because AS OF QUERY_ID syntax is invalid.
D is incorrect because USING QUERY_ID does not exist in Snowflake's SQL syntax.
E is incorrect because it attempts to filter by query_id directly, which is not how Time Travel operates.

Question #14:
Correct Answer: A
Explanation:

A is correct because the CREATE TABLE statement with AS OF is valid for restoring tables to a specific timestamp.
B is incorrect because RESTORE cannot directly restore to a new table.
C is incorrect because BEFORE TIMESTAMP is not valid for restoring tables.
D is incorrect because CREATE TABLE AT TIME is invalid syntax.
E is incorrect because FROM TIME is not a recognized clause in Snowflake.

Question #15:
Correct Answer: A
Explanation:
A is correct because it compares the current state of the table with its historical state by subtracting one from the other using the MINUS operator.
B is incorrect because COMPARE is not a valid SQL command in Snowflake.
C is incorrect because VERSION BEFORE TIMESTAMP is invalid syntax.
D is incorrect because EXCEPT cannot be combined with AS OF.
E is incorrect because it retrieves historical data but does not perform a comparison.

Question #16:
A team accidentally deleted critical data from a table in Snowflake. They need to create a clone of the table as it existed two days ago to recover the lost data. What SQL syntax is correct for this operation?
Options:
A. CREATE TABLE cloned_table CLONE table_name AS OF '2024-12-05 10:00:00';
B. CREATE OR REPLACE TABLE cloned_table AS CLONE table_name VERSION => '2024-12-05T10:00:00';
C. CREATE TABLE cloned_table CLONE table_name BEFORE (TIMESTAMP => '2024-12-05T10:00:00');
D. CREATE TABLE cloned_table CLONE table_name AT (TIME => '2024-12-05 10:00:00');
E. CREATE TABLE cloned_table AS SELECT * FROM table_name;

Question #17:
A database in Snowflake was accidentally dropped. The team used Time Travel to restore the database and now needs to create a clone of a specific schema from the restored database as it existed before it was dropped. Which command should they use?
Options:
A. CREATE SCHEMA cloned_schema CLONE restored_database.schema_name;
B. CREATE SCHEMA cloned_schema CLONE restored_database.schema_name AT (TIME => '2024-12-04 09:00:00');
C. CREATE OR REPLACE SCHEMA cloned_schema AS CLONE restored_database.schema_name AS OF '2024-12-04 09:00:00';
D. CREATE SCHEMA cloned_schema CLONE restored_database.schema_name VERSION => '2024-12-04T09:00:00';
E. RESTORE SCHEMA cloned_schema FROM restored_database.schema_name TO TIME '2024-12-04 09:00:00';

Question #18:

A developer wants to create a clone of an entire database as it existed at a specific query execution point in the past. What is the best way to achieve this?
Options:
A. CREATE DATABASE cloned_db CLONE original_db AS OF (QUERY_ID => 'query_id');
B. CREATE DATABASE cloned_db CLONE original_db AT QUERY_ID 'query_id';
C. CREATE DATABASE cloned_db CLONE original_db BEFORE (QUERY_ID => 'query_id');
D. CREATE DATABASE cloned_db CLONE original_db USING QUERY_ID 'query_id';
E. CREATE DATABASE cloned_db CLONE original_db;

Question #19:
A data engineer is tasked with cloning a table to a state it had at a specific timestamp. They also want to ensure that the cloned table does not inherit any changes made to the original table after the clone. What is the correct syntax?
Options:
A. CREATE TABLE cloned_table CLONE table_name AS OF '2024-12-06 12:00:00';
B. CREATE TABLE cloned_table CLONE table_name BEFORE '2024-12-06 12:00:00';
C. CREATE OR REPLACE TABLE cloned_table CLONE table_name AT TIME '2024-12-06 12:00:00';
D. CREATE TABLE cloned_table AS SELECT * FROM table_name VERSION => '2024-12-06 12:00:00';
E. CREATE TABLE cloned_table CLONE table_name VERSION AS OF '2024-12-06 12:00:00';

Question #20:
The team wants to clone a schema in Snowflake and create a new version of it as it existed one week ago, while preserving the current schema. What command should they use?
Options:
A. CREATE SCHEMA cloned_schema CLONE schema_name AS OF '2024-11-30';
B. CREATE SCHEMA cloned_schema CLONE schema_name BEFORE TIMESTAMP '2024-11-30';
C. CREATE SCHEMA cloned_schema CLONE schema_name VERSION => '2024-11-30';
D. CREATE SCHEMA cloned_schema CLONE schema_name;
E. CREATE OR REPLACE SCHEMA cloned_schema AS CLONE schema_name;

Answers and Explanations

Question #16:
Correct Answer: A
Explanation:
A is correct because the CREATE TABLE cloned_table CLONE table_name AS OF syntax allows cloning a table to its state at a specific timestamp.
B is incorrect because VERSION => is not valid in Snowflake.
C is incorrect because BEFORE (TIMESTAMP =>) is not a supported clause.
D is incorrect because AT (TIME =>) is invalid syntax.
E is incorrect because it clones the current state of the table, not a past state.

Question #17:
Correct Answer: A
Explanation:

A is correct because the CREATE SCHEMA cloned_schema CLONE restored_database.schema_name syntax clones a schema from a restored database.
B is incorrect because AT (TIME =>) is not supported for cloning.
C is incorrect because AS OF is not valid for cloning schemas.
D is incorrect because VERSION => is invalid syntax.
E is incorrect because RESTORE cannot be used to create clones.

Question #18:
Correct Answer: A
Explanation:
A is correct because CREATE DATABASE cloned_db CLONE original_db AS OF (QUERY_ID => 'query_id') is the correct syntax for cloning a database at a specific query point.
B is incorrect because AT QUERY_ID is not valid.
C is incorrect because BEFORE (QUERY_ID =>) is not a supported syntax.
D is incorrect because USING QUERY_ID is invalid.
E is incorrect because it clones the current state of the database, not a specific point in the past.

Question #19:
Correct Answer: A
Explanation:
A is correct because CREATE TABLE cloned_table CLONE table_name AS OF ensures the clone reflects the table's state at the specified timestamp.
B is incorrect because BEFORE is not valid syntax for cloning.
C is incorrect because AT TIME is not supported for this use case.
D is incorrect because VERSION => does not work for cloning tables.
E is incorrect because VERSION AS OF is not valid syntax.

Question #20:
Correct Answer: A
Explanation:
A is correct because CREATE SCHEMA cloned_schema CLONE schema_name AS OF allows cloning the schema to its state at a specific timestamp.
B is incorrect because BEFORE TIMESTAMP is not valid.
C is incorrect because VERSION => is invalid syntax.
D is incorrect because it clones the current schema state, not a historical state.
E is incorrect because CREATE OR REPLACE would replace the current schema instead of creating a separate clone.

Question #21:
A database administrator needs to recover a table that has exceeded its Time Travel retention period. The data has now moved to Fail-safe. What steps must be taken to recover this data?
Options:
A. Submit a Snowflake Support request to restore the table from Fail-safe.
B. Execute the RESTORE TABLE command with the AS OF TIME clause.
C. Perform an UNDROP operation on the table.

D. Use the Fail-safe table directly with a SQL query.
E. Recreate the table manually using backup data from Fail-safe.

Question #22:
A team has discovered that a critical table was dropped 10 days ago. Their Snowflake account has a Time Travel retention period of 7 days. What can they do to recover the table?
Options:
A. Use Fail-safe by contacting Snowflake Support.
B. Use the UNDROP TABLE command to recover the table.
C. Perform a CREATE TABLE statement using historical data from Fail-safe.
D. Query the data using Time Travel and reinsert it into a new table.
E. Run the RESTORE TABLE command with a timestamp within the Fail-safe period.

Question #23:
A company wants to ensure they can recover data beyond the Time Travel retention period. How can they utilize Fail-safe effectively in their disaster recovery strategy?
Options:
A. Enable Fail-safe for specific tables.
B. Rely on Snowflake Support to recover data from Fail-safe.
C. Extend the Time Travel retention period to cover Fail-safe.
D. Use Fail-safe for business continuity and implement external backups.
E. Query Fail-safe tables directly to retrieve data.

Question #24:
After a schema was dropped, a user realized they needed data from one of the tables in that schema. The Time Travel period has lapsed, and the schema has moved to Fail-safe. What should the user do to retrieve the data?
Options:
A. Use the RESTORE SCHEMA command with Fail-safe.
B. Open a Snowflake Support ticket to restore the schema.
C. Query the schema from Fail-safe using SQL.
D. Use the UNDROP SCHEMA command to recover the schema.
E. Extract data from Fail-safe through external data recovery tools.

Question #25:
A business is evaluating Snowflake Fail-safe as part of its disaster recovery plan. Which statements about Fail-safe are accurate?
Options:
A. Fail-safe ensures data recovery after the Time Travel retention period expires.
B. Users can directly query data from Fail-safe without Snowflake Support.
C. Fail-safe is designed for compliance and disaster recovery scenarios.
D. Data in Fail-safe is retained for an additional 7 days beyond Time Travel.
E. Fail-safe retention can be extended upon request.

Answers and Explanations

Question #21:
Correct Answer: A
Explanation:
A is correct because Fail-safe requires Snowflake Support intervention to recover the data.
B is incorrect because RESTORE TABLE works only during the Time Travel period, not Fail-safe.
C is incorrect because UNDROP can only be used within Time Travel.
D is incorrect because Fail-safe data is not queryable directly.
E is incorrect because users cannot manually access or recreate data directly from Fail-safe.

Question #22:
Correct Answer: A
Explanation:
A is correct because Fail-safe provides an option to recover data beyond the Time Travel retention period by contacting Snowflake Support.
B is incorrect because the UNDROP command works only within the Time Travel period.
C is incorrect because Fail-safe data cannot be recreated manually.
D is incorrect because Time Travel data is unavailable after its retention period expires.
E is incorrect because RESTORE TABLE cannot access Fail-safe data.

Question #23:
Correct Answer: B, D
Explanation:
B is correct because Fail-safe recovery is handled by Snowflake Support.
D is correct because Fail-safe is a last-resort option, and external backups provide additional assurance for disaster recovery.
A is incorrect because Fail-safe is not enabled per table; it applies automatically to all data.
C is incorrect because Fail-safe does not extend Time Travel.
E is incorrect because Fail-safe data is not directly queryable.

Question #24:
Correct Answer: B
Explanation:
B is correct because Snowflake Support can restore a schema from Fail-safe.
A is incorrect because the RESTORE SCHEMA command works only during Time Travel.
C is incorrect because Fail-safe data is not queryable.
D is incorrect because the UNDROP SCHEMA command is valid only within the Time Travel period.
E is incorrect because external tools cannot access Fail-safe data.

Question #25:
Correct Answer: A, C, D
Explanation:
A is correct because Fail-safe is a recovery mechanism after Time Travel ends.
C is correct because Fail-safe supports compliance and disaster recovery use cases.
D is correct because Fail-safe retains data for 7 days beyond Time Travel.
B is incorrect because Fail-safe data is not queryable directly by users.
E is incorrect because Fail-safe retention is fixed and cannot be extended.

Question #26:
Your organization needs to keep track of historical data for auditing purposes. You want to set a retention period that complies with your company's policies. What should you consider when configuring the retention period in Snowflake?
Options:
A. Retention periods in Snowflake cannot be adjusted.
B. The maximum retention period is 1 year for all Snowflake editions.
C. You can configure the retention period from 0 to 90 days, depending on your Snowflake edition.
D. All Snowflake editions support the same retention periods.
E. Time Travel retention periods are fixed at 30 days.

Question #27:
A team member accidentally deleted a table in your Snowflake environment. You need to recover the table using Time Travel. Which factors will determine the success of this recovery operation?
Options:
A. The retention period configured for Time Travel.
B. The amount of data stored in the table.
C. The number of concurrent queries running.
D. The Snowflake edition your organization is using.
E. The frequency of data updates to the table.

Question #28:
Your company has a policy to retain data for the maximum allowable period for compliance. Which configuration steps are needed to set up Time Travel to retain data for 90 days?
Options:
A. Configuring Time Travel retention period to 90 days.
B. Upgrading to a higher Snowflake edition if necessary.
C. Setting the default retention period in the account settings.
D. Manually creating a retention policy in the database.
E. Adjusting the table schema to accommodate the retention period.

Question #29:
The auditing department requires access to historical versions of a database for the last two months. How should you configure Time Travel to meet this requirement?
Options:
A. Set the retention period for Time Travel to 60 days.
B. Upgrade to a Snowflake edition that supports a 60-day retention period.
C. Enable Time Travel for each individual table.
D. Create clones of the database every 30 days.
E. Set up daily backups to an external storage.

Question #30:
You need to balance storage costs with the requirement to maintain historical data. What is the best approach to configure the retention period in Snowflake?
Options:
A. Configure the shortest possible retention period.

B. Set the retention period to 30 days by default.
C. Use a tiered approach, with different retention periods for different data.
D. Always use the maximum retention period available.
E. Regularly review and adjust retention periods based on data usage patterns.

Answers and Explanations

Question #26:
Correct Answer: C
Explanation:
C is correct because Snowflake allows you to configure the retention period from 0 to 90 days, depending on your Snowflake edition.
A is incorrect because retention periods in Snowflake are adjustable.
B is incorrect because the maximum retention period is not 1 year for all editions.
D is incorrect because different Snowflake editions support different retention periods.
E is incorrect because Time Travel retention periods are not fixed at 30 days.

Question #27:
Correct Answers: A, D
Explanation:
A is correct because the retention period determines if the data can be recovered.
D is correct because different Snowflake editions offer different retention period limits.
B is incorrect because the amount of data stored does not affect recovery.
C is incorrect because the number of concurrent queries does not impact recovery.
E is incorrect because the frequency of data updates does not determine recovery success.

Question #28:
Correct Answers: A, B
Explanation:
A is correct because you need to configure the retention period to 90 days.
B is correct because higher editions support longer retention periods.
C is incorrect because setting default retention in account settings alone is not sufficient.
D is incorrect because creating a manual retention policy in the database is unnecessary.
E is incorrect because adjusting the table schema is not required to accommodate retention periods.

.

Question #29:
Correct Answers: A, B
Explanation:
A is correct because setting the retention period to 60 days meets the requirement.
B is correct because some editions support longer retention periods.
C is incorrect because enabling Time Travel for each table is redundant.
D is incorrect because creating clones every 30 days is unnecessary.
E is incorrect because daily backups do not directly relate to Time Travel configuration.

Question #30:
Correct Answers: C, E

Explanation:
C is correct because a tiered approach can balance storage costs and historical data needs.
E is correct because regular reviews help optimize retention periods.
A is incorrect because the shortest possible retention period may not meet data requirements.
B is incorrect because a default 30-day period may not be optimal for all data.
D is incorrect because always using the maximum retention period can be costly and unnecessary.

Question #31: A data analyst wants to query historical data from multiple databases using Snowflake's Time Travel feature. The goal is to compare the state of a dataset across different databases at a specific point in time. Which of the following is required for this query to be successful?
Options:
A. The query must use the AT clause with the same timestamp in all databases.
B. The historical data must be replicated across all databases before it can be queried.
C. Time Travel can only query historical data from tables in the same database.
D. The AT clause can be used to query historical data across multiple databases without additional configuration.
E. Historical data can be accessed by specifying the database, schema, and table but must be explicitly restored before querying.

Question #32: A data scientist needs to analyze changes to a dataset across multiple databases using Snowflake's Time Travel. The data scientist queries a table in Database A and another in Database B, each using a point-in-time query. However, they receive an error stating that Time Travel is not supported across databases. What is the likely cause of this issue?
Options:
A. Time Travel is not supported for cross-database queries in Snowflake.
B. Time Travel must be enabled separately for each database before performing cross-database queries.
C. The query must use the AT clause with the same timestamp for all databases to work correctly.
D. Snowflake requires that all queried databases be in the same virtual warehouse.
E. The query needs to specify the historical timestamp in a separate AT clause for each database.

Question #33: You are performing an analysis of historical data across multiple databases in Snowflake. After running a Time Travel query, the data from one of the databases is not returned as expected. What might be the issue?
Options:
A. Time Travel data may not be available for the queried database if the retention period has expired.
B. You must query historical data across databases using the COPY INTO statement.
C. The data must be manually restored before it can be accessed through Time Travel.
D. Historical data is only accessible for tables, not for views or materialized views.
E. The warehouse associated with the query is suspended and cannot process historical queries.

Question #34: A data engineer needs to track historical changes to data across different Snowflake databases and analyze it for auditing purposes. They are querying tables in two separate databases at specific points in time. Which of the following practices will ensure a smooth and successful query execution?

Options:
A. Use the AT clause with timestamps for both databases and ensure that the historical data exists in both databases.
B. Use the AS OF clause with the same timestamp for all databases in the query.
C. Ensure that each database has a valid retention period for Time Travel to access historical data.
D. Use CLONE to create a snapshot of the databases before performing the query.
E. Time Travel queries should only be executed within a single database to avoid cross-database issues.

Question #35: You are tasked with comparing the state of a table in two different Snowflake databases as it appeared 7 days ago. You attempt to use Time Travel to retrieve the historical data but find that one of the tables does not return the expected results. What could be the reason for this issue?

Options:
A. The table in the second database does not have sufficient historical data retention.
B. Time Travel only works for tables that are less than 5 days old.
C. The databases must be in the same region for Time Travel queries to work across them.
D. Snowflake automatically restores the tables before any Time Travel query is executed.
E. The warehouse used for querying historical data needs to be manually restored before querying.

Answers and Explanations:

Question #31:
Correct Answers: A, D
Explanation:
A is correct because Snowflake's Time Travel requires using the AT clause with a specific timestamp in order to query historical data across multiple databases.
D is correct because Time Travel allows querying data across databases without additional configuration, provided the AT clause is used correctly.
B is incorrect because historical data does not need to be replicated across databases for Time Travel queries.
C is incorrect because Time Travel supports querying historical data from multiple databases if done correctly with the appropriate clause.
E is incorrect because historical data does not need to be restored before querying; Time Travel allows direct querying of past data.

Question #32:
Correct Answer: A
Explanation:
A is correct because Time Travel does not support cross-database queries in Snowflake. Queries involving multiple databases require careful management of data within a single database scope.

B is incorrect because Time Travel is not enabled across databases; it is specific to individual databases.
C is incorrect because using the same timestamp for all databases does not resolve the issue; the limitation is with cross-database support.
D is incorrect because Time Travel does not require databases to be in the same virtual warehouse for querying historical data.
E is incorrect because Snowflake does not require separate AT clauses for each database in cross-database queries, which is not supported.

Question #33:
Correct Answer: A
Explanation:
A is correct because if the retention period for Time Travel has expired, the historical data would no longer be available for querying. Snowflake typically allows a retention period of up to 90 days, depending on your configuration.
B is incorrect because Time Travel does not require using COPY INTO for querying historical data.
C is incorrect because Time Travel allows querying historical data without explicitly restoring it first.
D is incorrect because views and materialized views can also use Time Travel, provided the base table is eligible for it.
E is incorrect because Time Travel queries can be executed even if the warehouse is suspended, as long as the data is available.

Question #34:
Correct Answers: A, C
Explanation:
A is correct because using the AT clause with specific timestamps for each database is essential when performing Time Travel queries across multiple databases.
C is correct because the retention period for Time Travel must be valid for each database being queried; otherwise, historical data may be unavailable.
B is incorrect because the AS OF clause is not a valid syntax for querying across databases in Time Travel.
D is incorrect because CLONE is used to create snapshots of tables or databases but is not necessary for Time Travel queries.
E is incorrect because Time Travel can be executed across multiple databases if retention and access conditions are met.

Question #35:
Correct Answer: A
Explanation:
A is correct because if the retention period for the table in the second database is shorter than the requested Time Travel period, it will not return historical data.
B is incorrect because Time Travel can query data older than 5 days if the retention period allows it.
C is incorrect because the region does not affect Time Travel queries across databases; the limitation is with cross-database support.
D is incorrect because Snowflake does not automatically restore tables before a Time Travel query; it is a read-only feature for querying historical data.

E is incorrect because suspending a warehouse does not affect Time Travel queries, as the data is still available for querying.

Question #36

A Snowflake user has set different retention periods for two tables within the same database using Time Travel. The retention period for Table A is set to 7 days, while for Table B it is set to 14 days. The user needs to restore data from 10 days ago. Which table can the user restore data from?
Options:
A. Table A
B. Table B
C. Both Table A and Table B
D. Neither Table A nor Table B
E. Only Table A, but it will be incomplete

Question #37

You are managing a Snowflake database with multiple tables, each having different Time Travel retention periods. The retention period for Table X is set to 30 days, and Table Y is set to 5 days. A user attempts to restore Table Y to a timestamp that is 7 days old. What will happen?
Options:
A. The restore will fail because the data for Table Y is not available for that timestamp.
B. The restore will succeed because Time Travel allows querying data within the retention period.
C. The data will be restored, but with some missing records.
D. The restoration will apply to both Table X and Table Y simultaneously.
E. The restore will succeed, and the user will be charged for the restoration.

Question #38

A Snowflake administrator wants to preserve data history for Table A for 90 days, but the default retention for other tables in the database is 30 days. How can the administrator configure this retention?
Options:
A. Set the retention period for Table A to 90 days while leaving the default retention as 30 days for other tables.
B. Set the default retention for the entire database to 90 days.
C. Use a clone of Table A with a custom retention period of 90 days.
D. Use Time Travel on a per-query basis to extend the retention period for Table A.
E. Set the retention period for all tables in the database to 90 days to preserve Table A for that duration.

Question #39

You are tasked with ensuring that a table's data in Snowflake is available for Time Travel for exactly 14 days. You set this retention on the table. However, the table's data is deleted 12 days later. What will be the result when you try to query the data 15 days after the deletion?
Options:
A. The query will succeed because Time Travel always allows querying up to the retention period.

B. The query will fail because the data has exceeded the retention period.
C. The data will be partially restored, but some rows may be missing.
D. The query will fail, and an error message will indicate the retention period has been exceeded.
E. Snowflake will automatically extend the retention period for one more day.

Question #40

A Snowflake user has two tables: Table A and Table B. Table A has a Time Travel retention period of 10 days, and Table B has a retention period of 5 days. After 7 days, the user deletes records from Table B and attempts to use Time Travel to restore records from both tables to a point 6 days ago. What will happen?

Options:

A. The restore will succeed for both tables because Time Travel allows querying within the retention period.
B. The restore will fail for Table B because its retention period is only 5 days.
C. The restore will succeed for Table A, but not for Table B.
D. The restore will fail for both tables.
E. The restore will succeed for Table A, but Table B will only have partial data restored.

Answers and Explanations:

Question #36:
Correct Answer: B
Explanation:
B is correct because Table B has a retention period of 14 days, which covers the 10-day period needed for restoring data. A is incorrect because Table A only has a 7-day retention period, which would not allow restoration from 10 days ago. C is incorrect because the user cannot restore data from both tables if their retention periods do not overlap with the required timestamp. D is incorrect because at least one table has data available for restoration.

Question #37:
Correct Answer: A
Explanation:
A is correct because Table Y's retention period is only 5 days, so restoring data from 7 days ago exceeds that retention period. B is incorrect because Time Travel only works within the defined retention period, and the requested timestamp is beyond the available window. C is incorrect because the data would not be available for restoration from that point. D is incorrect because Time Travel applies to each table individually, not simultaneously. E is incorrect because restoring data doesn't incur extra charges unless additional services are invoked.

Question #38:

Correct Answer: A
Explanation:
A is correct because Snowflake allows setting custom retention periods for individual tables while leaving the default retention for others. B is incorrect because changing the database-wide default retention would affect all tables, not just Table A. C is incorrect because clones

do not affect retention periods; they inherit the retention settings from the original table. D is incorrect because Time Travel cannot extend retention on a per-query basis. E is incorrect because setting the retention for all tables in the database to 90 days is unnecessary for this use case.

Question #39:
Correct Answer: B
Explanation:
B is correct because once the data exceeds the specified retention period of 14 days, it is no longer available for Time Travel. A is incorrect because the data would no longer be available for restoration. C is incorrect because no data can be restored after the retention period ends. D is correct but too specific; Time Travel won't allow a query if the retention period is exceeded, so an error will occur. E is incorrect because the retention period will not automatically extend.

Question #40:
Correct Answer: C
Explanation:
C is correct because the restore will succeed for Table A as it has a retention period of 10 days, but Table B's retention period of 5 days will not cover the requested 6-day-old data. A is incorrect because the restore will fail for Table B due to its shorter retention. B is correct for Table B but wrong because it implies both tables will fail. D is incorrect because restoration will succeed for Table A. E is incorrect because partial restoration is not how Time Travel functions; if the data is within the retention period, it is fully restored.

Question #41
A Snowflake user shares data from Table A with another account using a Data Share. The data shared includes records from the past 30 days. The recipient needs to restore data from 35 days ago using Time Travel. What will happen?
Options:
A. The data cannot be restored because the data share only provides access to the latest version of the table.
B. The recipient can restore the data from 35 days ago if the data retention period of the shared table allows it.
C. The data will be restored, but the recipient will need to request the data owner to extend the retention period.
D. The restoration will fail because Time Travel is not supported for shared data.
E. The data will be restored, but some records will be missing.

Question #42
A Snowflake Data Share is configured to allow a recipient to access data from Table A, which has a retention period of 14 days. If the data is updated frequently, how can the recipient ensure they can still query the historical data from more than 14 days ago?
Options:
A. The recipient can access data from the past 14 days, but no further.
B. The recipient should configure their own Time Travel retention for the shared table to access older data.
C. The data provider should extend the retention period of the shared table beyond 14 days.

D. The recipient can create a clone of the shared table to extend the retention period.
E. The recipient will be able to query the table indefinitely without any issues.

Question #43
A Snowflake user shares a table that has Time Travel retention set to 7 days. The recipient tries to access data from 9 days ago via the data share. What will be the outcome?
Options:
A. The recipient will be able to access the data from 9 days ago if the data was not modified during that time.
B. The recipient will receive an error, as the data exceeds the retention period of 7 days.
C. The recipient can only query the current version of the data, but cannot access the historical data.
D. The data share automatically extends the retention period for shared data.
E. The recipient can request the data provider to restore the historical data for them.

Question #44
A Snowflake user wants to share a table with a 30-day retention period with an external party. The external party needs access to Time Travel data from the last 60 days. How can the external party ensure access to the required data?
Options:
A. The external party can only access the data within the 30-day retention period.
B. The external party can request the data provider to extend the retention period for the shared table to 60 days.
C. The external party can create a clone of the shared table to extend its retention period.
D. The external party can use a different Snowflake account with a longer retention period to access the data.
E. The external party can use Time Travel to restore data indefinitely for any shared table.

Question #45
A Snowflake Data Share is set up to share data with multiple external accounts. One of the recipients needs to restore historical data from 10 days ago. The data provider has set the retention period for the shared table to 5 days. What should the recipient do?
Options:
A. The recipient should access the data share and query the current data.
B. The recipient should request the data provider to extend the retention period for their specific use case.
C. The recipient will not be able to access any historical data because it is beyond the retention period.
D. The recipient can use Time Travel to restore data from the previous 5 days.
E. The recipient can create a clone of the shared table to access the historical data.

Answers and Explanations:

Question #41:

Correct Answer: B
Explanation:
B is correct because the recipient can restore data from 35 days ago only if the data retention period for the shared table allows it.
A is incorrect because Data Shares allow the sharing of historical data if the retention period is sufficient.
C is incorrect because extending the retention period is only possible for the data provider.
D is incorrect because Time Travel is supported for shared data, depending on the retention configuration.
E is incorrect because if the data retention has expired, it cannot be restored.

Question #42:
Correct Answer: C
Explanation:
C is correct because the data provider can extend the retention period beyond 14 days for the shared table, ensuring the recipient can access older data.
A is incorrect because the recipient cannot access data beyond the 14-day retention unless the provider extends it.
B is incorrect because Time Travel retention cannot be modified by the recipient.
D is incorrect because cloning does not change the retention period for the shared table.
E is incorrect because there are limitations on Time Travel access depending on retention periods.

Question #43:
Correct Answer: B
Explanation:
B is correct because the recipient will receive an error if they try to access data that exceeds the 7-day retention period. A is incorrect because accessing data from 9 days ago exceeds the retention period.
C is incorrect because the recipient can only query the most recent version of the data without Time Travel access to historical data.
D is incorrect because Data Share does not automatically extend the retention period for shared data.
E is incorrect because the recipient cannot request the data provider to restore data beyond the retention period.

Question #44:
Correct Answer: B
Explanation:
B is correct because the external party can request the data provider to extend the retention period to 60 days.
A is incorrect because the external party can only access data within the 30-day retention period.
C is incorrect because cloning the table does not extend the retention period for shared data.
D is incorrect because the external party cannot use a different account with a longer retention period. E is incorrect because Time Travel does not extend indefinitely for shared tables.

Question #45:

Correct Answer: B
Explanation:
B is correct because the recipient needs to request the data provider to extend the retention period for the shared table. A is incorrect because the recipient cannot access any data older than the retention period.
C is incorrect because Time Travel allows accessing historical data only within the defined retention period.
D is incorrect because the recipient cannot restore data from a time beyond the retention period.
E is incorrect because cloning the shared table does not extend the retention period for historical data.

Question #46
You need to query historical data in Snowflake using Time Travel for a specific table, sales_data, to retrieve the sales amount for each region and calculate the cumulative total of sales per region, ordered by transaction_date, for a point in time 5 days ago. Which SQL query would achieve this?
Options:
A.
SELECT region, transaction_date, sales_amount,
    SUM(sales_amount) OVER (PARTITION BY region ORDER BY transaction_date) AS cumulative_sales
FROM sales_data
AT (TIMESTAMP => '5 days ago')
B.
SELECT region, transaction_date, sales_amount,
    SUM(sales_amount) OVER (PARTITION BY region ORDER BY transaction_date ROWS BETWEEN UNBOUNDED PRECEDING AND CURRENT ROW) AS cumulative_sales
FROM sales_data
AT (TIMESTAMP => '5 days ago')
C.
SELECT region, transaction_date, sales_amount,
    SUM(sales_amount) OVER (PARTITION BY region ORDER BY transaction_date ROWS BETWEEN CURRENT ROW AND UNBOUNDED FOLLOWING) AS cumulative_sales
FROM sales_data
AT (TIMESTAMP => '5 days ago')
D.
SELECT region, transaction_date, sales_amount,
    ROW_NUMBER() OVER (PARTITION BY region ORDER BY transaction_date) AS cumulative_sales
FROM sales_data
AT (TIMESTAMP => '5 days ago')

Question #47
A Snowflake user wants to query the employees table and calculate the running total of the salary column, partitioned by department, for a historical state 3 days ago. The results should

include the employee's name, department, salary, and the running total. Which SQL query should be used?

Options:

A.
```
SELECT employee_name, department, salary,
    SUM(salary) OVER (PARTITION BY department ORDER BY salary DESC ROWS BETWEEN UNBOUNDED PRECEDING AND CURRENT ROW) AS running_total
FROM employees
AT (TIMESTAMP => '3 days ago')
```

B.
```
SELECT employee_name, department, salary,
    SUM(salary) OVER (PARTITION BY department ORDER BY salary ROWS BETWEEN CURRENT ROW AND UNBOUNDED FOLLOWING) AS running_total
FROM employees
AT (TIMESTAMP => '3 days ago')
```

C.
```
SELECT employee_name, department, salary,
    SUM(salary) OVER (PARTITION BY department ORDER BY employee_name ROWS BETWEEN UNBOUNDED PRECEDING AND CURRENT ROW) AS running_total
FROM employees
AT (TIMESTAMP => '3 days ago')
```

D.
```
SELECT employee_name, department, salary,
    SUM(salary) OVER (PARTITION BY department ORDER BY employee_name ROWS BETWEEN CURRENT ROW AND UNBOUNDED FOLLOWING) AS running_total
FROM employees
AT (TIMESTAMP => '3 days ago')
```

Question #48

You need to analyze the historical state of a transactions table 10 days ago and calculate the difference in the transaction_amount between each row and the previous row within each customer group. Which SQL query would accomplish this?

Options:

A.
```
SELECT customer_id, transaction_date, transaction_amount,
    LAG(transaction_amount, 1) OVER (PARTITION BY customer_id ORDER BY transaction_date) AS previous_transaction_amount,
    transaction_amount - LAG(transaction_amount, 1) OVER (PARTITION BY customer_id ORDER BY transaction_date) AS amount_difference
FROM transactions
AT (TIMESTAMP => '10 days ago')
```

B.
```
SELECT customer_id, transaction_date, transaction_amount,
    LEAD(transaction_amount, 1) OVER (PARTITION BY customer_id ORDER BY transaction_date) AS next_transaction_amount,
    transaction_amount - LEAD(transaction_amount, 1) OVER (PARTITION BY customer_id ORDER BY transaction_date) AS amount_difference
FROM transactions
AT (TIMESTAMP => '10 days ago')
```

C.
```
SELECT customer_id, transaction_date, transaction_amount,
    FIRST_VALUE(transaction_amount) OVER (PARTITION BY customer_id ORDER BY
transaction_date) AS first_transaction_amount,
    transaction_amount - FIRST_VALUE(transaction_amount) OVER (PARTITION BY
customer_id ORDER BY transaction_date) AS amount_difference
FROM transactions
AT (TIMESTAMP => '10 days ago')
```
D.
```
SELECT customer_id, transaction_date, transaction_amount,
    RANK() OVER (PARTITION BY customer_id ORDER BY transaction_date) AS
transaction_rank
FROM transactions
AT (TIMESTAMP => '10 days ago')
```

Question #49

You want to retrieve the historical state of a orders table 15 days ago and calculate the total amount spent by each customer across all orders up to that date, using a rolling window of 7 days. Which query would you use?

Options: A.
```
SELECT customer_id, order_date, total_amount,
    SUM(total_amount) OVER (PARTITION BY customer_id ORDER BY order_date ROWS
BETWEEN 6 PRECEDING AND CURRENT ROW) AS rolling_total
FROM orders
AT (TIMESTAMP => '15 days ago')
```
B.
```
SELECT customer_id, order_date, total_amount,
    SUM(total_amount) OVER (PARTITION BY customer_id ORDER BY order_date ROWS
BETWEEN CURRENT ROW AND 6 FOLLOWING) AS rolling_total
FROM orders
AT (TIMESTAMP => '15 days ago')
```
C.
```
SELECT customer_id, order_date, total_amount,
    SUM(total_amount) OVER (PARTITION BY customer_id ORDER BY order_date ROWS
BETWEEN UNBOUNDED PRECEDING AND CURRENT ROW) AS rolling_total
FROM orders
AT (TIMESTAMP => '15 days ago')
```
D.
```
SELECT customer_id, order_date, total_amount,
    LAG(total_amount, 7) OVER (PARTITION BY customer_id ORDER BY order_date) AS
rolling_total
FROM orders
AT (TIMESTAMP => '15 days ago')
```

Question #50

A Snowflake user wants to analyze the historical data of the products table 7 days ago and calculate the rank of each product by its sales_amount for that day. Which query will achieve this?

Options: A.

```sql
SELECT product_id, product_name, sales_amount,
    RANK() OVER (PARTITION BY product_id ORDER BY sales_amount DESC) AS product_rank
FROM products
AT (TIMESTAMP => '7 days ago')
```
B.
```sql
SELECT product_id, product_name, sales_amount,
    RANK() OVER (PARTITION BY product_name ORDER BY sales_amount DESC) AS product_rank
FROM products
AT (TIMESTAMP => '7 days ago')
```
C.
```sql
SELECT product_id, product_name, sales_amount,
    DENSE_RANK() OVER (PARTITION BY product_id ORDER BY sales_amount DESC) AS product_rank
FROM products
AT (TIMESTAMP => '7 days ago')
```
D.
```sql
SELECT product_id, product_name, sales_amount,
    ROW_NUMBER() OVER (PARTITION BY product_id ORDER BY sales_amount DESC) AS product_rank
FROM products
AT (TIMESTAMP => '7 days ago')
```

Answers and Explanations:

Question #46:
Correct Answer: A, B
Explanation:
A is correct because it uses the standard windowing function with the SUM to calculate cumulative sales over each region, ordered by transaction_date.
B is also correct as it specifies the rows to include in the window using ROWS BETWEEN UNBOUNDED PRECEDING AND CURRENT ROW, ensuring a cumulative total up to the current row.
C is incorrect because it specifies the wrong direction for the window, using ROWS BETWEEN CURRENT ROW AND UNBOUNDED FOLLOWING.
D is incorrect as it uses ROW_NUMBER() instead of a cumulative sum.

Question #47:
Correct Answer: A, C
Explanation:
A is correct because it calculates the running total of salaries by partitioning the data by department and ordering by salary.
C is correct as it also uses UNBOUNDED PRECEDING to include all prior records in the running total calculation.
B is incorrect because ROWS BETWEEN CURRENT ROW AND UNBOUNDED FOLLOWING calculates a rolling window forward from the current row, which is not appropriate for a running total.
D is also incorrect because the running total should not be calculated from employee_name.

Question #48:
Correct Answer: A
Explanation:
A is correct because it uses the LAG() function to calculate the difference between the current transaction amount and the previous one.
B is incorrect as LEAD() looks at the next row rather than the previous one.
C is incorrect because FIRST_VALUE() returns the first value in the window, which is not relevant for calculating differences between consecutive rows.
D is incorrect because RANK() does not calculate differences between rows.

Question #49:
Correct Answer: A
Explanation:
A is correct because it calculates the rolling sum of total_amount over a 7-day window, partitioned by customer_id and ordered by order_date.
B is incorrect because it defines a forward window (6 FOLLOWING), which is not appropriate for a rolling total up to the current row.
C is incorrect because it calculates a cumulative sum from the beginning of the window, not a rolling sum.
D is incorrect as LAG() does not provide a rolling window sum.

Question #50:
Correct Answer: A, C
Explanation:
A is correct because it ranks the products within each product_id partition, ordered by sales_amount in descending order.
C is also correct because DENSE_RANK() ranks products while handling ties by assigning the same rank to products with equal sales_amount.
B is incorrect because it ranks by product_name, which is not relevant to the desired rank based on sales_amount.
D is incorrect because ROW_NUMBER() would not handle ties properly.

MICROPARTITIONS

Question #1:
A Snowflake data warehouse is set up to store large volumes of data in a table that automatically uses micropartitions. After loading data into the table, the performance of queries is not as expected. What could be the primary reason for the issue?
Options:
A. The data was not properly compressed when loaded into Snowflake.
B. Micropartitions are automatically created, but manual clustering keys need to be defined for optimal query performance.
C. Snowflake does not optimize data in micropartitions for read-heavy operations.
D. The table has no primary key, affecting the creation of micropartitions.

Question #2:
A table in Snowflake has a large volume of data, and you notice the data is spread across multiple micropartitions. What feature allows Snowflake to ensure efficient query execution by only scanning the relevant partitions?
Options:
A. Columnar storage
B. Automatic pruning based on metadata (min/max values in micropartitions)
C. Data sharding
D. Indexing on micropartitions

Question #3:
You have loaded data into Snowflake, but queries are still taking longer than expected despite the data being spread across micropartitions. What is a potential reason for this, considering the automatic partitioning mechanism?
Options:
A. Data within micropartitions is not sorted by column value, leading to inefficient queries.
B. Micropartitions have become too small, causing too many partitions to be scanned.
C. The micropartitions were created but have not yet been optimized for data retrieval.
D. Snowflake doesn't use micropartitions for large data sets; it only works with small data.

Question #4:

You are querying a Snowflake table that has been loaded with millions of rows. The performance is poor even though Snowflake uses micropartitioning. What should be done to improve performance based on Snowflake's handling of data storage?

Options:

A. Manually define clustering keys to optimize data storage in the table.
B. Increase the size of the warehouse to handle large queries.
C. Decrease the retention period for Time Travel to reduce the number of micropartitions.
D. Convert the table into a star schema for better performance.

Question #5:

A Snowflake table uses automatic micropartitioning, and the data has a variable distribution across partitions. How does Snowflake handle the creation and organization of these micropartitions?

Options:

A. Micropartitions are created manually by the user and optimized for query performance.
B. Micropartitions are organized automatically by Snowflake, based on the size of the data and metadata.
C. Snowflake requires users to specify a partitioning strategy for large tables to optimize performance.
D. Micropartitions are only used for small data sets; large data sets are managed by other mechanisms.

Answers and Explanations:

Question #1:
Correct Answer: B, A
Explanation:
B is correct because Snowflake uses automatic clustering of data based on how the data is distributed across micropartitions. However, defining manual clustering keys can improve performance for larger datasets.
A is correct because Snowflake automatically organizes data into micropartitions, but query performance may still benefit from clustering keys.
C is incorrect because Snowflake does optimize data in micropartitions for both storage and query performance.
D is incorrect because Snowflake does not require primary keys for partitioning, though primary keys may be used for data integrity.

Question #2:
Correct Answer: B
Explanation:
B is correct because Snowflake uses metadata, including the minimum and maximum values of each column, to determine which micropartitions are relevant for a query, resulting in automatic data pruning.
A is incorrect because columnar storage optimizes the storage format and retrieval of data, but it is not the primary mechanism for pruning micropartitions.
C is incorrect because sharding is a concept not directly applicable to Snowflake's automatic micropartitioning.

D is incorrect because Snowflake does not require traditional indexing on micropartitions to optimize queries; it uses automatic pruning and columnar storage instead.

Question #3:
Correct Answer: A
Explanation:
A is correct because Snowflake's automatic partitioning works best when data is sorted in a way that minimizes the number of partitions to scan. If data within micropartitions is not sorted, query performance may degrade.
B is incorrect because while micropartitions can be small, Snowflake's metadata pruning usually prevents unnecessary scanning.
C is incorrect because Snowflake automatically optimizes micropartitions for efficient queries after data loading.
D is incorrect because micropartitions work with both small and large datasets; the issue here is more likely related to query execution or clustering.

Question #4:
Correct Answer: A
Explanation:
A is correct because manual clustering keys can improve query performance by organizing data in a way that minimizes the need for scanning large amounts of irrelevant data across micropartitions.
B is incorrect because merely increasing the warehouse size may improve compute resources but does not address the root cause of inefficient query execution.
C is incorrect because decreasing the retention period for Time Travel will not affect how data is partitioned and queried.
D is incorrect because converting the table to a star schema would require restructuring the data and is not directly related to optimizing micropartitions.

Question #5:
Correct Answer: B
Explanation:
B is correct because Snowflake automatically organizes data into micropartitions based on size and metadata. This helps to optimize query performance without the need for user intervention.
A is incorrect because micropartitions are not manually created by users; they are managed by Snowflake.
C is incorrect because Snowflake automatically handles partitioning; users don't need to define a partitioning strategy for large tables.
D is incorrect because micropartitions are specifically designed to handle large datasets efficiently and are used by Snowflake for both small and large datasets.

Question #6:
You are analyzing query performance in Snowflake and notice that the queries are performing slower than expected, even though you are using micropartitions. What could be the reason, considering Snowflake's columnar storage format?
Options:
A. The data is not properly compressed within the micropartitions.
B. The queries are scanning unnecessary columns due to the lack of column pruning.

C. The micropartitions are too large, and query performance suffers because Snowflake has to scan more data.
D. Snowflake does not optimize for query performance in columnar storage.

Question #7:
You are working with a large table in Snowflake, and your query performance is impacted by how data is being stored. Which feature of Snowflake's columnar storage should be optimized to ensure better query performance?
Options:
A. Ensuring that the data is partitioned by row to reduce data scanning.
B. Organizing data in a way that minimizes the need for full table scans by utilizing columnar storage and appropriate metadata.
C. Reducing the number of columns in the table to minimize scanning.
D. Ensuring that the table uses a star schema for faster querying.

Question #8:
A user reports slow performance on a Snowflake query that reads only a few columns from a large table. How can Snowflake's columnar storage help improve query performance for this workload?
Options:
A. Snowflake only reads the necessary columns from the micropartition, reducing the amount of data scanned.
B. Snowflake indexes the columns, speeding up access to them.
C. Snowflake reads all columns in the table to optimize query performance.
D. Snowflake stores all data as row-based storage to avoid columnar scanning.

Question #9:
You have noticed that some queries in Snowflake are scanning unnecessary columns from a large table, which impacts performance. How can you improve query performance with columnar storage?
Options:
A. Create a smaller, denormalized table with only the columns that are needed for frequent queries.
B. Ensure the queries are designed to select only the necessary columns, allowing Snowflake to use columnar storage more effectively.
C. Create indexes on the columns that are frequently used.
D. Use materialized views to store precomputed results.

Question #10:
A large dataset is loaded into Snowflake, and the data is stored in micropartitions. You want to optimize query performance by ensuring efficient use of Snowflake's columnar storage. Which of the following actions should you take?
Options:
A. Add clustering keys to the table to improve data access patterns within micropartitions.
B. Split the table into multiple smaller tables based on the column distribution.
C. Avoid using clustering keys, as they are unnecessary in Snowflake's columnar storage.
D. Continuously optimize the warehouse size to ensure better query performance.

Answers and Explanations:

Question #6:
Correct Answer: B
Explanation:
B is correct because Snowflake uses columnar storage, which allows it to read only the necessary columns during a query. If unnecessary columns are being scanned, it could be due to inefficient query design or missing column pruning.
A is incorrect because data compression within micropartitions does not directly impact query performance unless data is excessively uncompressed, which is rare in Snowflake.
C is incorrect because while large micropartitions can affect performance, Snowflake's automatic pruning ensures only the relevant partitions are scanned, even if they are large.
D is incorrect because Snowflake optimizes query performance even with columnar storage, and it is unlikely that this is the main cause of the issue.

Question #7:
Correct Answer: B
Explanation:
B is correct because Snowflake's columnar storage format allows data to be stored in a way that optimizes query performance by reducing full table scans. Proper use of metadata for column pruning also improves performance.
A is incorrect because Snowflake's storage does not rely on partitioning by row; partitioning is done at the micropartition level.
C is incorrect because reducing the number of columns might reduce the amount of data scanned, but it's more efficient to only scan relevant columns via column pruning.
D is incorrect because while a star schema may improve some types of queries, it is not the primary method for optimizing columnar storage.

Question #8:
Correct Answer: A
Explanation:
A is correct because Snowflake's columnar storage format ensures that only the necessary columns are read, which reduces the amount of data scanned and improves query performance.
B is incorrect because Snowflake does not index columns for query speed. It relies on metadata and columnar storage for performance.
C is incorrect because Snowflake uses columnar storage and reads only the necessary columns for queries, not all columns.
D is incorrect because Snowflake uses columnar storage by default, not row-based storage, to optimize query performance.

Question #9:
Correct Answer: B
Explanation:
B is correct because ensuring that queries select only the necessary columns allows Snowflake to take full advantage of columnar storage, reducing the amount of data that needs to be scanned and improving query performance.
A is incorrect because creating a smaller, denormalized table can improve performance in

some cases but is not always necessary when using columnar storage effectively.
C is incorrect because Snowflake does not require traditional indexing for columnar storage optimization.
D is incorrect because materialized views may improve performance for some queries, but they are not specifically tied to optimizing columnar storage.

Question #10:
Correct Answer: A
Explanation:
A is correct because clustering keys help Snowflake optimize data access patterns and improve performance, especially for large datasets stored in micropartitions.
B is incorrect because splitting the table into smaller tables may reduce storage overhead, but it will not optimize columnar storage or improve query performance.
C is incorrect because clustering keys are beneficial in Snowflake's architecture and improve query performance by organizing the data efficiently.
D is incorrect because continuously optimizing warehouse size is useful for compute performance, but it does not directly optimize columnar storage or query performance.

Question #11:
You are running a query in Snowflake that should only retrieve specific records from a large table. However, you notice that it is scanning more data than necessary. How can Snowflake improve this query performance through its micropartitioning and pruning mechanism?
Options:
A. Snowflake reads all the data from the table and then filters out the irrelevant records during query execution.
B. Snowflake utilizes metadata associated with micropartitions to prune irrelevant partitions before performing the query.
C. Snowflake scans all partitions but only reads the columns needed by the query.
D. Snowflake automatically indexes the table to ensure that only relevant data is scanned.

Question #12:
You have a large table in Snowflake and want to ensure that your queries run as efficiently as possible by minimizing the data that needs to be scanned. Which of the following actions will help Snowflake achieve efficient data pruning using micropartitions?
Options:
A. Create partitioning keys based on frequently queried columns.
B. Ensure that the table uses a star schema to optimize query performance.
C. Create clustering keys on columns with high cardinality to help Snowflake prune irrelevant micropartitions.
D. Regularly vacuum the table to ensure efficient data pruning.

Question #13:
You have a query that is performing poorly due to scanning a large number of irrelevant rows. Which feature of Snowflake's micropartitioning system helps improve performance in this case?
Options:
A. The ability to automatically perform data pruning based on the metadata associated with micropartitions, such as min and max values.

B. Snowflake only stores column data that is relevant to the query being executed.
C. Snowflake uses an indexing mechanism to ensure only relevant partitions are read.
D. Micropartitions store data by row, making it easier to perform pruning.

Question #14:
Your Snowflake database contains large tables, and you're looking to improve performance by limiting the amount of data that needs to be scanned during queries. How does Snowflake achieve this using its micropartitioning system?
Options:
A. By storing data in smaller partitions based on time intervals, making it easier to filter relevant data.
B. By using metadata such as the minimum and maximum values for columns, which allows Snowflake to prune irrelevant micropartitions.
C. By using clustering keys to organize the data physically, which helps Snowflake skip irrelevant partitions.
D. By creating indexes on columns to optimize query performance and reduce the data scanned.

Question #15:
You are working with a table that has several large micropartitions. Your query performance is suffering, and you want to optimize it by reducing the amount of data that needs to be scanned. How can Snowflake's data pruning mechanism help?
Options:
A. Snowflake will automatically scan all micropartitions but only read the relevant columns for the query.
B. Snowflake uses the metadata for each micropartition to automatically prune irrelevant partitions based on the query's conditions.
C. Snowflake requires the use of an index to perform data pruning effectively.
D. Snowflake will automatically reorganize micropartitions to ensure that all data is evenly distributed across partitions.

Answers and Explanations:

Question #11:
Correct Answer: B
Explanation:
B is correct because Snowflake uses metadata (such as min and max values for each column) associated with micropartitions to enable data pruning. This means Snowflake only scans relevant micropartitions, significantly reducing the amount of data processed.
A is incorrect because Snowflake does not read all data first and filter it later; it prunes irrelevant partitions from the start.
C is incorrect because Snowflake does not scan all partitions; it prunes irrelevant ones based on metadata.
D is incorrect because Snowflake does not use traditional indexing to filter partitions, but instead relies on its metadata pruning mechanism.

Question #12:
Correct Answer: C
Explanation:
C is correct because creating clustering keys on columns with high cardinality can improve data pruning in Snowflake, making it more efficient when scanning relevant micropartitions.
A is incorrect because partitioning keys are typically not directly used in Snowflake's pruning mechanism.
B is incorrect because the star schema does not specifically impact Snowflake's ability to prune irrelevant data during queries.
D is incorrect because Snowflake does not require manual vacuuming for pruning; it automatically handles pruning based on metadata.

Question #13:
Correct Answer: A
Explanation:
A is correct because Snowflake uses metadata, such as min and max values, to automatically prune irrelevant micropartitions during query execution, which reduces the amount of data scanned.
B is incorrect because Snowflake stores data in columnar format, not based on query relevance.
C is incorrect because Snowflake does not use traditional indexes to filter partitions.
D is incorrect because Snowflake stores data in columnar format, not row-based format, and uses metadata pruning for performance optimization.

Question #14:
Correct Answer: B
Explanation:
B is correct because Snowflake uses metadata, such as the minimum and maximum values for each column, to prune irrelevant micropartitions, improving query performance.
A is incorrect because Snowflake does not rely on time-based partitioning to achieve data pruning.
C is incorrect because clustering keys help optimize data storage and query performance but are not directly related to pruning irrelevant micropartitions.
D is incorrect because Snowflake does not use traditional indexes; pruning is handled by metadata.

Question #15:
Correct Answer: B
Explanation:
B is correct because Snowflake uses the metadata for each micropartition to automatically prune irrelevant partitions based on query conditions. This reduces the amount of data that needs to be scanned.
A is incorrect because Snowflake does not scan all micropartitions first; it prunes irrelevant ones upfront using metadata.
C is incorrect because Snowflake does not require indexes for pruning; it relies on metadata for efficient pruning.
D is incorrect because Snowflake does not automatically reorganize micropartitions; it uses metadata to prune unnecessary data.

Question #16:
You have a large dataset in Snowflake that is being automatically distributed across micropartitions. You notice that query performance is not as optimal as expected, and some queries are slower than usual. Which of the following features of Snowflake's automatic clustering mechanism can help improve the situation?
Options:
A. Snowflake automatically reorganizes data within micropartitions based on predefined indexing strategies.
B. Snowflake automatically redistributes data across micropartitions to ensure that frequently queried data is optimized for performance.
C. Snowflake uses automatic clustering to reorder data within micropartitions, optimizing queries that filter on specific columns.
D. Snowflake requires manual clustering to reorder data within micropartitions for better performance.

Question #17:
You are working with a large table in Snowflake that is constantly growing, and you want to ensure that its data is optimally organized for query performance without having to manage clustering manually. Which Snowflake feature helps with this?
Options:
A. Automatic clustering automatically reorders data within micropartitions based on query patterns.
B. You need to create manual clustering keys for Snowflake to reorder data based on query performance.
C. Snowflake automatically partitions data into separate tables based on size, optimizing query performance.
D. Snowflake automatically creates indexes on frequently queried columns to improve query performance.

Question #18:
You notice that performance on a Snowflake table has degraded over time. Upon reviewing, you realize that the table has grown large and the data distribution could be causing the performance issues. Which feature of Snowflake would help improve the organization of data in this table without manual intervention?
Options:
A. Automatic clustering, which helps to reorder data within micropartitions based on data access patterns.
B. Automatic indexing, which creates indexes on frequently queried columns to boost performance.
C. Partitioning data manually into smaller tables for better query performance.
D. Micropartitions automatically compressed to improve storage efficiency.

Question #19:
You have recently added a large amount of data to a Snowflake table, and you want to ensure that future queries are optimized. How can Snowflake automatically improve the organization of this new data without requiring manual clustering or partitioning?

Options:
A. Snowflake automatically clusters the new data within existing micropartitions based on columnar usage patterns.
B. Snowflake automatically indexes the new data to optimize query performance.
C. Snowflake requires you to define clustering keys to automatically optimize data.
D. Snowflake partitions the new data into separate storage locations for optimized query access.

Question #20:
You are managing a Snowflake table with a large amount of data, and you are concerned about its long-term performance as the dataset grows. What does Snowflake's automatic clustering feature do to help ensure data is stored and queried efficiently?
Options:
A. It automatically reorganizes data within micropartitions based on specific query patterns, ensuring better performance for common queries.
B. It manually partitions the data into smaller, more manageable chunks for improved performance.
C. It requires users to define clustering keys to improve query performance over time.
D. It compresses the data to reduce storage requirements.

Answers and Explanations:

Question #16:
Correct Answer: C
Explanation:
C is correct because Snowflake's automatic clustering feature reorders data within micropartitions based on query patterns, which helps optimize query performance.
A is incorrect because Snowflake does not rely on predefined indexing strategies.
B is incorrect because Snowflake doesn't redistribute data to optimize queries based on frequency; instead, it automatically reorders data.
D is incorrect because Snowflake handles data clustering automatically, not manually.

Question #17:
Correct Answer: A
Explanation:
A is correct because automatic clustering ensures that data is reordered within micropartitions based on how it is queried, helping improve performance over time without manual intervention.
B is incorrect because Snowflake's automatic clustering doesn't require manual clustering keys; it's done automatically.
C is incorrect because Snowflake does not partition data into separate tables; it distributes data across micropartitions for storage optimization.
D is incorrect because Snowflake does not create indexes automatically but uses clustering to optimize performance.

Question #18:
Correct Answer: A

Explanation:
A is correct because Snowflake's automatic clustering feature reorders data in micropartitions based on data access patterns, which helps improve performance without requiring manual intervention.
B is incorrect because Snowflake doesn't automatically create indexes; it uses clustering for performance optimization.
C is incorrect because manual partitioning is not necessary with Snowflake's automatic clustering.
D is incorrect because Snowflake's micropartitions are already compressed to optimize storage.

Question #19:
Correct Answer: A
Explanation:
A is correct because Snowflake automatically clusters new data within micropartitions based on usage patterns, ensuring better performance for future queries.
B is incorrect because Snowflake doesn't automatically index new data; it uses clustering for performance optimization.
C is incorrect because Snowflake handles clustering automatically and does not require users to define clustering keys.
D is incorrect because Snowflake does not partition new data into separate storage locations.

Question #20:
Correct Answer: A
Explanation:
A is correct because Snowflake's automatic clustering feature reorganizes data within micropartitions based on query patterns, helping to ensure efficient data storage and query performance.
B is incorrect because Snowflake does not partition data manually; it distributes and clusters data automatically.
C is incorrect because Snowflake automatically handles clustering without requiring users to define clustering keys.
D is incorrect because Snowflake uses automatic clustering to optimize query performance, not compression alone.

Question #21:
You are tasked with querying historical data from a table in Snowflake. You want to retrieve data from 7 days ago without restoring a backup. How does Snowflake's Time Travel feature leverage micropartitions to enable this?
Options:
A. Snowflake stores historical versions of data within the same micropartitions, allowing you to access data at any point within the retention period.
B. Snowflake stores historical versions in a separate table that is linked to the original table.
C. Snowflake stores data versions in a global index, making querying historical data faster.
D. Snowflake creates new micropartitions every time data is updated, without retaining past versions for Time Travel.

Question #22:
A user attempts to perform a query on historical data in Snowflake using Time Travel but encounters an error stating that the data is no longer available. What is the most likely reason for this error?

Options:

A. The data was deleted after the Time Travel retention period expired.
B. The user does not have the correct privileges to access historical data.
C. Snowflake no longer supports Time Travel for micropartitions.
D. The query was executed on a table that does not support Time Travel.

Question #23:
You are conducting an audit on a Snowflake table and need to retrieve data from 14 days ago. How can Snowflake's Time Travel feature assist in this situation, and how does it work with micropartitions?

Options:

A. Snowflake automatically archives all data versions in external storage, which can be accessed during Time Travel.
B. Snowflake keeps historical versions of the data within micropartitions and allows you to query them as long as they are within the retention period.
C. Snowflake performs a full restore of the table's historical state to enable Time Travel queries.
D. Snowflake only retains the latest version of the data within each micropartition, so historical queries are not supported.

Question #24:
You are restoring data to a previous state in Snowflake using Time Travel. How does Snowflake handle micropartitions in this case to ensure data consistency?

Options:

A. Snowflake rolls back the micropartitions to their state at the specified point in time, effectively restoring the table to the desired version.
B. Snowflake retrieves historical data from an external data warehouse and loads it into the table.
C. Snowflake rewrites the entire table to a new micropartition to maintain version consistency.
D. Snowflake automatically purges outdated micropartitions and creates new ones with the historical data.

Question #25:
You need to use Time Travel in Snowflake to query data as of a specific point in time within the past 30 days. Which of the following best describes how Snowflake utilizes micropartitions for Time Travel?

Options:

A. Snowflake stores all versions of data within the same micropartition, which can be accessed during the retention period.
B. Snowflake stores versions of data in separate micropartitions for each day, and you can query the data within each day's partition.
C. Snowflake only stores one version of each record within a micropartition and removes old data when Time Travel is used.

D. Snowflake maintains a snapshot of the data at each query, which is stored separately from the original micropartition.

Answers and Explanations:

Question #21:
Correct Answer: A
Explanation:
A is correct because Snowflake stores historical versions of data within the same micropartitions, allowing users to query data at any point within the retention period.
B is incorrect because historical data is not stored in a separate table but within the same micropartitions.
C is incorrect because Snowflake does not use global indexes for Time Travel queries.
D is incorrect because Snowflake retains past versions of data in micropartitions, making Time Travel possible.

Question #22:
Correct Answer: A
Explanation:
A is correct because the most likely cause of the error is that the data has been deleted after the Time Travel retention period expired, which is typically 1-90 days depending on the account settings.
B is incorrect because Time Travel access is available to users with the correct privileges.
C is incorrect because Snowflake continues to support Time Travel for micropartitions.
D is incorrect because all Snowflake tables support Time Travel, but retention limits apply.

Question #23:
Correct Answer: B
Explanation:
B is correct because Snowflake keeps historical versions of the data within micropartitions, which can be accessed as long as the data is within the retention period.
A is incorrect because Snowflake does not archive data externally for Time Travel; it is stored internally.
C is incorrect because Time Travel does not require a full restore; it allows querying historical data as it existed at a specific point in time.
D is incorrect because Snowflake retains multiple versions of data in the same micropartition, not just the latest.

Question #24:
Correct Answer: A
Explanation:
A is correct because when using Time Travel, Snowflake rolls back the micropartitions to their state at the specified point in time, ensuring data consistency and restoring the table to the desired version.
B is incorrect because Snowflake does not retrieve historical data from an external data warehouse.
C is incorrect because Snowflake does not rewrite the entire table to a new micropartition; it

restores historical versions within the existing micropartitions.

D is incorrect because Snowflake does not purge micropartitions during Time Travel; it allows querying historical data within the existing partitions.

Question #25:
Correct Answer: A
Explanation:
A is correct because Snowflake stores all versions of data within the same micropartition, which can be accessed during the retention period via Time Travel.

B is incorrect because Snowflake does not store versions of data in separate partitions per day.

C is incorrect because Snowflake retains multiple versions of data within each micropartition during Time Travel.

D is incorrect because Snowflake does not create separate snapshots for each query; the historical versions are stored within the same micropartitions.

DATA MODELING

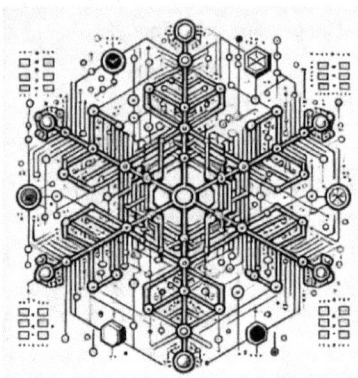

Question #1:
A retail company ingests product catalog data from multiple sources in JSON and Parquet formats. Analysts need to query the data to find products with specific attributes. How should the data be ingested and stored in Snowflake to maintain compatibility and efficient querying?
Options:
A. Use a VARIANT column for both JSON and Parquet.
B. Convert all JSON to Parquet before ingestion.
C. Store JSON and Parquet data in separate tables.
D. Use a structured schema for both formats.
E. Use semi-structured external tables for JSON and Parquet.

Question #2:
Your data pipeline ingests Avro-formatted event logs into Snowflake daily. The logs contain nested data structures, and the analytics team requires flattened data for better reporting. What steps should you take to ensure efficient loading and querying of these logs?
Options:
A. Store the raw Avro logs in a VARIANT column and use FLATTEN during queries.
B. Convert the Avro logs to CSV and load them into structured tables.
C. Use Snowflake's native Avro data support to ingest the logs into a VARIANT column.
D. Flatten the nested structure during the ingestion process into structured tables.
E. Use schema inference to convert Avro logs to JSON before loading into Snowflake.

Question #3:
An IoT application sends sensor readings as JSON payloads with varying structures. How would you leverage Snowflake's VARIANT column type to store this data, ensuring flexibility and scalability for queries?
Options:
A. Flatten the JSON data and store it in structured columns.
B. Store the entire payload in a VARIANT column.
C. Convert the JSON to CSV before storing.
D. Store the payloads in separate tables based on their structure.
E. Use external tables to store the JSON data.

Question #4:
You have a VARIANT column storing customer activity logs in a nested JSON format. The analytics team needs to query specific fields, such as "event_type" and "timestamp," for a weekly report. What is the best way to optimize this process?
Options:
A. Use FLATTEN in every query to extract specific fields from the VARIANT column.
B. Create a materialized view to pre-extract and store frequently queried fields.
C. Normalize the JSON data into structured tables before querying.
D. Store the data in separate tables for each field.
E. Use schema evolution to adjust fields dynamically.

Question #5:
A data engineering team receives unstructured JSON files daily, which contain inconsistent fields. They need to load this data into Snowflake without predefined schemas for ad-hoc exploration. How can the schema-on-read feature of Snowflake simplify this workflow?
Options:
A. Use a VARIANT column to store the JSON data.
B. Predefine schemas based on expected fields in JSON files.
C. Use external tables for JSON files with schema auto-detection.
D. Convert the JSON files to Parquet before loading into Snowflake.
E. Utilize Snowflake's auto-ingestion feature with flexible schema support.

Answers
Question #1
Correct Answer: A, C
Explanation:
A is correct because Snowflake's VARIANT column is designed to store semi-structured data like JSON and Parquet, allowing for compatibility and efficient querying.
C is correct because separating JSON and Parquet into different tables can help optimize queries and simplify data management.
B is incorrect because converting all JSON to Parquet could result in loss of flexibility for downstream processing.
D is incorrect because structured schemas are not ideal for semi-structured data.
E is incorrect because external tables are less efficient for querying than native Snowflake storage in this scenario.

Question #2
Correct Answer: A, C
Explanation:
A is correct because storing raw Avro logs in a VARIANT column and flattening the data during queries provides flexibility and preserves the original structure.
C is correct because Snowflake natively supports Avro format and can efficiently ingest nested data into VARIANT columns.
B is incorrect because converting to CSV could lose important hierarchical relationships in the data.
D is incorrect because flattening during ingestion removes flexibility for querying the original nested structure.
E is incorrect because schema inference for Avro is unnecessary with Snowflake's built-in Avro support.

Question #3
Correct Answer: B
Explanation:
B is correct because storing the JSON payloads in a VARIANT column provides flexibility to handle varying structures and ensures scalability for future queries.
A is incorrect because flattening the data before storage reduces flexibility for varying structures.
C is incorrect because converting JSON to CSV can lose important hierarchical information.
D is incorrect because storing payloads in separate tables creates unnecessary complexity.
E is incorrect because external tables are not required for this use case and could complicate querying.

Question #4
Correct Answer: B, C
Explanation:
B is correct because materialized views can optimize the querying of frequently accessed fields by precomputing and storing the results.
C is correct because normalizing JSON data into structured tables improves query performance for specific fields.
A is incorrect because using FLATTEN in every query is inefficient for repetitive access patterns.
D is incorrect because separating data into multiple tables can lead to redundancy and complex joins.
E is incorrect because schema evolution is not applicable to optimize querying existing fields.

Question #5
Correct Answer: A, C
Explanation:
A is correct because VARIANT columns in Snowflake support schema-on-read, enabling the storage of unstructured JSON data for ad-hoc exploration.
C is correct because external tables with schema auto-detection simplify data loading for files with inconsistent fields.
B is incorrect because predefined schemas are not necessary for schema-on-read functionality.
D is incorrect because converting JSON to Parquet removes the flexibility of querying JSON's hierarchical structure.
E is incorrect because schema auto-detection is part of external tables, not Snowflake's standard ingestion pipeline.

Question #6
Your organization ingests event logs in JSON, where fields like click_event and page_view vary across different data sources. The team wants to build exploratory dashboards with minimal preprocessing. How does Snowflake's **schema-on-read** capability assist in this scenario?
A. By automatically converting JSON fields into relational columns during ingestion.
B. By allowing raw JSON data to be queried directly without prior transformation.
C. By providing automatic JSON validation at the time of storage.

D. By supporting integration with third-party ETL tools for preprocessing.
E. By requiring predefined schema definitions for all incoming JSON fields.

Question #7
A VARIANT column in Snowflake stores nested JSON data representing customer orders. Each order contains an array of items, including their prices and quantities. How would you use the **FLATTEN** function to extract these items for analysis?
A. Flatten the VARIANT column to break nested structures into a relational format.
B. Use the FLATTEN function to create a duplicate copy of the VARIANT column.
C. Use FLATTEN to normalize the JSON data into separate Snowflake tables.
D. Apply FLATTEN to transform arrays into individual rows for querying.
E. Combine FLATTEN with JOIN to query arrays across multiple tables.

Question #8
An e-commerce database has a table with a VARIANT column storing JSON logs. The JSON includes nested fields like user_info and session_data. How can the **FLATTEN** function help transform these logs for visualization in a BI tool?
A. By converting the nested JSON into a tabular format for querying.
B. By extracting key-value pairs from the JSON and creating columns.
C. By splitting the JSON logs into separate Snowflake tables for BI use.
D. By dynamically creating views based on JSON content.
E. By enriching the JSON logs with additional metadata.

Question #9
A sales team needs to run highly selective queries on a Snowflake table containing billions of rows. Each query searches for specific customer IDs or transaction dates. How can enabling the **Search Optimization Service** improve query performance?
A. By clustering data in micro-partitions for faster access.
B. By creating optimized indexes on high-cardinality columns.
C. By enabling automatic re-clustering on selective query columns.
D. By precomputing results for common queries.
E. By partitioning the data physically by transaction date.

Question #10
Your organization maintains a Snowflake table with semi-structured data containing high-cardinality fields. The queries on this table frequently time out due to slow scans. How would the **Search Optimization Service** address this issue?
A. By indexing frequently queried fields for faster lookups.
B. By automatically compressing data to reduce scan times.
C. By reducing query execution overhead through caching.
D. By improving query performance on selective conditions with indexed access.
E. By creating query-specific partitions for optimized reads.

Answers and Explanations
Question #6:
Correct Answer: B
Explanation:
B is correct because Snowflake's schema-on-read capability allows teams to ingest raw JSON data and query it using SQL without requiring preprocessing or schema definition upfront. This

flexibility is ideal for exploratory analysis and dashboards.
A is incorrect because Snowflake doesn't automatically convert JSON into relational columns during ingestion.
C is incorrect because while JSON is validated syntactically, this isn't relevant to schema-on-read capabilities.
D is incorrect because ETL tools aren't required due to schema-on-read flexibility.
E is incorrect because Snowflake doesn't require a predefined schema for semi-structured data.

Question #7:
Correct Answer: A, D
Explanation:
A and D are correct because the FLATTEN function converts nested structures, such as arrays, in a VARIANT column into rows for easier querying, allowing for analysis of array elements.
B is incorrect because FLATTEN doesn't create duplicates of columns.
C is incorrect because it doesn't normalize data into separate tables but transforms nested structures within a table.
E is incorrect because FLATTEN alone doesn't enable cross-table joins.

Question #8:
Correct Answer: A
Explanation:
A is correct because the FLATTEN function extracts and transforms nested JSON fields into a relational tabular format, making the data suitable for visualization in BI tools.
B is incorrect because while FLATTEN can extract key-value pairs, it primarily transforms nested structures.
C is incorrect because it doesn't split data into separate tables but flattens structures within a table.
D is incorrect because FLATTEN doesn't dynamically create views.
E is incorrect because it doesn't add metadata to the JSON logs.

Question #9:
Correct Answer: A, C
Explanation:
A and C are correct because the Search Optimization Service creates optimized structures, allowing highly selective queries to bypass full scans and directly access relevant micro-partitions.
B is incorrect because Snowflake doesn't use traditional indexes.
D is incorrect because precomputing results isn't part of Search Optimization.
E is incorrect because Snowflake doesn't physically partition data; it uses virtual clustering.

Question #10:
Correct Answer: A, D
Explanation:
A and D are correct because the Search Optimization Service creates indexing-like structures that allow Snowflake to optimize performance for queries with selective filters on high-cardinality fields.
B is incorrect because data compression is standard but unrelated to Search Optimization.

C is incorrect because caching doesn't directly address query scan issues.
E is incorrect because query-specific partitions aren't part of Snowflake's architecture.

Question ##11:
A large Snowflake table containing website analytics data has billions of rows. The queries often filter by region and date. How would defining a manual clustering key improve query performance for such filters?
A) It increases storage usage by reorganizing data.
B) It optimizes data storage by grouping rows with similar values in a single micropartition.
C) It ensures that queries on other columns are automatically optimized.
D) It reduces the need for Time Travel functionality.
E) It makes it impossible to add new rows efficiently.

Question ##12:
A financial organization stores transaction data in a Snowflake table. Queries filtering by account_id and transaction_date are slow. How can manual clustering keys be applied to optimize these queries?
A) By clustering the table with account_id, transaction_date to ensure relevant data is grouped together in micropartitions.
B) By adding a new virtual column combining account_id and transaction_date and clustering on it.
C) By clustering the table with transaction_date, account_id for better query flexibility.
D) By removing clustering entirely and relying on Snowflake's automatic partitioning.
E) By enabling automatic clustering to handle all queries efficiently.

Question ##13:
A business analyst needs to run a query to analyze historical versions of a Snowflake table as of a specific date. How do micropartition snapshots enable this without duplicating data?
A) By storing previous versions of data within micropartitions and enabling Time Travel.
B) By creating separate physical tables for each historical version.
C) By storing historical data in a dedicated staging area.
D) By using clustering keys to retain old data structures.
E) By archiving data to external storage automatically.

Question ##14:
You accidentally deleted rows from a critical table in Snowflake. Explain how the micropartition snapshots feature can be used to recover the data without restoring from a backup.
A) By querying the table as of a previous time using the AT clause in a SQL query.
B) By restoring the table from external storage.
C) By cloning the table as of a historical timestamp using Time Travel.
D) By enabling micropartition snapshots retroactively.
E) By applying schema changes to rebuild the deleted rows.

Question ##15:
Your team maintains a permanent Snowflake table with Time Travel enabled for 7 days. A teammate accidentally overwrites some records. How can you recover the overwritten data using Snowflake features?

A) Use the UNDELETE command to restore the overwritten records directly.
B) Query the table using the AT clause to retrieve data before the overwrite.
C) Clone the table as of the timestamp before the overwrite occurred.
D) Restore the table from Snowflake's backup service.
E) Use micropartition snapshots to undo changes incrementally.

Answers and Explanations

Question #11:
Correct Answer: B
Explanation:
B is correct because manual clustering improves performance by organizing data in micropartitions to optimize queries on frequently filtered columns (such as region and date).
A is incorrect because while clustering can impact storage slightly, its main benefit is query performance.
C is incorrect because clustering does not automatically optimize all columns, only those specified in the key.
D is incorrect because clustering and Time Travel are independent features.
E is incorrect because new rows are handled efficiently by Snowflake even with clustering keys.

Question #12:
Correct Answer: A
Explanation:
A is correct because clustering by account_id and transaction_date groups related data, improving query performance.
B is incorrect because while adding a virtual column is possible, clustering directly on existing columns is more efficient.
C is incorrect because the order of clustering keys matters, and frequent filters should be prioritized first.
D is incorrect because removing clustering can degrade query performance for specific use cases.
E is incorrect because automatic clustering is useful but not a substitute for effective manual clustering.

Question #13:
Correct Answer: A
Explanation:
A is correct because micropartition snapshots enable Time Travel by retaining older versions of data within the same partition structure.
B is incorrect because Snowflake does not require creating separate tables for historical data.
C is incorrect because historical data is retained within the table, not moved to a staging area.
D is incorrect because clustering keys are unrelated to historical data retention.
E is incorrect because archiving data externally is not part of micropartition snapshots.

Question #14:
Correct Answer: A, C
Explanation:

A and C are correct because you can query the table using the AT clause for a specific timestamp or clone the table as of that timestamp, both leveraging Time Travel.
B is incorrect because Snowflake does not rely on external storage for recovery.
D is incorrect because micropartition snapshots are automatic and cannot be retroactively enabled.
E is incorrect because schema changes cannot recover data.

Question #15:
Correct Answer: B, C
Explanation:
B and C are correct because querying the table AT a previous timestamp or cloning it as of a specific time allows data recovery using Time Travel.
A is incorrect because Snowflake does not support an UNDELETE command.
D is incorrect because Snowflake does not provide direct "backup" services; it uses Time Travel for recovery.
E is incorrect because micropartition snapshots do not undo changes but provide a historical view for queries.

Question #16:
A data governance audit requires analyzing changes to a table over the past week. How does the Time Travel feature of permanent tables assist in fulfilling this requirement?
Select one or two answers:
A. Time Travel allows querying historical data without restoring backups.
B. Time Travel supports analysis by maintaining snapshots of the table for a configurable retention period.
C. Time Travel automatically replicates data changes to ensure availability for audits.
D. Time Travel eliminates the need for change tracking through schema constraints.
E. Time Travel increases performance by caching historical data in memory.

Question #17:
A Snowflake ETL pipeline uses a transient table to stage raw data before transforming it into a permanent table. What are the advantages and risks of using a transient table in this scenario?
Select one or two answers:
A. Transient tables offer better performance by skipping Time Travel.
B. Transient tables reduce storage costs by avoiding Fail-safe.
C. Transient tables are ideal for critical transactional data that requires high durability.
D. Transient tables cannot be recovered if accidentally dropped.
E. Transient tables allow for version control during ETL processing.

Question #18:
During a migration process, you temporarily load raw data into a transient table for validation. After successful validation, the table is deleted. Why might a transient table be preferred over a permanent table here?
Select one or two answers:
A. Transient tables are optimized for fast write and delete operations.
B. Transient tables do not incur Fail-safe charges after deletion.

C. Transient tables retain history for longer analysis during validation.
D. Transient tables provide high availability and replication for disaster recovery.
E. Transient tables are subject to strict access controls suitable for compliance.

Question #19:
You are running an ad-hoc analysis during a user session and need a temporary table to store intermediate results. What are the benefits of using a temporary table for this purpose?
Select one or two answers:
A. Temporary tables are automatically dropped at the end of the session.
B. Temporary tables can be shared across sessions for better collaboration.
C. Temporary tables reduce storage usage as they do not persist beyond the session.
D. Temporary tables ensure data visibility to all users in the same role.
E. Temporary tables are included in Time Travel for future recovery needs.

Question #20:
A data scientist creates a temporary table during a session to filter data for modeling. What happens to this table once the session ends, and how does this behavior benefit temporary data processing?
Select one or two answers:
A. The table is automatically dropped when the session ends.
B. The table remains available for subsequent sessions by the same user.
C. The table's lifecycle eliminates manual cleanup after analysis.
D. The table is retained for a limited period through Fail-safe.
E. The table's data is stored in Time Travel for up to seven days.

Answers and Explanations:
Question #16:
Correct Answers: A, B
Explanation:
A is correct because Time Travel allows querying historical data directly, which is invaluable for audits.
B is correct because Time Travel retains snapshots, enabling analysis of past states over the retention period.
C is incorrect because Time Travel does not replicate data; replication is a separate feature.
D is incorrect because Time Travel does not replace schema constraints; it provides historical data access.
E is incorrect because Time Travel does not cache historical data in memory, but stores it in Snowflake's underlying storage.

Question #17:
Correct Answers: A, B
Explanation:
A is correct because Transient tables skip Time Travel, improving write and query performance.
B is correct because Transient tables avoid Fail-safe charges, reducing storage costs.
C is incorrect because Transient tables are not ideal for critical transactional data due to lack of Fail-safe.
D is correct because dropped transient tables are unrecoverable, posing a risk in some

scenarios.
E is incorrect because Transient tables do not inherently support version control.

Question #18:
Correct Answers: A, B
Explanation:
A is correct because Transient tables are optimized for short-lived data, making them faster for migration tasks.
B is correct because deletion of transient tables avoids Fail-safe charges, making them cost-effective.
C is incorrect because Transient tables do not retain history for extended periods.
D is incorrect because Transient tables lack replication or high availability by design.
E is incorrect because Transient tables are not particularly suited for strict compliance access controls.

Question #19:
Correct Answers: A, C
Explanation:
A is correct because Temporary tables are automatically dropped at the session's end, requiring no manual cleanup.
C is correct because they reduce storage usage by not persisting beyond the session.
B is incorrect because Temporary tables are session-specific and cannot be shared across sessions.
D is incorrect because Temporary tables are not visible to other users, maintaining session-level isolation.
E is incorrect because Temporary tables are not included in Time Travel.

Question #20:
Correct Answers: A, C
Explanation:
A is correct because Temporary tables are dropped at the session's end, simplifying data lifecycle management.
C is correct because automatic cleanup eliminates the risk of orphaned tables after analysis.
B is incorrect because Temporary tables are session-specific and do not persist across sessions.
D is incorrect because Temporary tables are not part of Fail-safe.
E is incorrect because Temporary tables are not stored in Time Travel.

Question #21:
A Snowflake table contains columns for customer demographics and purchase history. Queries often focus on purchase history only. How would vertical partitioning improve query efficiency in this scenario?
A. By enabling faster scans of columns relevant to the query.
B. By replicating frequently queried columns across regions for better availability.
C. By reducing storage cost through compression.
D. By storing customer demographics in an external database.
E. By dynamically adjusting compute resources based on query demand.

Question #22:
A healthcare dataset has sensitive patient data and less-sensitive operational data. You want to separate the sensitive data for additional security measures. How can vertical partitioning help achieve this?
A. By encrypting specific columns during query execution.
B. By storing sensitive data in separate tables or schemas.
C. By restricting access to sensitive data using table-level access controls.
D. By physically separating sensitive and operational data for compliance.
E. By leveraging micro-partitions to separate sensitive data automatically.

Question #23:
A Snowflake warehouse frequently experiences high query latency during peak hours. How does Snowflake's scaling feature dynamically adjust compute resources to handle this workload?
A. By pausing underutilized clusters and reallocating them to other regions.
B. By automatically adding compute clusters to handle increased demand.
C. By scheduling queries during off-peak hours.
D. By limiting the number of concurrent queries.
E. By increasing the cluster size based on pre-configured rules.

Question #24:
Your team needs to run several resource-intensive queries simultaneously during a monthly reporting period. How would using multi-cluster warehouses improve performance without manual intervention?
A. By enabling additional clusters to handle concurrent workloads.
B. By segmenting queries to specific clusters based on their resource needs.
C. By reducing the number of queries run during peak times.
D. By ensuring larger clusters are used instead of multiple smaller clusters.
E. By pausing underutilized clusters to save costs.

Question #25:
A team is working with a Snowflake table containing billions of rows of sales data. They notice slow query performance when running detailed sales analysis. How can clustering keys improve query performance?
A. By sorting data within micro-partitions to align with query filters.
B. By dividing large tables into multiple smaller tables.
C. By compressing data to reduce query time.
D. By storing frequently queried data in a cache.
E. By replicating the table across regions for parallel processing.

Answers and Explanations
Question #21:
Correct Answer: A
Explanation:
A is correct because vertical partitioning separates data into columnar storage, allowing Snowflake to scan only the relevant columns (e.g., purchase history), significantly improving query efficiency.
B is incorrect because vertical partitioning does not replicate data across regions.
C is incorrect because while compression is a benefit, it is not related to query efficiency in

this context.
D is incorrect because storing demographics in an external database is not vertical partitioning.
E is incorrect because compute resources are not related to vertical partitioning.

Question #22:
Correct Answers: B, D
Explanation:
B and D are correct because vertical partitioning can store sensitive data in separate tables or schemas, providing physical separation and enhancing security and compliance.
A is incorrect because encrypting specific columns is not vertical partitioning.
C is incorrect because table-level access controls restrict access but do not physically separate data.
E is incorrect because micro-partitions do not automatically separate sensitive data.

Question #23:
Correct Answer: B
Explanation:
B is correct because Snowflake's auto-scaling feature dynamically adds compute clusters during peak times to handle higher demand, ensuring reduced latency.
A is incorrect because clusters are not paused or reallocated across regions.
C is incorrect because Snowflake does not schedule queries automatically based on usage.
D is incorrect because limiting queries would not address high query latency.
E is incorrect because Snowflake auto-scaling is not dependent on pre-configured rules.

Question #24:
Correct Answer: A
Explanation:
A is correct because multi-cluster warehouses dynamically scale by adding more clusters to handle concurrent workloads without user intervention.
B is incorrect because Snowflake does not assign queries to specific clusters based on resource needs.
C is incorrect because reducing the number of queries does not utilize multi-cluster warehouses effectively.
D is incorrect because using larger clusters is unrelated to multi-cluster functionality.
E is incorrect because pausing clusters does not enhance performance during peak periods.

Question #25:
Correct Answer: A
Explanation:
A is correct because clustering keys improve query performance by sorting data within micro-partitions to align with query filters, reducing the scan size.
B is incorrect because dividing tables is not related to clustering keys.
C is incorrect because compression reduces storage cost but does not improve query performance.
D is incorrect because Snowflake's caching mechanism is separate from clustering keys.
E is incorrect because replication does not impact clustering or query performance directly.

```sql
SELECT 'Good luck with your certification quest!' AS sincere_wishes,
    'You're already an asset to your company!' AS current_status
FROM TABLE(GENERATOR(ROWCOUNT => 1));
    -- Keep querying greatness!"
```

www.ingramcontent.com/pod-product-compliance
Lightning Source LLC
Chambersburg PA
CBHW071017240526
45469CB00006BD/1961